PERFORMANCE ANXIETY

D1167445

PERFORMANCE ANXIETY

Overcoming Your Fear In:

The Workplace
Social Situations
Interpersonal Communications
The Performing Arts

Mitchell W. Robin, Ph.d
Rochelle Balter, Ph.d

ADAMS PUBLISHING
Holbrook, Massachusetts

Published by
Adams Media Corporation, 260 Center Street, Holbrook, MA 02343

ISBN: 1-55850-441-9

Printed in the United States of America.

J   I   H   G   F   E   D   C   B   A

Library of Congress Cataloging-in-Publication Data
Robin, Mitchell W.
   Performance anxiety : overcoming your fear in the workplace, social situations, interpersonal
   communications, the performing arts / Mitchell W. Robin, Rochelle Balter.
      p.   cm.
   Includes index.
   ISBN 1-55850-441-9
   1. Speech anxiety—Treatment. 2. Stage fright—Treatment. 3. Rational-emotive psychotherapy.
   4. Self-help techniques. I. Balter, Rochelle. II. Title.
   RC552.S69R63   1994
   616.85'223—dc20   94-41706
                                                                                              CIP

This publication is designed to provide accurate and authoritative information with regard to the subject matter covered. It is sold with the understanding that the publisher is not engaged in rendering legal, accounting, or other professional advice. If legal advice or other expert assistance is required, the services of a competent professional person should be sought.
   — From a *Declaration of Principles* jointly adopted by a Committee of the American Bar Association and a Committee of Publishers and Associations

This book is available at quantity discounts for bulk purchases.
For information, call 1-800-872-5627.

*This book is affectionately dedicated to our readers:
performers whether they are professionals or "civilians."*

Table of Contents

PART 1

PART 2
SIXTEEN PRESCRIPTIONS FOR OVERCOMING
PERFORMANCE ANXIETY

Foreword

I probably would not have created Rational-Emotive Behavior Therapy (REBT) had I not been stricken with performance anxiety from day one until I was nineteen. I was phobic about speaking up to authority figures and, especially, about performing in public—which I avoided at all costs. Being bright, I was steadily asked to act in class plays, to debate with other youngsters, and to be chairman of public functions. I always made up excuses and copped out. Although I knew the answers to almost all the questions my teachers asked in my classes, I seldom volunteered and only spoke up when a teacher specifically called on me.

When I knew that I had to memorize a little poem—which I could easily do—and recite it in class the next day—which I religiously convinced myself I couldn't do—I told my mother I had a severe headache, sometimes put a thermometer against the radiator in my room to create a "fever," and stayed home "sick." Nothing could persuade me to get up in public and "make a fool of myself."

At the age of sixteen I became devoted to reading philosophy, including the self-help philosophy of Epictetus, Marcus Aurelius, Proverbs, Ralph Waldo Emerson, Bertrand Russell, and others, and by the time I was nineteen, I convinced myself that I could overcome my anxiety by thinking differently. I also read about the experiments of John B. Watson and his associates who desensitized children who feared harmless animals by giving them *in vivo* (live) desensitization in the presence of actual animals and soon had them petting these feared creatures.

So, following this kind of philosophic and behavioral therapy, I made myself *un*comfortable by giving many public talks and *un*easily encountering scores of "dangerous" women. Within months of forcing myself to do this therapeutic homework, I became a fearless public speaker and an intrepid encounterer of new partners. In fact, I became very adept at both these "risky" pursuits.

I also discovered, in the course of my speaking and social encounters, that if I concentrated strongly on the *message* I was conveying to the members of my audience, I nicely distracted myself from my anxiety. Thus, I saw that if I focused on "What am I talking about? How will I get my point across to my listeners?" I was not able to think too much of "How well am I doing? What terrible things will happen if I fail? How foolish will I be!"

I used my self-taught methods of overcoming my anxiety very successfully for a number of years and put them into my therapy techniques when I became a therapist at the age of thirty. But I still thought that psychoanalytic delving into my clients' early history was "deeper" and more effective than the cognitive behavior therapy I had used so well on myself. So I went for postdoctoral training in psychoanalysis.

What a mistake! After practicing psychoanalysis for a number of years, I saw how ineffective it was, looked around for a more efficient method, and created Rational-Emotive Behavior Therapy (REBT), the pioneering Cognitive Behavior Therapy (CBT) that is now very popular. Surprise, Surprise!—it included the philosophic and homework methods I had started using on myself to overcome my performance anxiety at the age of nineteen. It has added, over the years, many additional thinking, feeling, and behavioral methods.

That is what Mitchell Robin and Rochelle Balter show in the present book, *Performance Anxiety*. They have done a remarkably good job of showing what performance anxiety is, and how it is similar to other kinds of human anxiety and depression. They use Rational-Emotive Behavior Therapy (REBT) to explore what people think and what they imagine just before they make themselves panicked about public speaking, acting, personal encounters, and other "risky" performances. They accurately show their readers how they largely create their own anxiety and the self-defeating avoidance of "dangerous" situations.

Best of all, they give many REBT remedies for "stressful" conditions people encounter. REBT is the pioneering method of what Arnold Lazarus calls "Multimodal Therapy." From the time I created it in 1955 it has always included a number of thinking, feeling, and behavioral techniques—more, probably than the other cognitive-behavior therapies that followed it in the 1960's and that have become increasingly popular in the recent years.

Why are REBT and the other cognitive behavior therapies so widely used? Because over five hundred scientific experiments have tended to show that neurotic individuals have more and stronger irrational or dysfunctional beliefs than less disturbed individuals have. Several hundred studies have shown that when REBT and CBT are used with anxious, depressed, enraged, and self-hating individuals, they tend to become significantly less distressed.

Mitchell Robin and Rochelle Balter use REBT methods very adequately in this book, and particularly show the readers how to do cognitive, emotive, and behavioral exercises and homework assignments to overcome their needless fears. They have written a clear, highly understandable, and quite therapeutic manual that will be of great help to almost any reader who works at following their lucid instructions. See for yourself what a useful book this is!

Albert Ellis, Ph.D., President
The Institute for Rational-Emotive Therapy
45 East 65th Street
New York, New York 10021-6593

Acknowledgments

Writing a book (even with a co-author) may be a solitary experience but getting it published requires the efforts and cooperation of many people. The authors are grateful for the support, cooperation, and effort of many people who helped them with this, their maiden voyage as self-help authors. We would especially like to acknowledge our literary agents Carol Mann and Gareth Esersky who first approached us about writing this book. We would also like to thank Dick Staron of Adams Media Corporation for his unfailing support, enthusiasm, and patience with the "dumb" questions of novice authors.

As we began to put this book together many people helped us in ways too numerous to mention but we would like to single out Gary Pitz and Gertrude Fellner for their helpful comments and suggestions, and Rosemary Binnie for her resourcefulness in the library and most especially Herbert Goldman for his sharing with us the results of his research. We are also extremely grateful to Tyna Fox who took our initial chaotic tape recordings and transcribed them, in a timely fashion, into an "editable" first draft of this book. We would like to thank Beth Free for her help with locating "missing" chapters. We would like to call special attention to the very model of a modern copy editor, Alice Manning, whose efforts both in the aid of increasing clarity and in the proper use of commas helped to make this book better.

Writing a book and finishing it by a deadline usually means that some things have to "slide" or that others have to take up the slack. We would like to thank our respective spouses Gina (a.k.a. SWMBO), and Steve for their patience, support, and encouragement (nagging) during the 18 months that this book took to go from a suggestion to a finished product. We would like to thank them for their forbearance during the triumphs (finishing an acceptable proposal, signing the publication contract) and tragedies (discovering that one entire prescription had never been dictated but had only been alluded to on other tapes, the accidental reformatting of the hard drive) that characterize any new endeavor.

Most especially we would like to acknowledge the pioneering efforts of Dr. Albert Ellis, "grandfather" of cognitive/behavioral therapy and founder of the Institute for Rational-Emotive Therapy whose theories form the cornerstone of this book, and whose guidance, wisdom, and inspiration have helped in writing their first self-help book.

The Conventions for Reading This Unconventional Book

Before you begin to read this book, Rochelle and I would like to share some of the reasons we decided to write this book the way we did.

Pronouns

When we started to write this book, Rochelle and I decided to treat it as a dialogue between you the reader and ourselves. Therefore, we tried to write it as if you were sitting with us in either an individual session or a group workshop at the Institute for Rational-Emotive Therapy in Manhattan. The pronouns *I, we, you,* and *us* are used conversationally. *I* is used to refer to either Rochelle or me when one of us is writing about something that either one of us said to a specific client. *We* refers to both Rochelle and me, and our general approach to rational-emotive therapy. *You* refers to you our readers, the people to whom this book is dedicated. Sometimes you will read "all of us" or "we all," or another similar phrase. This is a reminder that all of us have certain ideas, perceptions, behavior, and emotions in common. No one is immune from them.

Case Histories

We have included many case histories throughout the book. These case histories are all composites of various clients that Rochelle and I have had. Each case is an amalgam of a number of typical cases and is not intended to represent any specific individual current or past client of either author or the Institute for Rational-Emotive Therapy. The cases cited do accurately reflect the thoughts, behaviors, and emotions of real people who have been successfully treated for performance anxiety.

We have tried to select issues representative of the wide variety of people who both experience and suffer from performance anxiety. Each chapter contains at least one or two typical cases, but no one chapter contains examples from all walks of life. We have found that people who suffer from performance anxiety tend to share certain beliefs, emotions, and behaviors. If you are a businessperson, you can read an actor example just as profitably as an actor can read one of the business examples.

Homework

Throughout the book you will find homework assignments being given. It is our experience that people are more likely to benefit from any kind of therapy—face to face or bibliotherapy—if they attempt to put the insights that they have gotten into daily practice. Write down your answers to the questions that we pose throughout the book, and try to do the homework assignments. It has been our experience that you will increase your chance of success if you do.

Language

People have asked us if all therapists use candid language, earthy metaphors, and dramatic examples. We cannot speak for all therapists, but we know from our own experience that our clients seem to respond well to our use of language, metaphor, and example. We have found that dramatic examples and earthy metaphors are most memorable. Our clients tend to recall them more readily and can therefore use them when needed. We tend to use candid language to more accurately reflect the emotional reality of our clients. While euphemisms may be fine in certain contexts, it may be self–defeating for a therapist to call a spade a shovel. When our clients are angry at themselves for making a mistake, they tell themselves they screwed up. They don't say, "Oh, darn, I made a boo-boo." We have discovered the importance of memorable words and language in our therapeutic practice. I guess you can say that Rochelle and I are not anti-semantic.

Coping Cue Cards

Another unusual feature of this book is the Coping Cue Cards. Each Coping Cue Card in Appendix B contains a wallet-sized summary of one of the sixteen prescriptions for overcoming performance anxiety. Please feel free to cut them out of the book and use them when needed. Each card can serve as a handy reminder of the issues that you are working on that are hindering your performance or preventing you from performing. Each card contains a review of one or more effective tools that you can use to help you act, think, or feel more effectively in a performance situation.

It has been our experience that when our clients have made up and used similar memory aids, they have made more rapid progress.

We wish you well, and hope that you learn how to overcome your fear of performance on the boards, in the boardroom, and in life.

PART 1

PART 1

Chapter 1
Our Greatest Fear

What do all of these people have in common?

- "The first time was a nightmare. But instead of getting easier, it seems to be getting worse."—Susan, age forty-five, a trial lawyer.

- "I don't know why anyone should have to be made to suffer like this just to get a lousy degree."—Norman, age twenty-three, a student.

- "I dread it each time I have to do it." – Rebecca, age thirty, a dancer.

- "It happens even when I order lunch."—Steve, age thirty-five, a middle-level manager.

- "I knew that being a parent would be difficult, but nobody warned me about this."—Marsha, age thirty, PTA member.

- "It's the feeling of the unexpected that gets to me."—Tony G., age forty-five, experienced character actor.

All of them suffer from performance anxiety.

When you get up to speak, do you feel sick to your stomach? When you think about performing, do you shake all over? If you are asked to perform in public, do you always say, "*No*, not me"? If you do, you too are probably suffering from some form of performance anxiety, and as you can see, you are not alone. Millions of people are called upon to perform in public each day. Some may be professional singers, dancers, and actors, while others are "civilian performers," including sales directors and managers, teachers and students. Most of these performers, both famous and unknown, will experience some degree of stress. For example, Carly Simon recalls that "I became so anxious that I started to have heart palpitations," and Sir Laurence Olivier reported being "frozen with terror" when performing in *The Master Builder* in London. Al Jolson's first-night jitters were described as "a sickening self–conscious coldness" the night he opened in *La Belle Paree.*

Some will be defeated by their performance stress, while others seem to thrive on it. What distinguishes the defeated from the thrivers? Can someone who experiences stress not be overcome by it? The answer is a resounding *yes*, as demonstrated by Broadway actress Stockard Channing, who is quoted as saying that she "feels like heading to the nearest airport" until a half hour before curtain and then becomes calm, or by Jean Stapleton, who also seems to be "on the brink" and then goes on to give a sterling performance. Those who are defeated by performance anxiety can be helped or, more importantly, can learn to help themselves to reduce their anxiety to more workable levels.

Many people suffer from performance anxiety. Others experience the symptoms of performance anxiety, and some—the fortunate few—may not know what we are talking about because they have never experienced any of it. In the United States, performance anxiety is our greatest single fear. Many people are so afraid of performing or speaking in public that they rate the mere possibility of public speaking as potentially far more frightening than the thought of dying.

Why is this so? What is your opinion?
Can you think of reasons why people would be so afraid of performing
that they would rate that fear higher than the fear of death?

Many possibly rate death as less frightening because they believe that death is final—"When you're dead, you're dead, and it's over"—whereas, they believe that they may have to perform every single day of their lives, and they would rather not have to do that. Many believe that performing exposes them to discomfort, and possibly ridicule and loss. They would do anything rather than put themselves at risk in that way. As a result, either they don't perform or they perform so badly that, paradoxically, they experience those dreaded negative consequences.

All the World's a Stage...

What is a performance? If you are a teacher, it may take the form of stepping in front of a class or giving a lecture to your colleagues. If you are a student, it may be taking a test, giving a speech, or even writing a paper. If you are an executive, it may be the opportunities you are offered to present information at committee meetings or at a conference. If you are a sales agent, it may mean approaching a customer or making a "cold call."

In every situation we have just described, people are *performing*. They are getting up in a public setting and allowing themselves to come under public scrutiny. We will refer to such people as *civilian performers*. Civilian performers can be differentiated from the more traditional professional performers—actors, singers, dancers, artists—who perform for the public by appearing on TV, on stage, or in films in order to make a living. The only difference between them, however, is that professional performers tend to realize that appearing in public goes with the territory and therefore it would be a good idea to be prepared and trained to be able to perform without anxiety. Civilian performers generally are surprised when they discover that public scrutiny is part of their lives. They are neither prepared nor trained for it. Both professional and civilian performers can experience performance anxiety, and both can be "done in" by it.

As Shakespeare wrote, "All the world's a stage, and all the men and women merely players." For our purposes, performing means doing something in the public eye, whether the performer is an entertainer who sings or acts for a living, or a professional businessperson who presents at conferences or meetings, or a pure civilian, an average human being who discovers, inconveniently perhaps, that he or she is suddenly called upon to speak in public, or to act in some way that he or she is not accustomed to. For some people this poses no problem. But many others experience performance anxiety, and the experience overwhelms them.

Performance Anxiety

What is anxiety? The dictionary defines *anxiety* as a pervasive sense of dread that something bad will occur and that we will be helpless or powerless to prevent it or to cope with it when it does come. Anxiety is typically experienced physically. The physical symptoms of anxiety include dry mouth, shaky hands, a trembling voice, rapid heartbeat, and a variety of other symptoms to be discussed later.

People can experience anxiety in a variety of settings; however, when you experience it as you are anticipating having to perform, preparing to perform, or in the midst of an actual performance, we call it *performance anxiety*. Performance anxiety is that sense of dread, accompanied by physical symptoms of distress, when having to perform. It may be a dread that the performance situation will overcome the performer or will put the performer at unimaginable risk. It may be a dread that the individual will not be able to function properly or that his or her ego and worth will be evaluated and the results may not be favorable.

People who suffer from performance anxiety experience both the dread and the physical sensations not only in performance settings but also when contemplating being in a performance setting. They experience anticipatory anxiety that is as real to them physically as the anxiety they experience when they are actually in the performance setting. Ironically, many people who experience performance anxiety never actually come face to face with the public while they perform, as do professional actors or public speakers, but rather experience the public indirectly. Writers and graphic artists, for example, never actually practice their craft under public scrutiny (as would a dancer), but they nonetheless experience performance anxiety. Their "public" may get to examine their work only after it is already completed, but the thought of eventual public scrutiny is an ever-present reality that can result in that same crippling sense of dread and physical discomfort.

People who experience performance anxiety may not be anxious at other times, but only when called upon to perform (whether professionally or incidentally). We also wish to call your attention to an important distinction between people who experience performance anxiety and people who *suffer from* performance anxiety. People who experience performance anxiety perform despite their physical and cognitive symptoms and may even incorporate them into their performance. They perceive these symptoms as the "cost of doing business" and may use them as a signal that they are charged up and ready to go on.

On the other hand, people who suffer from performance anxiety not only experience the physical and cognitive symptoms but also have another, more debilitating set of symptoms as well: procrastination, impaired performance, or nonperformance. As you can readily see, there is not one response called performance anxiety, but rather a continuum of physical, emotional, cognitive, and behavioral responses.

Physically

We all experience stress in response to immediate or anticipated danger. Additionally, we experience the symptoms of stress in response to real or perceived pleasure. This latter condition can be called *eustress*. When you experience eustress, you are experiencing the same physical symptoms, but you are not interpreting them as danger signals. Many of the physical symptoms that accompany anxiety also accompany pleasure. There are people who thrive on performing and think that it is the greatest thing. There are also people who like to sky-dive and fall out of airplanes. There are people who get a high from doing things that others think of as scary. How strongly we experience these symptoms is directly related to the strength of our perceptions. We will discuss this in greater detail in the next chapter.

What Are Your Physical Symptoms?

Here is a list of possible physical responses. First check off the ones that you are aware of when you perform. Then go back and rate them on a scale of 1 to 5, where 1 is mild or nondisturbing and 5 is very strong and incapacitating.

Physical Symptom Checklist

Symptom	Do I experience this?	Intensity
I am aware of my heartbeat when I perform.		
I am aware of my breathing when I perform.		
I am aware of muscle tension when I perform.		
I am aware of needing to urinate more frequently when I perform.		
I am aware of being light-headed/nauseous/dizzy when I perform.		

Emotionally

We may experience a variety of emotions, from pleasant to unpleasant, as a result of being in a performance situation. People who experience performance anxiety not only feel anxious but may also feel embarrassed about their anxiety, and annoyed about experiencing both anxiety and embarrassment. People who suffer from performance anxiety not only feel anxious, but also tend to experience a constellation of negative emotions, including depression, self-downing, low self-esteem, anger, and panic. However, you could also experience joy, elation, pleasant anticipation, or happiness as a result of being in performance situations.

What Are Your Emotional Responses?

Here is a list of possible emotional responses that people experience when they perform. Check all of those that apply to you. Then go back and pick out the three emotions that you most frequently feel when you are called upon to perform and rate those three on a scale of 1 to 5, where 1 is mild or nondisturbing and 5 is very strong and incapacitating.

Emotional Response Checklist

Emotions	Do I Experience This?	Intensity
Joy		
Elation		
Happy anticipation		
Concern		
Anxiety		
Dread		
Fear		
Panic		
Anger		
Depression		
Low self-esteem		
Self-downing		

The various emotional responses that people have, as well as the intensity of their physical symptoms, are dependent upon the way people think about and perceive the quality of the performance situation.

Cognitively

Whether you only experience the symptoms of performance anxiety or suffer from performance anxiety depends on how you think about both the performance situation and your physical and behavioral response to it. If you think, "Oh, well, I feel shaky; that's too bad, but I will just have to deal with it," you will neither stop yourself from performing nor perform poorly. If, however, you think, "Oh, my God! I am shaking! This is intolerable. I can't shake. Only stupid, worthless people do that. I hate it that I shake, and I hate having to be placed in situations that make me nervous," you probably will either perform poorly or stop yourself from performing.

What Are Your Cognitions

Following is a list of possible thoughts that people have when they are called upon to perform. Check all that apply to you. Then go back and rate the frequency with which these thoughts occur to you. 5 = they occur at every performance opportunity; 4 = they occur only at "important" performance opportunities; 3 = they seldom occur to me; 2 = they never occur to me; 1 = I am not aware of what I am thinking.

Behaviorally

The most common behavioral response to performance anxiety is procrastination—people put off or try to delay their performance. People who suffer from

What Are My Cognitions?

Cognition	Do I Experience This?	Frequency
Oh, boy, an opportunity to do what I like doing.		
I can't wait to meet this challenge.		
I am not very good at this, but if I take advantage of this opportunity, I probably will improve.	✓	5
I hate doing this. Why should I have to be put in this position?		
I'm not ready yet. I must not perform until I am.	✓	5
I must not experience any physical discomfort when I perform.	✓	5
I can't stand the hassle of performing.		
I can't stand the physical discomfort I experience when I perform.	✓	5
It's the end of the world (or at least very bad) if I don't do perfectly, or at least very well.		
It's the end of the world (or at least very bad) if I am seen as less than perfectly competent and prepared.		
I feel totally worthless (or at least bad about myself) when I believe I have done poorly or not achieved my "personal best."	✓	5
I feel totally worthless (or at least bad about myself) when I feel any discomfort.	✓	5
I feel totally worthless (or at least bad about myself) when others rate me as performing poorly.	✓	5

performance anxiety not only procrastinate but try to avoid performing entirely. If they are forced to perform, they tend to perform poorly; that is, they do a bad job of acting, singing, dancing, or speaking in public. They are so overwhelmed by their physical experiences and their self-damning thoughts that they incapacitate themselves and do not do as good a job as they could have, given their current level of ability.

What Is Your Behavioral Response?

Here is a list of possible behavioral responses that people can make as a result of being called upon to perform. Read them and then pick your three most frequent responses.

Behavioral Response Checklist

Behavior	Frequency
Do it immediately	
Make a commitment to do it and meet the commitment	✓
Start to prepare	
Procrastinate, but do it eventually	✓
Procrastinate indefinitely	
Refuse to do it, but eventually give in	
Refuse to do it	✓

Let's review our checklists. We will start with the physical symptoms. Look at the checklist you just filled out. What symptoms did you check off? Remember that we said that anxiety is often accompanied by dry mouth, rapid heartbeat, palpitations, etc. Do you experience any of these? There are also emotions that accompany these. When you filled out your checklist, what did you write down as your emotional accompanying symptoms? Do you find that you get anxious and fearful? Do you find that you get angry or depressed? If you do, what other emotions do you experience as a result of feeling angry or depressed? Do you self–down? Do you get sad? And when you do that, what kinds of thoughts do you have? Do you want to run from the situation and say, "I shouldn't be here"? Do you say, "Oh, I can't stand this and I don't want to go on and do this thing that I have to do?" Are you so overwhelmed that you just hide and don't perform? No matter what degree of symptoms you checked off, this book is designed for you. We will cover everything on our diagnostic checklist and help you learn the necessary skills to cope with them effectively.

It is interesting to note that whether we perform poorly or avoid performing altogether, we provide ourselves with additional things to think about, and so the cycle continues. Since we performed badly last time and we recall our self-damning thoughts and unpleasant physical symptoms, we begin to dread the next performance opportunity, fearing that those same responses will return—and inevitably they will return—unfortunately at a stronger level.

Can we break this cycle? Can we learn to perform without fear, or at least without being incapacitated by our physical distress and our self-damning thoughts? Happily, the answer is a resounding *yes!* In the next few chapters you will be given more information about both the physical aspects of stress and the thoughts that create and later exacerbate anxiety. You will also be introduced to some of the basic principles of cognitive-behavioral psychology. The rest of the book is devoted to showing you how to use those principles to help yourself perform without fear.

Before you read any further, take the self-test on the following pages.

Performer's Self-Test

Scenario 1

Imagine that you are about to get up to perform. You are reasonably well pre-pared. You are rested, and you had a bite to eat about half an hour ago.

    a. How do you feel *physically?*

        i. Fine. I am not aware of any disturbing physical symptoms.

        ii. Fine. However, I do notice that my mouth feels dry and some of my muscles are tense.

        iii. Not so good. I am aware of many disturbing physical symptoms.

        iv. Terrible. I have too many disturbing physical symptoms.

        v. Out of control. My physical symptoms are running away with me.

    b. How do you feel *emotionally?*

        i. Elated

        ii. Alert and concerned

        iii. Worried and anxious

        iv. Frightened

        v. Panicked

    c. What is your most persistent *thought* as you are about to perform?

        i. I am really going to enjoy this.

        ii. I think I am prepared enough. If not, there is always tomorrow.

        iii. I hope everyone won't notice how scared I am. If they did, I couldn't take it.

        iv. I wish I wasn't here. It will be awful.

        v. I wish I wasn't here. My future is on the line. I may not get another chance. If I screw this up, I will prove to everyone how incompetent I am.

    d. How well do you *expect to do?*

        i. Very well.

        ii. As well as I can, given my current level of proficiency.

        iii. OK, as long as I can keep my jitters under control.

        iv. Poorly. But maybe I'll do OK if I can only concentrate and be in perfect control.

        v. Terribly. I never do well in these situations.

Scenario 2

You are in the middle of a performance when you notice that you are having trouble concentrating.

    e. Now how do you feel *physically?*

        i. Fine. I am not aware of any disturbing physical symptoms.

    ii. Fine. However, I do notice that my mouth feels dry and some of my muscles are tense.

    iii. Not so good. I am aware of many disturbing physical symptoms.

    iv. Terrible. I have too many disturbing physical symptoms.

    v. Even more out of control. My physical symptoms are running away with me.

f. Now how do you feel *emotionally?*

    i. Elated

    ii. Alert and concerned

    iii. Worried & Anxious

    iv. Frightened

    v. Panicked

g. What is your most persistent *thought* as you perform?

    i. I am really enjoying this. But I had better shift my attention back to the task at hand.

    ii. I hope I won't allow myself to get too distracted. But distractions are part of being human.

    iii. I don't like it when I get distracted. Everyone will notice how scared I am. I can't stand this.

    iv. I hate it when I get distracted. No one else ever allows their attention to drift. Now I am bound to screw up.

    v. I hate it when I get distracted. I must never allow myself to get distracted. Everyone now knows I lost my place and is either laughing at me or feeling sorry for me. I wish I were dead.

h. Now how well do you *expect to do?*

    i. Very well.

    ii. As well as I can, given my current level of proficiency.

    iii. OK, if I can keep my distractibility under control.

    iv. Poorly. But maybe I'll do OK if I can only concentrate and be in perfect control.

    v. Terribly. I never do well in these situations.

Scenario 3

You have just finished performing and people are coming over to talk to you. Most of them are telling you that you did a good job, but one or two have criticisms.

i. Now how do you feel *physically?*

    i. Fine. I am not aware of any disturbing physical symptoms.

    ii. Fine. However, I now notice that my mouth feels dry and some of my muscles are tense.

    iii. Not so good. I am aware of many disturbing physical symptoms.

    iv. Tired. I had too many disturbing physical symptoms.

    v. Exhausted. My physical symptoms are still running away with me, and I have trouble concentrating on what is going on around me.

j. Now how do you feel, *emotionally?*

    i. Elated. I am having a performer's high.

    ii. Pleased that I have gotten a good response.

    iii. Concerned that I might not have done as well as I would have liked to do.

    iv. Anxious—what if the people who are congratulating me are lying?

    v. Panicked.

k. Now what is your most persistent *thought?*

    i. I really enjoyed that. I hope I get a chance to do it again.

    ii. I really like to hear the response of people afterwards, but I'd better not take anything they say too seriously. I know I still need to work on some stuff.

    iii. That wasn't so bad. I wish I didn't get uncomfortable and distracted, but I really like the response afterward.

    iv. I hate this whole process. Maybe I should rethink my goals in life.

    v. Get me out of here. I will never again put myself in this position.

l. Now, how well did you *actually do?*

    i. Very well.

    ii. As well as I could, given my current level of proficiency.

    iii. OK, I guess. But I really need to keep my "distractibility" and tension under control.

    iv. Poorly. I rarely do well in these situations.

    v. Terribly, as I knew I would.

Scenario 4

You are being asked to perform sometime in the near future. You don't know what kind of a crowd it will be or how many people will be there. You are being given some time to prepare, but not enough to be overtrained or "perfect."

m. Now how do you feel *physically?*

    i. Fine. I am not aware of any disturbing physical symptoms.

    ii. Fine. However, I do notice that my mouth feels dry and some of my muscles are tense.

    iii. Not so good. I am aware of many disturbing physical symptoms.

    iv. Terrible. I have too many disturbing physical symptoms.

    v. Out of control. My physical symptoms are running away with me.

n. Now how do you feel *emotionally?*

    i. Very happy

    ii. Pleased

    iii. Concerned

    iv. Anxious

    v. Panicked

o. Now what is your most persistent *thought?*
    i. This is going to be fun. I always enjoy a new challenge.
    ii. I am glad they asked me. I like the opportunity to "show my stuff."
    iii. Oh-oh—do I really want to go through that again?
    iv. I hate this whole process. Maybe I should rethink my goals in life.
    v. Get me out of here. I will never again put myself in this position.

p. Now how will you *respond?*
    i. "Thank you very much; I'd love to."
    ii. "Let me check my calendar. I think I might be free."
    iii. "I am not sure I can do it. Do you have someone else you could use? If not, I'll be glad to."
    iv. "I will be out of town on that date. I am booked for the foreseeable future."
    v. "No, thank you."

Performer's Scoring Key

There were sixteen questions, a through p. Each one had five choices, i through v. Each choice is worth its own value. For example, if you chose the first response for question A, give yourself 1 point; if you chose the third response, give yourself 3 points, etc. Now, go back and figure out your **total score** on the **self-diagnostic test.**

Total scores on the *performer's self-diagnostic test* range from 16 to 80. If you scored between 16 and 32, you probably do not have performance anxiety. If you scored between 33 and 48, you probably have some performance anxiety, and you may have trouble achieving some of your performance goals because of it. It is our experience that most people normally score between 16 and 48. However, if you scored 49 or higher, you probably have moderate to severe performance anxiety and will probably experience trouble achieving many of your performance goals. If you scored between 48 and 64, you probably have moderate performance anxiety. However, if it is properly channeled, moderate anxiety can sometimes be redirected so as to enhance performance rather than detract from it. If you scored 65 or higher, you probably have severe performance anxiety, and you may want to consult a professional after you have read this book.

Symptom Scores

You can also figure out your **symptom scores.** The *performer's self-diagnostic test* can be broken down into four **symptom scores:** physical discomfort, emotional response, cognitive response, and behavioral response. If you wish, you can see which of your symptoms need the most work. The **physical discomfort symptoms** questions a, e, i, and m. The **emotional response** questions are b, f, j, and n. The **cognitive response** questions are c, g, k, and o. The **behavioral response** questions are d, h, l, and p. Again, you can add up your scores for each subscale.

The scores for each subscale range from 4 to 20. It has been our experience that most people normally score between 4 and 8. A score between 9 and 12 on any subscale suggests that you may have a problem with that symptom. A score of 13 or higher reveals greater disturbance; that particular symptom bears working on.

Emergency Performance Situation Triage

If you are reading this book because you are either experiencing performance anxiety or suffering from performance anxiety, read on. Read the chapters and prescriptions in order. However, if you are reading this book in hopes of dealing with an upcoming performance situation that is looming on the horizon and that you are experiencing anxiety about right now, use your scores on the subscales to guide your reading. Read the remainder of Part 1, and then read the prescriptions that target your specific symptoms.

Emergency Performance Situation Triage Chart

If You Scored High On	*Read Chapters 2 through 5, Plus*
Physical discomfort	Prescriptions 1, 2, 3, 4 + 5, 15*
Emotional response	Prescriptions 5, 6, 7, 8 + 1, 15*
Cognitive response	Prescriptions 13, 14, 15, 16 + 1, 15*
Behavioral response	Prescriptions 9, 10, 11, 12 + 1, 15*

* Finish the book when the emergency is over

We have used these techniques, and the theories that underlie them, with our clients and have found that they are generally useful. Remember, however, that when we use them with our clients, we typically work with these clients for many weeks, and occasionally months, reviewing and rehearsing these techniques so that they are well ingrained. Some people grasp them quickly and experience the benefits of them immediately. Others understand the principles involved and realize that they could work, if applied, but initially have trouble applying them.

It has been our experience that if you read this book, understand the concepts, and regularly practice the principles involved, you probably not only will experience some relief but will also be well on your way to overcoming your performance anxiety and performing without fear.

Chapter 2
"Why Are My Butterflies Like Elephants?"

An actress named Gwen once told me, "I know that when people perform, they experience butterflies in their stomach, but how come *my* butterflies always feel like elephants?" When she said that, she was very much afraid of how bad she would feel when she had to get up to perform. She thought that all of her physical symptoms were danger signals. They were red flags signaling that she was going to get very sick. She feared that she would be overcome by the experience, and she therefore avoided the activities that "made her sick." She did not ever want to experience those elephants walking around in the pit of her stomach. Gwen thought that normal people, unlike herself, had only very minor symptoms. What she did not realize was that the more afraid of her symptoms she became, the bigger they felt. The butterflies grew into elephants as she watched. She did not realize that stress is not a danger signal. Stress is normal! Everybody who is alive experiences stress.

If you don't experience the physical symptoms of stress occasionally, something is amiss. Stress is the body's normal reaction to new and unexpected situations. Stress is also the body's normal reaction to situations that you have learned to perceive as anxiety-ridden, unpleasant, or frightening. Not experiencing the symptoms of stress may actually endanger you, since you may not be alerted to situations that require a different level of attention.

Remember that some stress is normal. When Gwen said that her butterflies were elephants, she was aware that people experience stress, but she thought that she **shouldn't be** experiencing "such an abnormally high level of stress." Gwen therefore made her symptoms worse. She wasn't getting sicker; she was just experiencing her symptoms more vividly. We helped Gwen understand that she couldn't avoid the stress reaction entirely, but that she could learn to cope with it once it occurred and could reduce its impact on her.

One of the goals of this book is to help you learn to live with your symptoms without being overwhelmed by them. Some of your symptoms, like Gwen's, may very well diminish or even disappear as you learn to perceive them differently.

What again is stress? Stress is your reaction to a unique, frightening, or conditioned "stress situation." A conditioned stress situation is a situation that you have learned to perceive as stressful. If, when you were a child, you were told that getting up and speaking was frightening and that anyone would be afraid to do it, you probably learned to see speaking in front of a group as stressful. You therefore possibly experience symptoms of stress when you need to speak in public. Does everyone see public speaking as dangerous? No, but if you have learned to perceive it as dangerous, you will then experience the symptoms of stress.

What are the normal symptoms associated with stress? They include the following: rapid heartbeat, shallow breathing, and a change in blood pressure. Your pupils may become dilated, and therefore the world may suddenly seem very bright. Your mouth may become dry, but you may also sweat. Your hands and all your muscles may twitch, and you may find yourself trembling. You may find that your pulse is racing and that your heartbeat appears to be louder and more rapid than usual.

You may experience bowel and/or bladder distress, and as a result you may either have to go to the bathroom more frequently or feel that you are about to vomit. You may experience a heightened sense of nausea or dizziness. You may discover that your hair stands up on end, which is known as pilomotor activity.

Chart 1
Stress*

I. *Stress defined*

    A. It is *normal!*

    B. It is the body's automatic response to novelty, emergency, or familiarity.

II. *Components of stress and their consequences*

    A. *Physical*

       1. Increase in heartbeat

       2. Increase in respiration

       3. Change in blood pressure

       4. Dry mouth

       5. Wet palms

       6. Body sweats

       7. Pupils dilate

       8. Muscle tremors

       9. Gastrointestinal motility

      10. Bowel and bladder distress

      11. Pilomotor response

      12. Penile and nipple erection

---

*The following is adapted from M.W. Robin, "Overcoming Performance Anxiety: Using RET with Actors, Artists, and Other 'Performers,'" in *Innovations in Rational-Emotive Therapy*, ed. W. Dryden and L. Hill (Newbury Park, Calif.: Sage, 1993).

B. *Psychological*
   1. Distress
      a. Anxiety
      b. Fear
      c. Panic
   2. Eustress
      a. Pleasurable anticipation
      b. Joy, happiness, etc.
      c. Elation, ecstasy, "natural high"
C. *Social/Behavioral*
   1. Distress
      (1) Avoid the situation
      (2) Delay/procrastinate
      a. Anxiety
      (1) Perform poorly
      b. Fear
      (1) Avoid the situation
      (2) Delay/procrastinate
      (3) Perform poorly
      c. Panic
      (1) Avoid thoughts about the situation in any of its forms
      (2) Avoid the situation in any of its forms
      (3) Avoid people connected with the situation who might get you to perform
   2. Eustress
      a. Pleasurable anticipation
      (1) Prepare
          (a) Enjoy the process of preparation
          (b) Anticipate the pleasant outcome
      (2) Procrastinate (*Note:* This undesirable outcome can occur if your fantasy about doing well or having fun is highly rewarding and the effort of actual preparation is perceived as "too much of a hassle")
      b. Joy, happiness, etc.
      (1) Enjoy the process of performing
      (2) Enjoy the people you are with or the situation you are in
      c. Elation, "natural high"
      (1) Whoops, shouts, cheers

You may also experience other symptoms of heightened arousal that are unique to you, but that you usually experience when you are in stressful circumstances. All of these symptoms are normal. You are **supposed to have them,** and indeed, animals that have similar reactions have a better chance of survival than those that do not react to stressors in this way. Therefore, you may want to remind yourself, even before you read the rest of this book, not to frighten yourself when you experience the physical symptoms of stress. They are not always a red flag of danger, but may rather be the yellow flag of being alive.

Let us add some words of caution. If you experience some of the above symptoms that are *not* usually in your repertoire of stress responses, you should check with your physician to ensure that these symptoms are not indicative of physical illness. For example, having a dry mouth along with frequent urination could signal the beginning of diabetes. Rapid heartbeat and increased blood pressure can also signal health problems. Therefore, if you have any doubts, call your physician and have your symptoms checked.

Remember, stress does not necessarily signify danger, but it is a warning that your body and mind give you that something might be happening that's frightening to you. Humans and animals seem to have this early warning system, which helps them to survive. You may recall Hans Selye's *fight or flight* theory of stress from your school days. This theory states that when an organism senses danger, its body systems prepare to deal with the situation. Selye called this reaction the General Adaptation Syndrome. He described the syndrome as having three stages: an alarm or alerting reaction, a stage of resistance, and the last stage, exhaustion. When Selye first proposed his theory in the 1930s, the only physical systems thought to be involved in this response were the pituitary and adrenal systems. However, later research indicated that almost every chemical system in the body is involved in the stress reaction.

Let's take an example of the *General Adaptation Syndrome.* Let's say that Elsa the lion is standing calmly in the jungle when she senses danger. It could be another beast of the jungle or a natural event such as a fire. Elsa's senses become very keen, and her body prepares to deal with the danger. Once she either gets out of the situation or the danger passes, there is down time during which the overstressed systems that prepared her to get out of danger go back to their resting state. Similar things happen to humans. However, in humans, the stressor does not have to be real danger, it can be a perception of unpleasantness or danger. In humans, *the General Adaptation* response, including the exhaustion stage, can be triggered by situations that you know are not really life-threatening but that you perceive as frightening and unpleasant. Your neurotransmitters (e.g., catecholamines, endorphins, etc.) may be affected. Catecholamines are known to be related to suppressed immune function in laboratory mice. Some evidence exists that this is also true for humans. Suppressed immune function means that you are more susceptible to disease. Increased endorphins such as epinephrine and norepinephrine have been associated with increased levels of blood cholesterol in humans.

You may react to a situation you perceive as threatening as if you were a deer in a forest fire: You will want to get away from the threat as quickly as possible. Many people, unfortunately, perceive speaking in public or other performance situations as their own personal forest fire. They convince themselves that the most useful response is to get out of the danger zone. This is okay if you are never in a situation where you are required to speak or perform in public. What if you are in a profession where being in the public eye and performing is necessary, such as acting, singing, dancing, teaching, or presenting papers? If you are in one of these situations, running away is harmful. If you are an executive trainer, leaving the threatening situation is not okay. If you are trying to break into an industry and need to go through job interviews, running away is not okay.

It Is Not Okay, but You Are Okay Doing It!

When we describe certain outcomes as "okay" or "not okay," we mean that they do or do not result in your accomplishing your long-range goals. While there is no rule of nature, logic, or law that says you *must* accomplish your goals, we assume that you strongly desire to do so, and therefore self-defeating thoughts, emotions, or behaviors are "not okay" within that context. However, keep in mind that your worth as a person does not have to be affected when you do things that short-circuit your long-range goals. It is bad enough that you might choose to avoid a potentially useful, although stressful, situation without your also telling yourself that you are a bad person as a result. We will explain why this is so, both in the next chapter and routinely throughout the rest of the book. For the time being, we would just like you to remember that while certain of your thoughts, emotions, and behaviors may not be helpful to the accomplishment of your long-range goals, you are still basically okay despite your doing, thinking, or feeling them.

How can you tell whether your fear is helpful or self-defeating? First, it would be a good idea to evaluate the situation you are in. Suppose you are camping in the woods and you smell smoke. The first thing to do is to look around you for the source of the smoke and see if it is coming from your cooking source, from one of your fellow campers' cigarettes, or from something larger. It would also be a good idea to contact the local ranger station if possible or to listen to your radio for fire warnings. If you see smoke coming from above and/or hear a warning, then your fear is rational and you need to take the steps necessary to protect yourself.

Let's say, however, that you become terrified when you need to get up and speak at a meeting. How would you evaluate the situation? What are the real threats involved in this situation? Is the situation life-threatening, in reality? Are you going to be physically endangered if you stutter or do poorly? Is your future, *as evaluated by objective means*, on the line or at risk because of one presentation that may or may not go badly? Is this a realistically life-threatening situation, or are you making a campfire into a forest fire?

Is there a way that you can put out the forest fires related to your irrational fears? When you smell the smoke and start shaking, you can say to yourself, "I must be really afraid of this, and the first thing that I need to do is evaluate the situation." You can use this book to work on this and other problems.

Let's go back to the forest for a moment. What if, when you walk into the forest, you encounter a large, hairy animal, such as a bear? Hopefully, you would sensibly retreat from the bear. Unfortunately, for many people who experience performance anxiety, any public performance becomes a big, hairy animal. Is it that way for you? If it is, is your first inclination to run as far away from the performance situation as possible? The choice is yours. You may want to start to ask yourself, "Do I need to see this as a grizzly bear, or would I be better off seeing it as a large teddy bear?"

Find a Useful Level of Stress

Hans Selye taught us about fight or flight and showed that under conditions of perceived danger or real danger, the normal response is either to fight back or to run away if the danger is too great. J.D. Dodson gave us another way of looking at stress. He said that for every activity that we encounter, a certain **level** of stress is necessary and useful. Too much stress does us in by incapacitating us. Too little stress does us in by boring us. The Yerkes-Dodson theory teaches us that a life without stress is a life without accomplishment. Every task you have to face requires a level of stress that is appropriate to the task. If you are climbing stairs, you need to have enough energy to get to the top. If you are fighting a forest fire, you need to have enough energy to fight it. If you treat the stairs like a forest fire, you will probably be overcome, overwhelmed, or frightened. If you treat the forest fire like a flight of stairs, you will probably be burned to death. People who demand that they never experience any stress, interestingly, find that they don't get their jobs done. They don't know, or can't seem to see, the difference between the forest fire and the flight of stairs. Circus trainers know this to be true: Animals that are stressed are motivated to learn. Circus trainers stress their animals by keeping them hungry. If the animal is too hungry, it becomes exhausted and goes to sleep. If the animal is not kept hungry enough, it loses its curiosity. Just enough hunger keeps the animal motivated to engage in new activities.

In each case cited, we saw that physical stress was necessary for accomplishment. If you are like most of the people who are reading this book, you too wish to accomplish a variety of things. You may want to perform on stage. You may want to speak in public. You may want to conduct effective seminars. You may want to be able to express your views at a PTA meeting. You may want to be able to get up in class and give a speech, or give your first presentation to the board of directors at your company.

The stress you feel can defeat you if you add additional stress to your normal stress. You alone create the additional stress for yourself. Every event that's new is stressful. Remember, your body prepares for anything that is unusual as if it were responding to an emergency. Until you have had a chance to learn from your experience, you don't know if you are responding to a forest fire or a flight of stairs. You don't know if it's a grizzly bear or a teddy bear.

Unfortunately, some of you, because of your experiences, both in the past and currently, have learned to see performing in public as a grizzly bear or a forest fire. You may have been laughed at, you may have been criticized—or you may have been called a "listener."

Charles S., a middle-aged social worker, recalled being in a third-grade singing class waiting to be classified by vocal type. He heard a boy being classified as a tenor, a girl being classified as an alto, and someone else being classified as a soprano. When his turn came, he was classified as a "listener." He recalled asking, "What does that mean? Where do I sing?" and could vividly remember his humiliation when his voice teacher explained, "Oh, no, no, you don't sing—you sit and listen to everyone else because you sound so bad."

Experiences like the one Charles described, while not necessarily toxic or deadly, are certainly unpleasant. Charles concluded that he was embarrassed beyond belief and decided that he should never be placed in that position again. Today, Charles won't ever sing in public or even in the privacy of his shower because he doesn't like the sick feeling he gets when he recalls his earlier embarrassment.

How you evaluate both the situation and your body's response to it can either enhance your coping or detract from it. People who suffer from performance anxiety tend to think in ways that detract from their coping ability. Like Gwen and Charles, they turn their butterflies into elephants. Others may experience the same set of physical symptoms, but say to themselves, "Boy, how exciting! Look how excited I am! Look how juiced I am!" They then perform with all of the excitement they feel. Some performers, like the great diva Maria Callas, believe that unless they get so worked up that they throw up before a performance, they are not sufficiently prepared. Callas' nausea never stopped her from singing, but singing certainly was not as much fun for her as it might have been. She was, however, able to overcome and cope with her symptoms of stress, and indeed learned to believe that without her symptoms, she could not perform. She was probably right, because she needed a certain amount of stress in order to do her job of being a leading diva.

How much stress do you need to do your job? Remember, the answer is not zero. The question is not how much stress you would like to experience, but how much stress is necessary to accomplish the task at hand? People who are comatose are not involved. If you are not involved, you won't accomplish anything.

You probably need less stress to mail a letter than you do to present in court, but you need some level of stress even to mail a letter. If you tend to be anxious and also react badly to stressful situations, you may require more energy to mail a letter than others do. You may see even the task of mailing a letter as tremendously frightening and therefore experience a heightened sense of danger.

Most of us, however, do not find mailing a letter dangerous. Some of us would not even consider mailing a letter something to think about. It might be seen as a minor hassle. You may be in your cozy, warm apartment, and you have to get dressed and go downstairs, find the letter box, and maybe find the stamp. Since all of those activities are hassles, your body probably responds appropriately by charging up: Your heartbeat increases, your stomach starts to churn, and you may discover you suddenly have to go to the bathroom before you put on your coat. All of this energy is expended just to mail a letter. What must it be like if you perceive the hassle of finding the stamp and mailing the letter as dangerous? What must it be like if you are suddenly confronted not with a letter to mail, but with a major audition for the job of your life? What must it be like if you perceive the audition as not only an important audition, but the biggest opportunity and the most important chore you could ever have? Many theatrical performers evaluate auditions in just that way, and therefore they don't see it as "just another audition." They tell themselves, "If I get this job, my life will change immeasurably. This is my do or die, make or break audition." They are like the people in

Michael Bennet's musical *A Chorus Line,* who sing about how incredibly and inconceivably important it is to get a particular job. Some thrive and sing and dance appropriately, and others become so frightened that they don't even leave the house.

Civilians may equally see certain events as more than just hassles. It is a hassle to make a cold sales call. You have to gear yourself up to do it. But if you suddenly begin to think not "Oh, well, it's a hassle; too bad," but rather, "I can't stand this; I shouldn't have to do this; how dare I be placed in a job where I have these inconveniences," you may discover that not only do you experience the physical symptoms, you experience them as extraordinarily strong and debilitating. While it may very well be true that at certain times in life there are "do or die," "life or death" events that take place, is taking an exam a life-or-death, once-in-a-lifetime activity? Is calling for a job interview a do-or-die, once-in-a-lifetime, if-I-don't-do-it-I'll-die activity? What we will be doing in the following chapters is helping you to appropriately evaluate the events in your life.

Chapter 3
Anxiety, Shame, Embarrassment, and Guilt

Anxiety Comes in Many Forms

The Case of Carla R: Carla R., age twenty-five, was a budding attorney who refused to bloom. She couldn't bring herself to take the bar exam. She was a good enough student, but she hated exams—in any form. She managed to do well in school, but the "personal cost was too high." Every time she took an exam, she was laid up in bed for a week afterwards," and that was just for a midterm—finals were much worse. Imagine what it would be like for me if the exam were life or death...as the bar exam is!" She hated the fact that she was so anxious, but she knew she couldn't do anything about it: "That's just the way I am; I am not generally anxious, but I do get overwhelmingly anxious whenever I have to take a test."

Setting the "Anxiety Reaction" in Motion

For people in their late forties and older, the face of anxiety is personified by Don Knotts, who played the deputy on the Andy Griffith show and who as an actor on the old Steve Allen show gave "man in the street" interviews in a shaky voice with a blur of fidgets and tics. He was the archetype of the anxiety neurotic, afraid of everything, including his own reactions. His character was endearing. It was vulnerable, and comic, because it was overdrawn. Anxiety, however, is neither endearing nor funny.

While anxiety often prepares you to scan the environment for potential danger, it may also so unrealistically broaden that definition that everything appears to be dangerous. Anxiously scanning the horizon may assist you in preparing to cope with danger by helping you anticipate possible frightening scenarios and the manner in which you might handle them. Anxious scanning, however, could also undermine your ability to cope with danger by presenting various terrifying scenarios that have no solutions.

Answering the "What-If" Question

Anxiety, for those who suffer from it, is experienced as a never-ending series of "what ifs":

- What if I am called upon to speak today?
- What if I look too old?

- What if I shake when I get up to read?
- What if I have unexpected expenses?
- What if I get the promotion or the part?
- What if I don't get the promotion or the part?

Just asking yourself "what if" sets the anxiety reaction in motion. If you believe that you can answer the "what-if" question with a resounding "No big deal!" or "Piece of cake!" you do not experience anxiety, but rather some positive or calming emotion. If you believe that you can answer the "what-if" question with a realistic but heightened awareness of your need to prepare for the anticipated problem areas, you do not experience anxiety, but rather an emotion called concern. If you believe that you have no answer to the "what-if" question, or that any answer will create more and larger problems, you will experience anxiety. If your answer places your physical or social comfort or self-worth on the line, then you may experience a sense of dread and impending doom that is called anxiety.

When the "what-if" question is followed by additional and even more urgent "what ifs," then the accompanying sense of dread is experienced as even more dreadful. You may now become convinced that the potential consequences to you will be at least unacceptable, and at worst unendurable. At this point the anxiety reaction takes on a life of its own and has certain predictable consequences.

People who suffer from anxiety will

1. Find that they can't perform as well when they are anxious, which only tends to increase their anxiety.
2. Tend to postpone or procrastinate about doing things that make them anxious.
3. Postpone indefinitely doing things that make them anxious.

What are your most persistent "what ifs?"
How do you handle them?

Discomfort Anxiety and Ego Anxiety

Anxiety comes about because people ask themselves "what if?" Many people who are anxious answer the "what-if" question with predictions regarding their physical or social comfort or security. They can also answer the "what-if" question with predictions about themselves, their worth, or their esteem. Albert Ellis has named the latter ego anxiety, and the former discomfort anxiety.

Discomfort Anxiety

Answering the "what-if" question with a list of potential dangers to your comfort or physical security is called discomfort anxiety.

The Case of Rev. G.: Rev G., age thirty-five, was a newly ordained minister who was about to be given his first pulpit. When he was in the seminary, he had experienced odd moments of anxiety, but he was able to keep them under control with prayer and by immersing himself in his studies. He typically reassured himself that his nervousness, his sweaty palms, his cottony mouth, his upset stomach occurred because he was inexperienced. He also assumed that once he was ordained and going about the Lord's work, he would be unafraid and no longer nervous. However, as the day approached for him to take his first pulpit, the "worst thing in the world happened." While he was preparing his first sermon, he once again began experiencing all those "dreadful physical symptoms." "What if I can't stop this feeling? What if it happens when I am in the pulpit? What if these feelings incapacitate me?" Rev. G. not only started his anxiety reaction in motion, he fueled it by concluding that his physical symptoms were intolerable and incapacitating, and must be avoided at all costs.

Discomfort anxiety occurs for two reasons:

- We dread the possible consequences of the physical symptoms we experience in specific situations.
- We dread the possible consequences of being hassled.

In what situations do you experience discomfort anxiety?
What is at risk for you?

Ego Anxiety

While people can, and do, set the anxiety response in motion by asking "what-if" questions and answering them with a list of potential dangers to their comfort or physical safety, many people also set the anxiety response in motion by perceiving that their worth, value, or esteem may be at irreparable risk.

> *The Case of Maria J.:* Maria J., age nineteen, wanted to be an opera singer. She had a vibrant soprano voice, but she was fearful of taking classical training because "nobody in my neighborhood had ever even seen an opera, let alone sung in one." She believed that if she even spoke to her parents about her desires, they would reject her. She further believed that her neighbors would consider her desire to be an opera singer as foolish, and she didn't want to appear foolish. As a result, Maria experienced ego anxiety. Anxiety answered her "what-if" question for her. She thought, "What if I became an opera singer? Well, if I took lessons, people would think I was foolish. Therefore, I would be doubly foolish: I would risk not only potential failure but also being thought a fool. I couldn't stand being thought a fool. I couldn't tolerate losing my family and friends' respect. I couldn't take my parents' rejection."

Ego anxiety comes about as a result of believing that your worth as a human is on the line in certain, or all, activities. Many situations are typically associated with ego anxiety:

- Speaking in public
- Going for auditions
- Going for a job interview
- Making cold calls

These are all occasions in which some people may experience ego anxiety because they are placing their worth on the line. They may see themselves as being at risk because of it. As a result, rather than anticipating ways of coping with the potential negative consequences, Maria J. focused on the irrevocable damage to her worth that revealing her desires would bring and therefore stopped herself before she even began.

In what situations do you experience ego anxiety? List them now!

Many people suffer from ego anxiety, as was readily obvious in Maria's case. They equate failing at a task with failing as a person. They see threats to their esteem rather than challenges to their current level of ability. The unpleasant possibility of losing a job becomes the even more threatening possibility of losing their self-worth. As a result, people who suffer from ego anxiety cope with their anxiety by removing the possibility of danger, rather than learning how to cope with the danger. This means that they do not even try to do things that might place their worth, value, or esteem in jeopardy. On the face of it, this solution seems like an effective coping strategy. As a client once remarked, "You can't get eaten by a shark if you stay out of the shark's mouth." In reality, this strategy effectively stops you from attaining the very thing you desire—success in reaching your goal.

You can't sing in the opera if you avoid lessons, training, and auditions. You can't be a practicing attorney if you don't take the bar exam. You can't be a manager without encountering hassles. In fact, you can't accomplish anything if you avoid the very things you need to do to succeed.

> *The Case of Tony L.:* Tony L. was an actor who had had some successes but was by no means a superstar. He had just been asked to audition for a new play when he began to experience anxiety. "I shouldn't have to audition. Auditions are a hassle that I shouldn't have to be put through. What if the director asks me to improvise? I hate improvs...you don't know what to expect. I usually dry up and start to get headaches. I hate this whole process."

Tony was experiencing discomfort anxiety and as a result began to plan ways to avoid the audition; however, he knew that if he did, it might be potentially damaging to his career. Tony, like Rev. G., Carla, and the others in this chapter, was experiencing anxiety because of his conclusion that the situation he was in not only "caused him" to feel uncomfortable and hassled but also placed his ego as well as his comfort, security, and safety at risk.

Underlying ego anxiety is a belief that one's ego, self-esteem, or self-worth is damageable. The damage typically is perceived as being emotional rather than physical, namely, shame, embarrassment, or guilt.

What happens to you when you think that you might experience shame, embarrassment, or guilt as a result of being in a performance situation? If you are like the clients we work with, you will probably attempt to avoid the situations in which these highly unpleasant emotions might be experienced. If the situations have possible legal consequences, as robbery or murder does, you would be wise to avoid them. However, if the situations are performance-related, such as speaking in class, taking an exam, auditioning for a part, or accepting a new and unusual role, you may unfortunately tend to avoid them as well.

What produces these emotions? Just as anxiety results from asking "what if" and concluding that something is at risk, shame, embarrassment, and guilt may come about as a result of your talking to yourself and concluding that you have broken some rule.

Shame on You

What is shame? What do you feel ashamed about? Many people feel ashamed when they don't do as well as they supposedly should. Imagine yourself being told, "Shame on you, a big four-year-old wetting your pants." "Shame on you; didn't you know any better than to scribble on the wall?" "Shame on you, a big girl like you not helping your mother."

"Shame on you" occurs when you or others assume that you *should be* more competent than you currently are. It occurs as a result of an expectation of personal competence based upon your age, status, or experience. You tell yourself that you should be competent in some area because you are old enough to be competent, or because you have had the proper training to assure competence, or because everyone else in your position appears to be competent. Shame, like anxiety, can defeat you, especially when you have your own personal unrealistic shoulds. We'll talk more about that in future chapters.

What happens to you when you discover that you are not as competent as you think you *should be*? What happens to you when you start the anxiety reaction and ask "what if" and conclude that you might appear less competent to yourself and to others? If you are like our clients, you are probably now experiencing both anxiety and either shame, embarrassment, or guilt.

Ooooh, I'm So Embarrassed!

Embarrassment comes about as a result of thinking that your shame, which is personal and private, is about to be made public. You tend to get embarrassed when someone is seeing you behave in a way you would prefer them not to. Joan G. experienced embarrassment at birthday parties when she sang "Happy Birthday." She believed that anyone should be able to sing that simple song, and therefore if she sang off key, as she usually did, it was not only shameful but embarrassing. She especially hated it when she "had to sing" in front of others, who would therefore discover how terrible she sounded. As a result, Joan rarely went to birthday parties in order to avoid feeling ashamed or embarrassed. Ironically, this stratagem was unsuccessful because Joan now discovered that she felt ashamed of not going to the parties: "After all, I am a grown-up. A grown–up shouldn't let a silly thing like a birthday party get her down!"

If you, like Joan, believe that you *should* know how to sing a "silly song like 'Happy Birthday'" and *must* sing well in every and all conditions, not only will you feel personal shame because you didn't do the job that you *should have* done, but you will also feel publicly embarrassed. Even if you do something well, it won't stop people from thinking critically, if they have a mind to. You know that when you stop yourself from singing, or from any other similarly "shameful and embarrassing" act, you're just trying not to offend. But you're not joining in and having fun, and you're possibly limiting your opportunities. As a vocal coach in one of our workshops once said to us, "If you're going to sing off key, at least sing loud, so we can all hear you and help you." Where is it written that you should be singing perfectly? Since you're not a professional singer, you probably shouldn't be singing perfectly.

In fact, even professionals don't sing perfectly all the time. While they'd like to sing perfectly all the time, reality intrudes. They sing with colds, they sing with fevers, they sing with tension. Many times they overcome all of those things and sing beautifully, but, as any reviewer will point out, even the best singers have bad days. And if their shame, embarrassment, or guilt stopped them, we would never have any performers, ever. If the only possible response to a bad performance were shame, guilt, or embarrassment, we would all stop singing, stop acting, and stop speaking; we would become a nation of vegetables. As you may have noticed, vegetables don't sing. Your job, if you choose to take it, is to be a human and not a vegetable.

Thou Shalt Not...!

Shame is personal, embarrassment is public. Guilt is something else again. Guilt comes about as a result of violating major social rules, whether they are real or imaginary. Guilt comes about because we have learned that when we violate these rules, the moral, legal, and social consequences are potentially enormous. For example, people who have been raised to believe that there is an omniscient and omnipotent G–d tend also to believe that certain actions will provoke G–d's wrath. Therefore, they would be well advised to avoid those actions. Guilt, for these people, comes about when they intentionally, and in some cases unintentionally, break these very important rules. Those of you raised in the Jewish or Christian tradition, for example, tend to be aware of the Ten Commandments, and you probably try to avoid breaking these Commandments, not only to avoid G–d's wrath but also to avoid feeling guilty. In fact, most people who have been brought up to live as solid citizens within their culture have some sense of the actions that provoke guilt. As a result, they tend to inhibit those behaviors, and avoid the situations that provoke quilt.

Guilt can therefore be a very useful social tool. If feeling guilty or anticipating that you might feel guilty will prevent you from killing someone, it is worthwhile to feel guilty. However, is there a rule that says you must not sing off key? Is that a major social/spiritual taboo that will bring down the wrath of G–d? Is that one of the Ten Commandments, or is it one of *your* commandments? Do you have a rule that says that you must always be competent, or that says that you must not ever make a mistake? What happens when you violate a personal commandment—do you feel guilty?

What are your personal commandments? Make a list.

We are going to ask you to list your own personal ten commandments. You may find this amusing or annoying, but do you have your own private list? Think of them as your own personal "thou shalt nots" or "I shall nots." "I shall not" or "I must not..."

Many of our clients include these in their list:

- I should never feel uncomfortable.
- I should never make mistakes.
- I should always avoid hassles.

If you believe the last of these commandments, when a hassle occurs, you will probably want to avoid it. You may initially feel good because you have obeyed that commandment, but paradoxically, you will tend to feel worse and worse as time goes on. By obeying your personal commandment of avoiding hassles, you will also avoid opportunities to be successful. You may not go to auditions, or prepare your income tax on time. If you're in a business situation, you may choose not to attend meetings when it would be a good idea for you to do so. Initially this may feel good, because you're not guilty of violating your own personal commandment. However, as time passes, you may feel quite guilty because you have violated an even stronger personal commandment that states, "I should do what's good for me in the long run." This form of guilt not only is experientially greater but also subjects you to a "double whammy." Not only may your guilt increase but it may be accompanied by depression and self–downing because you have deprived yourself of the opportunity to succeed.

The secret is to learn the difference between avoiding behaviors and emotions that might land you in jail and avoiding behaviors and emotions that may initially feel bad but that are ultimately life-enhancing. One of the objectives of this book is to help you recognize when you're feeling appropriate guilt and when you're feeling inappropriate guilt.

Appropriate guilt occurs when you realize that if you were to break some major taboo, the legal, social, and personal consequences would be considerably negative. As a result of this expectation of personally, socially, or legally negative consequences, you might sensibly decide to stop yourself from breaking the taboo, such as deciding not to commit a murder or not to take what doesn't belong to you. Culturally appropriate guilt also includes recognizing that you probably will feel "guilty" if you even consider the possibility of breaking the taboo. Most people, sensibly, do not like the experience of feeling guilty, and so they attempt to stay within the confines of their culture in thought, word, and deed, despite the fact that doing so can be a hassle. This is especially true for people who have been taught by their culture that bad thoughts are equal to bad deeds. However, most people realize that there are significant social, personal, and legal benefits to be gained if they stay within the culturally acceptable limits.

It is important to realize that these limits are prescriptions for culturally acceptable behavior, not implacable demands that declare that you have no choice except to behave in the acceptable way. These limits could be read in the following way: "We strongly prefer that you not violate the taboos. However, we fully realize that as a person who has free will, you can choose to violate them no matter how strongly we would prefer that you didn't. Please be aware, however, that if you exercise your freedom of choice in ways that we disapprove of, we will probably exercise our freedom of choice and punish you."

Is guilt ever inappropriate? Yes. Inappropriate guilt comes about when you punish yourself for violating your own idiosyncratic "rules." While many people do not like to break their own rules, it comes as a shock to them that some of their rules function as taboos and that therefore they will feel guilty when they break them.

The Case of John Q.: John Q, age eighteen, had just started college when he was asked to try out for the debating team. He had never debated any topic, except with his parents, and he had never thought of himself as a scholar, let alone a speaker. He knew from past experience that whenever he spoke to strangers, he got nervous. As John began to consider the request, he noticed that he became anxious and shaky. He began saying to himself, "Wow, wasn't that interesting. I wonder if I should accept this offer...No, I shouldn't accept. If I did, I would have to speak up in public. I am not good at that. I don't like doing things I am not good at. I shouldn't have to be placed in this situation when I am only a freshman. This should be offered only to older students. I don't think I am smart enough to be a debater. If I accepted, people might think that I think I am very smart. I know better than to push myself forward."

John was beginning to feel guilty. He felt guilty because he was contemplating committing the culturally appropriate sin of pride. He also was feeling guilty because some of his idiosyncratic taboos were being challenged: Thou shalt not do things thou art not good at. Thou shalt not think of thyself as a person capable of "scholarship." Thou shalt not push thyself forward.

John's guilt was inappropriate, culturally as well as personally. There were no taboos in John's cultural community against "pushing oneself forward," nor were there taboos against making mistakes or trying to become good at something that was initially difficult. Lastly, there were no taboos against scholarship; in fact, the contrary was more common. When John created these personal commandments for himself, he inappropriately changed his desires into commands and set in motion a series of self–defeating emotions and behaviors that would only serve to reduce his chances for success and happiness—two outcomes he was trying to achieve.

Do you, like John and Joan, experience inappropriate guilt?

In the next chapter, we will not only teach you how to recognize when you are experiencing inappropriate guilt but also demonstrate to you how some of your thoughts can get you into serious emotional trouble if you allow them to remain unchallenged.

Chapter 4

"There Is Nothing Either Good or Bad, but Thinking Makes It So." *Hamlet*, Act II, scene 2

The Case of Sam G.: Sam, age fifty-two, had always wanted to be an actor. As a young man he had had fantasies of performing, but he thought that he could never support a family on an actor's salary, and so he had settled for a "sensible" job. He kept that sensible job his entire adult life, refusing to even consider more adventurous alternatives because "they would make me feel uncomfortable." When he saw an audition notice for a community production of *The Crucible*, which called for a number of men in his age range, he wanted to audition, but as he thought about going to the audition, he experienced an overwhelming sense of shame. He believed that if he got the part, his friends and coworkers would tell him that he was acting irresponsibly. If he didn't get the part, it would prove that his childhood fantasies should never have occurred. Furthermore, he said that he did not want other people "to make me feel stupid."

Many performers, in all walks of life, tell us that other people or situations control their emotions and behaviors:

- "The critic was in the audience, and that's what made me foul up."
- "My boss came into the presentation, and she made me nervous."
- "I realized that I was shaking, and after that I couldn't continue."
- Children, after an accident, have been known to say, "See what you made me do."
- Lovers say, in the words of an old song title, "You made me love you."
- Parents respond to their children's behavior by saying, "You make me feel so _____" (fill in the blank).

These beliefs are common to our culture and many other cultures. Thinking this way appears to be a worldwide phenomenon. Sam's response, therefore, was not unusual. He did not want others to "make him" feel ashamed or stupid, nor did he want others to "make him" think that he was behaving irresponsibly. He believed that the situation he was in and the people with whom he interacted "made him" behave and feel as he did. As a result, Sam let his dreams wither and did not take the risks essential for his own happiness and personal growth. Sam waited for other people to give him permission to have his fantasies. He became a connoisseur of other people's responses. If other people approved of his ac‑ tions, he was happy; but an unkind word could cause him to tremble.

Sam came by his fearfulness honestly. Popular culture, as conveyed by the mass media, teaches us that we have no control over, or responsibility for, our ac‑ tions or our emotions. We are constantly being bombarded with the point of view that we are *fragile goods*—that an unkind sentence or an ill-considered action can leave us permanently scarred. This point of view is in direct contrast to earlier teachings that can best be summed up by the old childhood chant "Sticks and stones may break my bones, but words can never hurt me." Unfortunately, it now appears that many people are more willing to agree with a comment attrib‑ uted to Dorothy Parker, "Sticks and stones may break my bones but words will break my heart."

The current point of view is just that: the *current* point of view. People's points of view about the world and how they function within it seem to be fairly de‑ pendent upon the era in which they live. If you take out your own views and ex‑ amine them, you may find that they have been shaped by your parents, friends, teachers, coworkers, and the media. Some of the points of view that you are pre‑ sented with lead to emotional well-being, but others may lead to emotional dis‑ turbance. In our experience, people who endorse the older version of "sticks and stones" are less likely to upset themselves than those who endorse Dorothy Parker's version. The latter group tends to be more apprehensive about the world and may perpetually scan the emotional horizon, anxiously awaiting the thing that will do them in. As you may recall from the previous chapter, this is ex‑ actly the way people who are suffering from performance anxiety respond. They are fearful that they will become involved in a situation where both their comfort and their self-worth will be on the line, and that they will be incapable of salvag‑ ing either one.

People generally tend to feel more disturbable, fragile, and victimizable when they are taught and *believe* that they are at the mercy of uncontrollable malevo‑ lent forces. If you think this way, you may very well feel helpless, and you will probably place the responsibility for your emotions and actions in other people's hands.

People do not all have the same reactions. Threat, like beauty, is in the eye of the beholder. You may perceive getting up to speak as threatening, exciting, or just a chore. The possibility of failure may be perceived as a horrible event to be avoided at all costs, a stimulating challenge to be worked through, or no big deal. The differing responses that people have to these and other events is dependent not upon the situation, but upon the person's *beliefs* about the situation.

There Are Two Kinds of Beliefs: Rational and Irrational

The situations you find yourself in, even the good ones, are provocative. They provoke you to respond. You can respond to provocations through actions, emo‑ tions, or thoughts. You may often respond reasonably well and feel reasonably good emotionally, and you may, as a result, think that you are "okay," or a good person. However, there will also be occasions when you do not respond reason‑ ably well, or not as well as you would have liked. There will also be occasions for which you cannot make predictions, because these situations are new, and you therefore have no way of predicting how well or poorly you will respond. How do you respond to these provocative, new situations? What emotions do you experience? What actions can you take? Write down your answers to these questions on a piece of paper.

Your answer to these questions is generally based upon your response to one last question, i.e. what are you thinking? How do you perceive the situation you are in? Write your response to this question on the same piece of paper. People generally think about situations in one of two ways: rationally or irrationally. Rational thinking (rB) is logical and factual, and typically can be proven to be true in a noncontestable way. Irrational thinking (iB) is not logical and not factual, and typically cannot be proven in a noncontestable way.

Let us examine a case in point to see how these criteria can be used:

> During final exam week, you see your teacher walking down the hall. You stop and smile and nod hello. The teacher walks right by you with a frown on her face.
>
> What is the most rational observation you can make?
>
> a. You have failed your exam and the teacher does not want to tell you.
> b. The teacher seems not to like you any more.
> c. The teacher is unhappy.
> d. The teacher knows something bad concerning you.
> e. Your teacher walked right by you with a frown on her face.

If your choice was e, you are correct. You have grasped the criteria for rational thinking. While choice e may appear to be nothing more than a simple description of the event that just occurred, it is nevertheless the most rational observation:

- It is factual—the teacher *did* walk by with a frown on her face.

- It is logical—it follows from the observables and *adds nothing to the situation*.

- It is provable in a noncontestable way—there is no controversy over what she did. Others who were there with you at the time saw the same thing. You do not need to get into the teacher's head or point of view. No one doubts that the teacher walked by frowning.

The other choices are neither factual nor logical. They cannot be proven without contest. You have no proof or evidence to support any of them. How can anyone really know if the teacher is trying to protect you from bad news, or indeed has had some bad news concerning you? How can you know if the teacher is unhappy without mind reading? Even if you know her pretty well, you can't really know what's on her mind. The very idea of mind reading is controversial. The authors of this book, who have more than half a century of psychological experience between them, cannot read minds. Mind reading is not included in any standard psychology curriculum.

Let's try another example:

> Susan, a new lawyer, has just had an accident that has confined her to a wheelchair. She has been given a case that requires her to appear in court. She knows that public speaking was not one of her strengths in school. She has never been in

court before, and she is still coming to terms with the intricacies of using her wheelchair.

What is the most rational observation Susan can make?

    a. I will never be able to do the job—there are too many strikes against me.

    b. I am about to experience many challenges.

    c. I have bitten off more than I can chew.

    d. My life is filled with obstacles, and it will continue to be that way forever.

    e. It is really inconvenient that I have to make my first court appearance while I am still learning to manage the chair, but life is rarely convenient.

If you chose either b or e, you have gotten the idea about what makes up a rational thought.

- Susan has no evidence that she will never be able to do the job.

- She won't know if she has bitten off more than she can chew unless she goes through with this experience and makes that discovery.

- While Susan is undoubtedly experiencing many hassles right now, there is no evidence that is nonchallengeable that the hassles that she is presently experiencing are obstacles, or that they will remain obstacles indefinitely.

Again the most rational response is the one that Sergeant Friday in the *Dragnet* TV series would request—"Just the facts, ma'am." People who think rationally tend to stick to the facts and do not offer editorial comment. All the other choices in the two examples offered above are filled with editorial opinion. *If Susan is to accomplish the immediate goals before her, presenting her first case* **and** learning to handle the wheelchair, she needs to be able to stay relatively calm and unafraid.

Choices b and e merely restate the basic facts, require little or no fortune telling or mind reading, and therefore do not require proof to support them. Susan *is* going to experience some challenges. She has not presented in court before, she is not yet an accomplished public speaker, and she is still learning how to use the chair. These situations, by definition, are challenges to her current level of **experience** *and nothing more!* She could also legitimately, and rationally, respond to these events by calling them inconvenient because it might be preferable to experience these challenges one at a time. She might have preferred new challenges to have come at a time when she was better prepared to meet them. However, how often does life provide us with challenges at a convenient time? The description of these life events, by themselves, is not enough to provoke dysfunctional responses. Dysfunctional responses occur when you editorialize.

Leave Editorializing Where It Belongs: In the Newspapers

What do we mean when we say that people editorialize? Do we mean that they are pontificating about something presented to us by the media, such as a news story? Do we mean that they are all journalists expressing opinions regarding the state of the society in which we live? No! What editorializing means, in this context, is that they are embellishing the situation and not reporting "just the facts." Rather than reporting what has happened, they are commenting about it and thereby adding to it. What they are adding, however, cannot be proved. Do you find that you embellish rather than just state the facts?

Let's look at a common example of this type of editorializing:

> You and two friends are going to the movies. On the way to the theater, you witness a fender-bender-type accident. Two cars enter the intersection at the same time from different directions and collide at fairly slow speed, resulting in some body damage to each vehicle. The police come on the scene to take an accident report, and you and your friends are asked to give eyewitness accounts. Circle the most appropriate response below.
>
> a. The two cars entered the intersection and collided.
> b. Car A was probably speeding before it got to the intersection.
> c. The second car was driven by someone who is younger/very old, and the driver must have been careless.
> d. If the intersection had been lit better, the accident would not have occurred.

If you chose a, you are not an editorializer. The other responses all involve some degree of commenting on or embellishing the situation. Response a is the only response that states the facts without adding anything to the situation. If you arrived at the intersection at the time of the accident, how would you know if a car had been speeding previously? How could you prove that the age of the driver had anything to do with that person's driving habits? Unless you have a guaranteed reliable and operational crystal ball, which is very doubtful, how could you prove in a nonchallengeable manner that lack of lighting caused the accident? Remember, editorializing usually upsets straight thinking rather than enhancing it.

Let's discuss another type of editorializing. An editorial can also be an opinion that reflects the biases of the holder. Some opinions are based on fact, and some are based on prejudice. It is ironic that many people treat themselves as if they were their own minority group. They hold opinions about themselves, their worth, and the possibility of their own success that would do a bigot proud. Their own personal bigotry gets directed at themselves, with predictably disastrous results. They feel worthless, and they get in their own way by engaging in self-defeating behaviors. If they could learn to get rid of their personal bigotry and give up their self-directed vendetta, they might live happier lives and achieve more of their goals.

If Susan were to believe, "I will never be able to do the job—there are too many strikes against me," it is likely that she would end up creating a self-fulfilling prophecy. As a result, she might help herself to fail. It is bad enough that she is being challenged at an inconvenient time. If she were to irrationally believe that she would never succeed or that she has bitten off more than she can chew, it would only result in her feeling depressed or anxious and therefore procrastinating or becoming immobilized. Have you ever helped yourself to fail?

The Thinking/Feeling Connection

People's emotions result from the kinds of thoughts they think. People who think rationally tend to experience emotions that help them live their lives in productive or functional ways. For example, you may experience joy, sorrow, irritation, or concern when you are thinking rationally. On the other hand, people who think irrationally tend to experience emotions that are unproductive or dysfunctional. Emotions such as manic elation, depression, rage, and anxiety tend to be dysfunctional or unproductive because you often can become immobilized by these feelings and as a consequence have trouble accomplishing your goals.

You may have noticed that we call certain emotions functional or productive, and others dysfunctional or unproductive. It is not our desire to cast stones at people who experience certain emotions, but merely to call attention to the consequences of feeling these emotions. You may also have noticed that we included both positive and negative emotions as part of both the productive and nonproductive outcomes. This is because, unlike the movies, life doesn't always have happy endings. Many people unfortunately believe that they should never experience negative emotions and that to do so is either a sign of weakness or a danger signal. This is an irrational belief. This particular irrational belief underlies many forms of anxiety, including performance anxiety. The belief that one should not experience negative emotions paradoxically leads to stronger emotional upset than would experiencing the emotions you may be trying to avoid. We will discuss this particular belief, and ways of dealing with it, in many chapters throughout this book. For the time being, remember: Negative emotions are natural, normal, and part of being human, even though they are unpleasant. Learning to cope with negative emotions in productive ways is one sign of maturity.

Do you remember Sam, who was attempting to audition for *The Crucible*? What negative emotions was he experiencing, and how well was he coping with them?

We could describe his emotions as both fear and anxiety. We could additionally predict that if Sam continued to feel these emotions and as a result indefinitely postponed his dreams, he would also feel depressed. Anxiety, fear, and depression are classified as dysfunctional when they stop you from realizing your long cherished goals. Therefore, we can conclude that Sam was not effectively coping with his negative emotions.

What was really stopping Sam? Was it the recognition that he had an opportunity to finally fulfill his dreams of auditioning and thereby possibly getting a part? Was it his resulting fear and anxiety, or was it the way he perceived the situation and its consequences?

What do you think Sam was telling himself? Our experience shows that his perceptions caused him to feel the way he did. He thought or *said to himself,* "If I did get the part, people might disapprove and think that I was foolish. If I don't get the part, it will only show how unrealistic my fantasies were and that I never should have had these fantasies in the first place."

As you can readily see, Sam's thoughts were very much related to his feelings. When Sam thought that he would appear foolish and that it would be horrible to be seen as foolish, he had no alternative except to feel anxious and fearful. However, while his emotions may be very related to his thoughts, he does have alternative ways of perceiving the situation. Emotions evolve as a result of your thinking about, perceiving, and evaluating the situations you are in. Once you think a dysfunctional thought, your emotions are likely to be dysfunctional as well. If you reevaluate the situation and think about it differently, and possibly rationally, your emotions will probably be functional and appropriate as well. Remember that functional and appropriate does not always mean pleasant. If the situation you are in is unpleasant, pleasant feelings would not be appropriate.

Let's take another typical situation:

Steve, a thirty-five-year-old executive, is about to order lunch. He is looking at the menu when he panics.

- Does everyone in the world experience panic while looking at a menu?
- Do you?
- Why did Steve panic?
- What happened to him while he was looking at the menu?
- What was he thinking?

Steve found himself in a situation that was all too familiar to him. He was not going to be alone at lunch. He was being joined by some coworkers and his supervisor. He was trying to choose what he would eat for lunch.

- Now, would you feel panic in this situation?

Steve "knew" that he had trouble making decisions. He thought that if he made the wrong decision, he might appear foolish.

- What emotions would you be experiencing now if you were Steve?

Steve also thought that if he appeared foolish, as reflected by his decision as to what to order for lunch, his coworkers would lose respect for him and he might even be denied promotion. He began to fret about the possible dire consequences to his career. He imagined himself being fired, and also posited that he would never be able to get another job. He then began to berate himself for his timidity because he knew that "real executives" were fearless decision makers. Since Steve was not good at decision making, he convinced himself that he would never succeed.

- If you thought like Steve, would you also feel panic?
- Did the menu *make* Steve panic?

The situation in which Steve found himself was provocative. It provoked his thinking. Some of his thinking was rational—logical, factual, and truthful. Some of his thinking was irrational—illogical, unfactual, and not truthful.

Steve's rational thoughts:

- I have trouble making decisions.
- If I make the wrong decision, I *might* appear foolish.
- If I appear foolish, *some* of my coworkers *might* lose respect for me, and this *might* influence my career.

Steve's irrational thoughts:

- I must never appear foolish.
- I must control the way people think about me.
- If people think badly of me, I will fail.
- All successful executives are fearless decision makers.

- No successful executives ever appear foolish to their coworkers or superiors.
- Any failure would be an unmitigated disaster.
- If I failed, I could never recover.

Steve's rational thinking did not get him in trouble. It is probably true that he has trouble making decisions in many areas of his life. It is equally true that many people (but not all) who have this problem experience career difficulty. It is also true that people who make the wrong decision *may* appear foolish to others, and that this *might* also affect their careers. If Steve had thought only these thoughts, he might have used them to motivate himself to take corrective action without panic.

Steve also had some irrational thoughts that were stronger and intensely more provocative. He devoutly believed that all foolish people are failures. This is insupportable. Even a casual perusal of the news, shows us that people of power and stature often do foolish things on a daily basis. If it were inevitable that the consequence of foolishness were failure, then there could not be successful people in the world because ultimately we all will do some foolish things over the course of our lifetimes.

Steve also strongly believed that he could avoid appearing foolish. This too is insupportable. We have all had the experience of doing something well, only to be told that someone else thought our actions were not as good as we thought. We can *try* to behave in a sensible way, but we can't *guarantee* that everyone will see our actions as sensible. We can never prove that we can control the thoughts and evaluations of others.

Steve's thoughts about executive fearlessness were equally irrational, as was his belief that if he was fired, it would be the end of the world. It is neither logical, factual, nor provable that all executives are fearless, or that all people who get fired remain unemployed for eternity (even in a bad economy).

Irrational Beliefs Come in Four Flavors

Steve's irrational thoughts about the situation he was in are examples of a few of the kinds of irrational thinking that get people into trouble. All of the different types of irrational thinking can typically be grouped under four headings: demandingness, awfulizing, low frustration tolerance, and global rating of self and others.

1. *Demandingness* refers to a constellation of beliefs that can also be called "musts."

- The world *must* be the way I want it.
- My body *must* respond as I want it to.
- I *must* never experience any unpleasantness or hassles.

What were Steve's musts?

Steve demanded that he must not have problems making decisions. He further demanded that he must never appear foolish and that others must not think him foolish. He thought that if he did appear foolish, he must not suffer any negative consequences.

2. *Awfulizing* refers to assuming that bad events are more than bad—they are awful or catastrophic, or may even signal the end of the world.

   - It would be terrible if I shook in public.
   - It was awful that the critic came to that particular performance.

   Was Steve indulging in awfulizing?

   Steve was an awfulizer as well. Not only did he demand that he never have difficulty or appear foolish, but he also thought that it would be awful if he appeared to have difficulty or appeared foolish to others. He awfulized about both the short- and long-term consequences of his apparent aberrant behaviors.

3. *Low frustration tolerance, or LFT,* refers to a constellation of beliefs that assume that hassles and inconveniences are not to be endured. The hallmark of an LFT sentence is the phrase "I can't stand it."

   - I can't stand it when things go wrong.
   - I can't stand it when I am uncomfortable.
   - I can't stand it when I have to perform.

   Does Steve have LFT?

   Steve's LFT takes the form of telling himself that he couldn't stand both the pressures of making a decision and the probable consequences of making a bad one. He also experienced LFT about having to be placed in situations in which any decision making was required, including making even minor decisions such as ordering lunch.

4. *Global rating of self and others* refers to a constellation of beliefs that assume that one's entire worth or value is determined by a single and possibly singular deed.

   - If I fail at this task, I am a total failure.
   - My boss criticized me. He is a total louse.
   - Since I passed the exam, my self-esteem has been greatly enhanced.

   Does Steve rate himself globally?

   Steve believes that he will be totally ineffective if he makes a bad decision. He believes that others would rate him as totally bad and worthless if they either discovered his poor decision-making capabilities or found out how anxious he was about decisionmaking. He also assumes that all executives are perfect decision makers and therefore are totally effective at all times, which automatically reinforces his thoughts that he is ineffective.

Not everyone endorses all of the types of irrational thinking in every situation he or she is in. Since Steve tended to be globally anxious, his repertoire of types of irrational thinking was larger than most. You may discover that you are a specialist in one type of irrational thinking, rather than being a generalist like Steve. Nevertheless, we have found that people who experience dysfunctional emotions in specific situations tend to be endorsing their unique type of irrational beliefs. What are your favorite irrational beliefs? You may want to go back to the list of feelings and thoughts regarding new situations that you wrote down earlier and see if any of the thoughts you listed fit into the four categories of irrational thinking.

Examine the following chart to see if you experience the same set of consequences as our clients do when you endorse one or more of the most common irrational beliefs. It has been our experience that most, although not all, of our clients typically experience these specific types of disturbance when they tenaciously cling to these particular irrational beliefs.

Chart 1
Common Irrational Beliefs (iB's) and Their Consequences

iB's	Consequences		
	Emotion	*Behavioral*	*Physical*
Demands	Anger	Violence, inappropriate outbursts, shunning, quitting	
	Frustration	Aggression, procrastination	
	Depression	Withdrawal, changes in eating and sleeping patterns, lack of concentration, crying, lack of sexual or other pleasure, sexual dysfunctions, suicidal thoughts	
Awfulizing	Anxiety	Avoidance	S T R E S S
	Fear	Withdrawal	
	Panic	Running away	
LFT	Anxiety	See above	
	Frustration	Procrastination	
	Anger	See above	
Global Rating	Depression	See above	
	Shame	Self-downing, procrastination	
	Embarrassment	Procrastination	
	Guilt	See depression	

Performers, like other people, tend to endorse a variety of irrational beliefs that contribute to their emotional disturbance. The following chart lists many irrational beliefs that performers tend to endorse:

Chart 2
Common Performance-Related Irrational Beliefs (IBs)*

I. *Demands*

A. I must perform perfectly.

B. I must be perfectly prepared.

    a. I'm not ready yet—I must not perform until I am.

C. I must be seen (heard, etc.) as I perceive myself to be, i.e., perfectly prepared and competent.

    1. I must not be seen/heard as the observer (casting director, critic, audience) prefers to see/hear me.

D. I must not reveal too much of my self to others via my act, performance, speech, art work, etc.

E. I must not experience any discomfort in performance.

F. I must not experience any discomfort in preparation for performance.

G. I must not experience any discomfort while thinking about preparing or performing.

H. I must be acclaimed after my performance, audition, etc.

    1. All my hard work in preparation, audition, performance, etc., entitles me to the effortless recognition and acclaim that I must have.

    2. Any delay in acclaim is intolerable.

I. I must achieve stardom, fame, etc., quicker than at my current rate of progress.

J. My life must not change in any undesirable way as a consequence of my performance.

II. *Low Frustration Tolerance*

A. I can't stand the hassle of...

    1. Preparing.

    2. Practicing.

    3. Auditioning.

    4. Waiting for a reply.

    5. Possibly being rejected.

    6. Possibly being accepted.

    7. Performing.

    8. Having to develop a track record/reputation.

    9. Having to live up to my reputation.

    10. Having to meet the public.

*This chart is taken from M.W. Robin, "Overcoming Performance Anxiety: Using RET with Actors, Artists, and other 'Performers,'" in *Innovations in Rational-Emotive Therapy*, ed. W. Dryden and L. Hill (Newbury Park, Calif.: Sage, 1993).

B. I can't stand the physical discomfort I experience when I...
   1. Meet the public.
   2. Have to deal with unpleasant people.
   3. Think about performing.
   4. Prepare.
   5. Practice.
   6. Audition.
   7. Get rejected.
   8. Get accepted.
   9. Perform.

III. *Catastrophizing*
   A. It's the end of the world if...
      1. I don't do well (perfectly).
      2. I am seen as less then perfectly competent and prepared, i.e., I
         a. Get a bad rating.
         b. Get negative comments.
         c. Get a bad review.
         d. Reveal my "secret-self."
      3. Experience any discomfort.

IV. *Global-Rating*
   A. The World is Utterly Terrible because...
      1. Its requirements are too hard.
      2. Its requirements are too inconvenient.
      3. It has rules at all.
   B. I am Totally Worthless When...
      1. I believe I have done poorly or not achieved my "personal best."
      2. I feel any discomfort.
      3. Others rate me as performing poorly.
   C. Others are Completely Rotten/Stupid When...
      1. They rate me negatively and I don't deserve it.
      2. They rate me positively and I don't deserve it.
      3. They don't understand/give me credit for my hard work, preparation, and anxiety.

All human beings think both rationally and irrationally about their lives. We are capable of both logical and illogical thought. Dr. Albert Ellis, our friend and teacher, whose work infuses this book and provides the foundation upon which it rests, reminds us that people are born thinking irrationally but later either learn or discover how to think rationally. We typically learn to think rationally because we discover that the consequences of rational thinking are usually more personally desirable and beneficial than the results of irrational thought.

Shakespeare was right —there *is* nothing good or bad but thinking makes it so. It is how we think that *determines* how we feel—not the situation we are in, not our past, not our parents, and certainly not anything over which we have no direct control. Nothing *forces* us to feel or act the way we do.

The Good News About the Awful Past

We frequently meet people who tell us that they were taught, as children, that they were stupid or were destined to be failures, and that that is why they think and feel as they do. "I can't help it. This is the way I think. I was taught that if I did something stupid, I am a totally stupid person. My mother taught me that losers quit and quitters lose. How can I help the way I think?"

We are bombarded by messages and information all day long. You automatically filter out some of these messages, yet you keep and pay attention to others. The ones you pay attention to are the ones that you believe are helpful to your functioning or survival at a particular time in your life. Many children unhappily discover that in order to survive in their particular homes, not only do they need to listen to negative messages about their worth, they also have to act as if they believed them. The more they act in accordance with their parents', or other important people's opinions of them, the more they come to internalize those opinions and believe them to be true.

The longer you practice these beliefs, and the longer they go unchallenged, the more likely you are to see yourself as a victim of a hostile and unforgiving world. People forget that, alongside the negative messages, they probably also heard some positive ones. If this happened to you, you may have ignored those instances or discounted them as being unimportant. You may have *chosen* not to be affected by the positive messages, possibly because they were so unusual, or possibly because they appeared to be false. You may discover that parental teachings about Santa Claus or the Easter Bunny, while benign or delightful, are largely irrelevant to your life and daily existence. Therefore, you may begin to selectively perceive only those instances that support your growing conviction that you, and the world you live in, are pretty awful.

While the picture, for those who made this discovery, seems pretty bleak; the outlook is *not* grave. The good news about the awful past is that as humans, we *learned* to think in both adaptive and maladaptive ways. Even if most of your thinking is currently unproductive, and even if you have a biological tendency to continue to awfulize or indulge in other irrationalities, *You can learn to think clearly about the past, present, and future and therefore not only feel better but get better!*

"But wait," we hear you saying, "I can't help the way I feel, think, and act—I was taught to be the way I am by my parents, or by my friends, or by the **prejudiced world we all live in**. No matter how much I try to think, act, or feel differently, I still live in a world that is very mean and that controls me in very real ways."

No one denies that the world you live in, good or bad, has some effect on your thoughts, feelings, and actions. However, its effect, good or bad, is in direct proportion to the amount of power you hand over to it. The world you live in, and the people in it, affects you by provoking you, not by controlling you.

You are reminded daily of the volatility of some adolescents who engage in antisocial behavior and then blame their victims. One case in particular stands out: One teenage boy stabbed another, who was a stranger to him, because he was "being looked at"! If you believe that merely being looked at doesn't *force* a teenage hoodlum to stick a knife into the observer and that he can, and should, learn to exercise some self-control, you may possibly be willing to examine the belief that others force you to think, feel, and act the way you do.

There is no inevitable way to think about things. You generally are not powerless over your thoughts, emotions, and actions. You can learn to overcome your habitual ways of thinking, feeling, and acting. If you have been practicing unproductive, irrational thinking for decades and have therefore been suffering from performance anxiety for years, *you can learn to overcome your performance anxiety and perform without fear.*

The means to this end are presented, in detail, in the next set of chapters. However, the approach we will take can be summarized simply:

1. Learn to take your emotional temperature. Are your emotional and behavioral responses functional or dysfunctional?
2. Learn to identify your irrational thoughts.
3. Learn to challenge your irrational thoughts.
4. Replace your irrational thoughts with more effective or productive thoughts.
5. Practice, practice, practice until this new way of thinking is second nature.
6. Tolerate relapses and plateaus until you achieve your goal.

Chapter 5
Tools of the Trade

In the previous chapters, we've looked at what performance anxiety is and discussed how it affects us emotionally, behaviorally, physically, and cognitively. We've described what stress is, and various physical responses to stress. The rather interesting and peculiar ways in which people who make themselves anxious think have also been described.

What do we do with all of this? How do you respond to it? What can you do when you make yourself anxious? Cognitive-behavioral psychology, e.g., rational-emotive behavioral therapy (REBT), outlines a number of approaches that can be effective, if people use them. What can you do to help yourself when you've suddenly discovered that you're anxious? You may have made yourself anxious by thinking, "Oh, this is terrible; I can't stand it," or by thinking, "If I don't get this job, it will be the end of the world." When you think these thoughts, you make yourself very uncomfortable. You may also discourage yourself from making future efforts to reach your goals.

The good news is that you don't have to feel discouraged or anxious. You can make yourself not only feel better but get better in any situation you create inside your head. The technique is called *disputing*. This technique, as originated by Albert Ellis and used herein, means arguing with yourself. What we're going to teach you to do is to diffuse the thoughts that upset you. Disputing will help you to think differently about the situations you're in, so that you can improve your performance and achieve your goals.

Arguing with Yourself Doesn't Always Mean You're Crazy
There are three types of disputes. The first type of dispute is called the empirical dispute. You are cast as Sergeant Friday in *Dragnet*. You may remember Sergeant Friday from an earlier chapter. He is the detective who asks for only the facts, without embellishment, and nothing more. You're going to ask yourself, "What are the facts?" Earlier in the book, we said that people who think irrationally don't use good evidence. What evidence do you have for thinking the way you do? When you say to yourself, "Oh, God, I will never get another job if I don't get this one," is that totally true? Do you really intend to convince yourself that there are no other jobs on the face of the earth except this one and that therefore if you don't get this one, the job market will dry up entirely? What you probably mean is that this is the job you most desire in all the world, and it would be nice if you could get it. This is certainly true, but it's not the only job. If you think to yourself, "If I make a mistake when I'm speaking, I will never be able to recover and peo-

ple will think I am totally and completely moronic," you will be quite upset and may end up engaging in self-downing. What evidence do you have for this thought? What are the facts of the case? Is it true that everyone in the world will think you're stupid? What evidence do you have for that? Most people would consider this kind of evidence, *mind-reading*. How do you know what your listeners are thinking? If they don't have the bad sense to tell you what they're thinking, why choose to believe that they want to spend their time condemning you and that they will never allow you to recover? What do you think about at conferences? Are you always thinking about the speaker? How do you know that your listeners are thinking about you? Can you prove that you are never going to recover even if you do a poor job and your listeners take note of it?

The best response that you can make, as we said before, is to stick to the facts. You may have made a mistake, and that is certainly true. Indeed, you may feel uncomfortable. That is equally true. You would prefer not to have made that mistake. Those are the facts! When you add additional information, editorialize, or think illogically, you'd be well advised to make your next response a dispute.

Take Your Emotional Temperature!

How do you know when to dispute? One way to know is to take your emotional temperature. How do you feel after you think illogically or irrationally? You usually feel worse. Your emotions often take a nosedive. You begin to experience those emotions that we have called dysfunctional because they do you in and stop you from achieving your desired goals. In other words, you experience anger or rage, anxiety, depression, or inappropriate shame, embarrassment, or guilt. To take your emotional temperature, ask yourself, "How am I feeling emotionally, right now?" If your answer is "depressed" or one of the other dysfunctional emotions, it is time to dispute!

Imagine yourself speaking in front of an audience and making an error. You suddenly experience discomfort, and possibly panic; you certainly are not feeling good. Even though it seems like it's going to take you minutes to recover from this, in the next fifteen seconds, you could take a calming breath and then say to yourself, "Wait, calm down. Humans make mistakes all the time. I have no idea what they are thinking, and I can recover." Then go right back into your presentation. This may seem like an eternity, but people who have done this report that they can do it in under ten seconds. As you get better at disputing, you will probably be able to do it in even less time. If you read the above sentences aloud and time it, you will discover that this takes very little time to say. People will not know that you are saying this to yourself. No one will care. Your listeners will only see you doing your job of speaking in public.

Sergeant Friday to the Rescue!

Empirical disputing (factual disputing) asks for rules, asks for evidence, and asks for facts. You can ask yourself, as we do, "Where is it written that you have to behave the way you want to behave?" Where is it written that you must be perfectly calm at all times and in all situations? The most general dispute that we can give you is to ask yourself, "Where is it written that if you're doing something new, you should do it perfectly?" Most people who are unaccustomed to performing do it imperfectly. In fact, the odds are very good that when you first start out doing anything new, you will do it clumsily and with errors. You're expected to make mistakes. When you catch yourself making one, rather than disturbing yourself by thinking, "I shouldn't be doing this—oh, how terrible; oh, how awful; I'll never recover," it would be better to think, "There I am being human, making mistakes, but at least I'm showing improvement. At least I'm capable of learning." If, however, you think, "This is the end of the world. I'll never be able to do it," remember that you have no evidence that you'll never be able to do it. You probably thought that about learning to tie your shoelaces when you were a child. You probably finally learned to do that. As a child you may have believed that you would never be able to ride a bike, but many of you learned to do that, too. There are many things that you thought you never could do that you eventually learned to do. The evidence, therefore, is much stronger for your ability to learn than for your ability to be incompetent or your inability to learn.

When you make a statement that has no support behind it, you make yourself feel bad. You are doing this to yourself, but, happily, you can stop. You can't control other people's actions, but you can always control your own. You can learn to say, "Wait, I don't have to think that way. What's my proof for the things I'm thinking? Where's it written that I have to think or feel the way I'm thinking or feeling?" Begin to change not only your thoughts but the emotions that occur as a result of your thoughts and the behaviors that go along with those emotions.

Is This the Proper Tool for the Job?

The second type of dispute is the pragmatic, or practical, dispute. It asks a very basic question: "How is this thought or action helping me accomplish my goal?" When you think, "I'll never get good at performing in public" or "I'll never learn this dance routine" or "I'll never learn to speak without stuttering," how does this help you to accomplish your goal of learning to speak, dance, or perform in public? *Never* means that you can't ever or never will accomplish what you want to accomplish and that there's no hope. It's more likely that you will eventually learn the skills you need. How does it help you to tell yourself that you never will? Does it enhance your pleasure or your opportunity for success? Undoubtedly, it does not. What it does do is make you feel miserable. *Never* becomes a self–fulfilling prophecy. If you say, "I never will," you may want to give up. If you stop trying to do something, you really never will do it. Therefore, by predicting a dire future, you're almost ensuring it. A better response for you to make would be to predict eventual success after much clumsiness. More evidence exists for this type of prediction than the "never" prediction.

You can dispute your behaviors just as you can dispute your beliefs using the practical dispute. Procrastination is a behavior you can dispute. What is procrastination? Procrastination is delaying what inevitably needs to be done to accomplish a goal. How does it help you to delay when you are preparing to deliver a speech? How does it help you to delay getting head shots ready, if you are an actor or an actress? How does it help you accomplish your goal? Nine times out of ten, the answer is that it doesn't help at all. Procrastination usually makes matters worse. What's your alternative? You could irrationally tell yourself, "Here I go again doing things that are stupid. Why do I always do these dumb things?" or you might equally irrationally say, "Having to do these things is too much. I can't stand all these hassles. I hate how I feel whenever I am faced with a hassle."

What would be a more truthful and therefore more practical and helpful statement? The thought that "This is a hassle, but not an impossible nightmare" is more useful. "I don't help myself in the long run when I procrastinate. Maybe I'd better remind myself that I can stand the discomfort of doing what needs to be done" is more useful. The pragmatic or practical dispute alerts you to the fact that you are using the wrong tool to accomplish your task.

You Can't Perform Brain Surgery Using Inadequate Tools!

I once worked with a businessman who had the goal of learning to be an effective and well-respected manager. During one of our sessions, we worked on his "flash pot" anger. Whenever anything went wrong, from the most significant to the most trivial, he would explode. I asked him how this anger was helping him to accomplish his goals of being effective and well respected. He replied, "It doesn't, but how am I going to get people not to make mistakes unless I yell at them?" I again asked him how his yelling *prevented* his coworkers from making errors. He said, "It doesn't, but if I can't yell, I don't know what else to do."

His behavior was ineffective because he was not only thinking irrationally, he was also using an ineffective tool to do the job. To persist in using an ineffective tool is equally self-defeating, and I pointed this out to him. I used the analogy of a brain surgeon who had developed a new technique. I asked him, if he needed a brain surgeon would he go to one who could only perform the operation by going in through the rectum. His response was a shocked, "But you can't do that!" I replied, "*Exactly*, and when you yell at your employees to get them to not make mistakes, you are performing rectal brain surgery!" Over time I got him to stop yelling, to dispute his irrational thoughts, and to develop a more effective managerial style.

Let Pollyanna Help You Build a New Frame for Your Picture

Another practical approach is called *reframing*. When you reframe something, you put it in different surroundings or a different context. It is certainly unpleasant not to be offered the part you wanted, but at least you got some role in the play. It is not pleasant to discover that you don't have sufficient dexterity to play the guitar like Andrés Segovia, but it is certainly pleasant to discover that you are playing better than you did last week, or that you are playing better than others who have had the same number of lessons. When you reframe your situation in this way, you may be able to shed some lightness upon the doom and gloom that you are temporarily experiencing.

Some people call this approach behaving like Pollyanna because they are acting like the little girl in Eleanor Porter's novel who played the "glad game." She would get people to see that their lives weren't so bad after all. For example, she might say to someone with a broken leg, "Don't feel sad; at least you have a leg to break. There are people who have no legs, you know." To someone who had no legs, she might have responded, "Don't feel bad; you have the use of both your arms, and your brain is still functioning—and there is lots you can do with them." While these sentences may sound a bit saccharine in a world of pervasive cynicism, they are true nonetheless, and if you used them, you might, like Pollyanna, feel glad. It is also interesting to note that Pollyanna has been supported by research scientists. In 1981, Dr. Thomas Wills developed a theory called *down-*

ward comparison. He discovered that people tend to feel happier if they compare themselves to others who have less than themselves. If the idea of acting like Pollyanna sends you screaming to the refrigerator to get a lemon to suck on, remind yourself that reframing and downward comparison are better tools than doom, gloom, or procrastination. You could also remind yourself, as some of us did in the 1970s, "If life hands you a lemon—make lemonade!"

Reframing can also be accomplished when you reconsider the language you use and go from "hot" language to "cool" language. Describing things as "terrible," "awful," and "the end of the world" may seem like an appropriate thing to do, but it generally results in your feeling increasingly worse and out of control. Try substituting instead the cooler language of "unfortunate," "inconvenient," "unpleasant," or "disappointing" and see what happens to your emotions. Many of our clients have taken great delight in attempting to tease us with such sentences as:

- "Gee, Mrs. Lincoln, it is most unfortunate that your husband was shot."

- "I am so sorry that they had to remove your leg…It must be rather inconvenient for you."

- "It must be very frustrating to have been rejected."

While these cooler sentences may seem to miss the emotional mark by trivializing the magnitude of the situation; in reality they are more helpful than their hotter alternatives. It *is* highly unfortunate when someone dies. It *is* very inconvenient not to have both legs. It *is* frustrating to be rejected. Making it more than that may seem satisfying for a moment, but to call things tragic, horrible, and awful only intensifies the pain and distress you feel without helping you solve the problem presented by the situation. The pain and suffering you may feel in performance situations can also be ameliorated by choosing appropriate but cooler substitutes for your experience.

Try to Lower Your Emotional Thermostat

Hot Phrases	Cooler Phrases
It would be *horrible* if I didn't get the job or part.	It would be *disappointing (frustrating)* if I didn't get the job or part.
It would be *depressing* to be given a bad review.	I would be *very sad (unpleasant)* to be given a bad review.
I couldn't stand it if I stuttered when I spoke.	*I wouldn't like it* if I stuttered while I spoke, but I could take it.
I feel *overwhelmed* when I have to get up in public.	I feel *challenged* when I have to get up in public.

It is ironic that many of us in the 1990s are cautious about the kind of language we use when we talk to someone else, but not when we talk to ourselves. We have been told, and we believe (rightly or wrongly), that the language we use might at the least meet with the disapproval of the listener, and at worst "maim" or "permanently scar" the emotions of the listener. Many of us, therefore, choose politically correct language in order to be sensitive to the needs of the listener.

While the authors of this book do not wish to be insensitive to the responses of those people who have been subjected to language that they would have much preferred not to hear (and that is currently illegal in some states), we do wish to point out that not everyone experiences the same emotions in response to words spoken by others. Some people are enraged when they are confronted by politically incorrect language, others are disappointed, and still others are amused or saddened by the speaker's stupidity. Some consider the source of the information and gauge their reaction accordingly.

The irony is that while people appear to experience a diversity of responses when hearing others speak and may or may not be disturbed by what they say, the words we speak to ourselves appear to have a much greater power to disturb us. The author's research and clinical experience provide ample evidence to support the belief that when we speak to ourselves irrationally, or use hot phrases, we generally disturb ourselves, get ourselves angry or depressed, and typically immobilize ourselves. If we call someone with red hair "Red," that person may not like it, may be amused by it, or may be proud that someone has given him or her a nickname. When we call ourselves "hopeless" or say to ourselves that we "can never be happy" unless a certain thing occurs, we do not seem to amuse ourselves but only seem to make ourselves **miserable.** Perhaps we should be as careful about how we speak to ourselves as about how we speak to others.

There are many alternative ways of thinking and behaving. First, it would be best to recognize when your thoughts or actions are doing you in. You can do this by utilizing pragmatic disputing, empirical disputing, or philosophical disputing, which is a more "elegant" way to think.

What Does the "Old Philosopher" Say?

The third type of disputing is the philosophical dispute. You may not realize it, but you have a philosophy of life. We have never met anyone who didn't have a philosophy of living, even if he or she didn't call it that. Philosophers provide us with definitions about the world, interpersonal relations, and individuals. Plato, for example, defines birds by their ability to fly and concludes that a *good* bird is one that flies very well. He also considers man to be a creature capable of thought and concludes that a *good* man is one who thinks very clearly. You may believe that life should be easy, and therefore conclude that a difficult activity is not (or should not be) part of life. That's a philosophy about how life should be. You may also hold cherished beliefs about how you *should* behave towards others, or how others *should* behave towards you.

For example, you may have a philosophy that assumes that intelligent people need to apply effort only to accomplish truly difficult things. You may also assume, philosophically, that having to apply effort to accomplish an "easy" thing is proof that you are not being an intelligent human. Therefore, if you encounter difficulty with a task that others find easy, your philosophy may create a problem for you: You may be "forced" to conclude that either you are not very intelligent or you are not human.

You may believe that you're supposed to do things effortlessly. That's another philosophy. You may believe that good deeds always should be rewarded. You may believe that a little work deserves a big payoff. These are all philosophical positions. You may believe that if you have a little failure, it means total failure, and that you will never be happy.

In reality, even if you failed at many things in life, you could probably still be happy and still be successful. The philosophical dispute helps you to look at your hassles in light of your total life philosophy and to place them in the proper perspective without giving them too much weight. Our tendency as humans is to magnify the events in life that are rated as unfavorable. Let's say that you are a dancer who has just auditioned for a major touring company. While executing the final routine for the choreographer, you slipped and missed a jump, so that you landed clumsily rather than gracefully. Is this the end of the world, or is it just an error made during an audition? If you tell yourself, "This is the worst thing that could have happened, and I will never get a job as a dancer again," you will probably feel miserable. You could use the empirical dispute to challenge this, or you could use the philosophical dispute. The empirical dispute (Sergeant Friday to the rescue) asks for proof or evidence that you could never get another dance job again. If you use the philosophical dispute (imagine, *me* a philosopher), you might ask, "Could I live a satisfying life even if I don't get this important job or dance with this company ever?" This dispute puts the audition into its proper perspective in your life. If you never got this job, you could probably still be happy. You might not be as happy, as successful, or as contented as you assume you would have been had you gotten what you wanted most, but you could still experience some happiness, some contentment, and some success. Would you rather experience some success or no success? Our suspicion is that most of you would say that some *is* better than none. If you agree that some is better than none, you are already beginning to change your philosophy. You have begun to question your assumptions about what makes up a *satisfying* life.

Does a satisfying life contain only getting exactly what you want in all situations? Could you be *satisfied* with other results? You get yourself in trouble if your philosophy is too narrow. Life is very complex and has many components. Do you intend to tell yourself that you have only one component or that your *entire* happiness is predicated on the attainment of one goal? We call that kind of philosophical reasoning an *irrational equation*. An irrational equation places all of your eggs in one basket and as a result *guarantees* that you can never be happy, successful, or contented!

A Sampler of Irrational Equations Guaranteed to Make you Anxious!

I = my work
I = having people dependent upon me
My worth = getting *everything* I want
My happiness = getting *everything* I want
My worth = acting perfectly
My happiness = acting perfectly
Effort = anxiety

What are your irrational equations?

You may notice that the left side of the equation equals the right side, so therefore if the right side of the equation isn't achieved, the left side = *zero!* You are saying that if, for example, you don't work or if you lose your job, you don't exist! Do you really want your existence to hinge on only one element? If people are no longer dependent upon you (as may occur when your children leave home), **do you cease to exist?** If you cannot achieve perfection (as you undoubtedly cannot), does your *total* worth, happiness, success, or ego cease to exist? If your philosophy contains these irrational equations, then every time you invoke them, you place your worth, happiness, contentment, success, ego, etc., at risk. As a result, you will continue to experience anxiety, panic, or other dysfunctional and self-defeating emotions.

When you challenge these irrational equations and conclude that your worth, ego, success, happiness, etc., is multi-dimensional, you are well on the way to developing a more effective, satisfying, and life enhancing philosophy of life. Is your total happiness in life dependent on achieving only one goal, or are there many things that contribute to your total happiness? If you believe the latter, then the loss or failure of one objective doesn't destroy your entire happiness. Is your total personhood dependent on only one activity, or are there many things that go into the making of a person? Again, if you believe the latter, then when you screw up one activity, your entire personhood, self, or ego is less likely to collapse.

- You *could* be *happy* if you only achieve some of your goals—maybe not as happy, but still somewhat happy.

- You *could* be *successful* if you are imperfect—maybe not as successful, but still somewhat successful.

- You *could* still *exist* even if you fail, are imperfect, change roles, or don't get everything you want. You never disappear or cease to exist, even though the *quality* of your existence may change.

Thinking More Effectively

Once you have disputed your thinking by examining the evidence for your belief, reconsidering the usefulness of your belief, or challenging your philosophy, it is time to replace your dysfunctional beliefs with ones that will be more helpful. Research has shown that people who think more clearly tend to experience less emotional disturbance than those who do not. Substituting a more effective rational belief for a less effective irrational belief will not only help you feel better but, if you continue practicing your new belief system and incorporating it into your daily life, will help you "get better."

Rather than saying, "I can't stand it when...," try substituting, "I don't like it when..., but I can tolerate it." Remember, you can stand or tolerate most things, even when they are highly unpleasant. When you tell yourself that you can't stand something, it means that you will actually die when confronted with it. While this may be true if you are in the jaws of a man-eating tiger, it is highly unlikely that being in the jaws of a performance situation is equally deadly. When you tell yourself that the two experiences are equal, you only increase your disturbance and immobilize yourself. Therefore the more effective belief is, "While it is true that I dislike performing, and I am uncomfortable doing it, it is only uncomfortable, and I can stand it. I can also, over time, possibly learn to be less uncomfortable when I perform."

Rather than saying, "I must have the approval of practically everyone," try substituting, "While I would like to have people's love and approval, I don't need it in order to exist." Remember, there is no evidence or rule of nature that states that you *must* be liked by everyone. There is also no evidence or rule that states that you, or anyone else for that matter, will cease to exist without love or approval—even though your life *might* not be as pleasant as it would have been if you had love or approval.

New Beliefs for Old

Old, Irrational Beliefs	*New, More Effective Beliefs*
I must be perfectly prepared. I must not perform until I am.	I realize that perfection is impossible. While I would like to be better prepared, I also realize that I don't have to be.
I must not experience any discomfort in a performance.	It is unrealistic to demand that I experience no stress. All humans experience some stress in everything they do.
I can't stand the hassle of preparing.	While preparing is a hassle, I can stand it.
I can't stand the physical discomfort I experience when I meet the public.	I can stand the discomfort, even though I don't like it. I may be very uncomfortable, but when I tell myself I can't stand something, my body reacts by preparing for an emergency. Meeting the public is *not* something life-threatening or dangerous.
It's the end of the world if I get negative comments or reviews.	Getting a negative comment or a bad review is certainly unfortunate, but it is not the end of the world. Many people get bad reviews and still are alive and performing.
It would be awful if I experienced any discomfort while performing.	While I certainly don't enjoy feeling uncomfortable, it is not the end of the world if I do.
My esteem is damaged beyond repair if I have done poorly or not achieved my "personal best."	Even though I don't like to do poorly, I can accept myself when I do, and work to improve my performance in the future.
I feel totally worthless when others rate me as performing poorly.	Even if others rate me poorly, it doesn't mean I must lose self–respect or esteem. I can still value myself.

In summary, what we have examined are the three major types of disputes: the empirical dispute that requires looking at only the facts without commentary or embellishment; the pragmatic-practical dispute that questions the usefulness of what you are telling yourself; and the philosophical dispute that places your thoughts in proper perspective within your life philosophy. We have also examined some of the more effective beliefs that you could substitute for your irrational beliefs.

Following is the case of John G. Read this case. Identify the beliefs that are not working for John (his irrational beliefs) and write out the dispute for each. Label each dispute as to whether it is empirical, pragmatic, or philosophical. What more effective beliefs could John substitute for his irrational ones?*

*You can check your answers at the end of this chapter.

The Case of John G.: John G., age forty-two, hated to be kept waiting—for anything. His wife, half–jokingly, referred to him as a "Type A" personality. John had a horror of delay. He hated wasting time. He despised others who made him late. He believed that lateness was a sign of weakness, and he despised being seen as weak. He also believed that he was too important to be made to deal with such trivial matters as waiting in line or other people's fallibility. He knew that when he was forced to deal with those kinds of trivial issues, he was again wasting time, and that time once wasted could never be recovered.

It is obvious that John G. could be described as an angry person—he would have been the first to admit that he didn't suffer fools gladly. What is less obvious is that John was also extremely anxious. His "what-if" questions concerned hassles and delays—"What if I experience a hassle of some kind?" "What if I am late?" He answered the "What-if" question by concluding that encountering any hassle or lateness would so potentially undermine his comfort that he would not be able to function properly. He perceived hassles as having a cumulative effect. The discomfort associated with the first hassle would be magnified by having to experience any other hassle, and the total was bound to do him in. He was convinced that everybody was as hypervigilant and condemnatory as he was, and therefore that he deserved to be rated poorly. John was not only vigilant about detecting potential hassles, so that he could cope with them before they got out of hand, but hypervigilant because he had a dread and horror of losing self-worth.

Once he started thinking about the potential dire consequences to his worth and esteem, John would become increasingly anxious. He tried to avoid situations in which he would encounter hassles or delays, but found that he could not. Other people were always getting in the way, and since it was impossible to avoid other people, short of becoming a hermit, he dreaded going to work or going out to do routine chores. (What were John's iBs? What disputes could you use? What more effective beliefs could John experiment with? Check your answers at the end of the chapter.)

Please Remember to Breathe!

Another tool in our anxiety prevention/stress reduction tool kit, along with effective thinking, is effective breathing. In previous chapters we have described shallow, rapid breathing as a symptom of stress and anxiety. When you are distressed, you tend not to get enough oxygen, and your body signals you that you need to correct that problem. One of our most basic needs is the need for oxygen, and so you sensibly try to take a big breath. Unfortunately, many people do not know how to breathe properly so that they can really take a big breath, and as a result they take a series of rapid, shallow breaths that only increases their distress by making them light-headed.

What Kinds of Breathing Do You Do? Try This Self-Test!

Let's do a self–diagnostic test to see what kind of breathing you do. Read the instructions first, then go back and try the test.

- Stand in front of a mirror, or ask a friend to observe you.
- Place your left hand on your upper chest and place your right hand on your lower abdomen.

- Take as big a breath as you possibly can, hold it for a slow count of three, and let it go. ("Swallow the room" and then count "1 Mississippi, 2 Mississippi, 3 Mississippi.")
- Slowly let the breath go through pursed lips. (Cool off a spoonful of soup.)
- Repeat this exercise again, but now *pay attention to which hand is moving.*

Is it your upper hand or your lower hand? You may have discovered that your lower hand moves in and out as you breathe. If this is true, then you are breathing properly (diaphragmatically), and you already have this useful tool in your tool kit. Did you discover that your upper hand and shoulders hiked up into the air as if you were trying to carry the world on your shoulders. If that was the case, you were taking a shallow breath. Shallow breaths do not help you calm down and relax, even though it may feel good to lift your shoulders. All a shallow breath does is help you hyperventilate and feel increasingly lightheaded and cold.

> *The Case of Jane L.:* Jane was getting up to present her annual report at a board of directors meeting of a large corporation. Jane began to notice that she was feeling scared. Not only was she scared, she was anticipating being embarrassed because she realized that she might not have included everything that she should have included in the report.

Imagine that you are in Jane L.'s place and that you are feeling ashamed and embarrassed and frightened. Vividly imagine this scenario. Now check how you are breathing as you imagine this. If you are breathing rapidly or if you suddenly feel that it is hard to breathe, you are responding just like Jane did. She too had difficulty breathing, and rather than saying to herself appropriately, "Now is the time to calm down; let me grab a breathe;" she said, "oh my God, I cannot even breathe, oh my God, I'm not going to be able to continue, I'll faint. I won't be able to do my presentation, and people will think I'm very stupid or crazy." These thoughts only served to further her distress, because once she thought them, her body cooperated and cranked up the volume of her discomfort.

What could Jane have done to reduce the volume of her discomfort?

- She could have disputed her irrational beliefs.
- She could have taken a calming/cleansing breath and started breathing properly.

A calming/cleansing breath is one that encourages you to breathe diaphragmatically. You can take this kind of breath at any time or (as we would recommend) use it routinely. You can use it when you are on stage or when you are at the speaker's platform and you suddenly realize that you are drying up. You can use it when you are getting yourself anxious, nervous, ashamed, or embarrassed. You can take a calming/cleansing breath, dispute, and continue.

How do you take a calming/cleansing breath?

When you're stressed, your body wants to take in oxygen, and so what you tend to do is breathe rapidly to try to get oxygen in. However, many of us also feel muscular tension when we're stressed, so we hunch our shoulders and lift them as we take this breath. What happens then is this: The diaphragm, which is a membrane below your lungs, rises instead of falling and does not allow the lungs to fully inflate. Ideally, what should happen when you're trying to take a deep breath is that your diaphragm drops, allowing the lungs to reach their full potential. When we take a shallow breath or a shoulder breath, what we do is lift our shoulders, lift the diaphragm, and make the lungs collapse.

In order to take a diaphragmatic breath, you need to drop the diaphragm, not raise it. Read this next section first, then try it on your own.

- Lie down on a couch or bed somewhere. If you have no couch or bed and are reading this in your office, lie down on the floor. (This is an ideal time to dispute your belief that a grown-up should not lie down on the floor.)

- Take a very light object, such as a tissue box, and place it on your lower abdomen.

- Breathe in through your nose and try to make the box rise. We sometimes refer to this technique as pop-the-box. (If your tissue box sinks, rather than rises, you know you're breathing incorrectly.) As you breathe in through your nose, try to push your abdomen out. Feel your muscles in the lower abdomen constrict below your stomach, which is what it feels like.

- As you breathe in, push the box up; as you breathe out, let the box slowly sink.

Another way of learning to breathe correctly is to stand up against the wall, with your back flat against the wall. Now, put the back of your head against the wall and slowly arch your back away from the wall. Take a breath. As you breathe, just breathe normally. If you watch your abdomen, you will discover that it goes up and down properly. When you inhale, it goes up; when you exhale, it goes down. What you are doing is breathing properly. However, while this shows you how to breathe, it's a rather uncomfortable position to maintain for very long. So, do it once or twice until you see what your body looks like when it's breathing properly and then try lying down again.

Practice popping the box. Lie down, put a tissue box or a very light paperback book on your abdomen, and watch it go up and down. Breathe through your nose when you inhale, and as you breathe in, expand your lower abdomen and watch the tissue box rise. As you breathe out or exhale, purse your lips, blow up a balloon, and let the air out through pursed lips—quietly, silently. When we teach this in our workshops at the Institute, this is a rather quiet moment, a silent breathing exercise. We typically don't hear people "swooshing" or "phphphping," nor do we hear them grunting or groaning. This is not a weight-lifting contest. You don't need to grunt or groan, nor is it necessary for you to do this exercise forcefully. You want to inhale slowly. Allow yourself a slow count of three or four as you inhale. You also want to exhale slowly and quietly. Allow yourself a slow count of three or four while you exhale. These slow counts are useful when you are practicing or when you are using it as a calming exercise. When you are active, you will just breathe diaphragmatically without the pauses.

You want to breathe diaphragmatically not only when you are lying down, but also when you are walking in the street or when you are talking or singing. You will discover that if you learn to breathe diaphragmatically, you will feel better after most exercises. You will feel better as you walk. You will feel better as you talk. You will feel better as you sing because you are breathing properly. As a vocal coach once said to me, "It's the best aerobic exercise you can do sitting down or standing up."

Amazingly, many singers and actors who breathe properly on stage breathe improperly off stage; they are shocked to discover that what they learned to do as performers would be a good idea for them to do as civilians. They use diaphragmatic breathing only to help them support a note when they sing, or to help them not run out of air when they speak on stage. However, they don't use it when they are doing things they perceive to be stressful, and as a result they hyperventilate and increase their stress.

In the next chapters, when we look at prescriptions for combatting performance anxiety, we will come back to this breathing exercise and add to it. But for now, remember that one of the tools you can use is that of proper breathing by taking a calming/cleansing breath.

Have You Had a Shamectomy?

The *shame attack* is another tool originated by Albert Ellis. Shame attacks get us to challenge our notions about what is shameful and embarrassing. Remember that shame comes about when you believe that you are not as competent as you *should* be, and embarrassment comes about when you deal with your shame publicly. You feel shame when you expect yourself to perform well and you do not. You may experience embarrassment when someone is seeing you behave in a way you would prefer them not to. See most people would prefer to sing on key. When you suddenly sing off key, if people look at you and say, "Don't you know how to sing?" you may very well be embarrassed. If you believe that you should know how to sing and must know how to sing under all conditions, not only will you feel personal shame because you didn't do the job that you should have done, but you may feel public embarrassment as well.

Shame is personal; embarrassment is public. Shame attacks are also public. When we ask you to do this behavior, which you might perceive as shameful, we want to remind you to *never* **do anything illegal, or anything that would cause you culturally appropriate guilt, or anything that would cause you or someone else to be physically harmed in any way**. To do a shame attack, try to do an age-inappropriate behavior in a public place.

Remember that the purpose of shame, embarrassment, and guilt is to get you to avoid doing things. If it helps you avoid a criminal act, then we would encourage you to feel ashamed, embarrassed, and guilty. However, if it stops you from living your life in a happy and zestful way, then maybe it would be a good idea to examine your rule book—even if you offend the ears of a poor, unsuspecting listener when you sing "Happy Birthday" poorly at a birthday party.

When you stop yourself from singing in that setting, you not only stop yourself from having the fun of joining in the party, you may also paradoxically provoke a situation in which people around you are saying, "Look at that poor, scared soul," which is what you were trying to avoid in the first place. Remember that people will think as they want to, not as you want them to. Therefore, it would be better for you to do what will add zest and joy to your life, and not be overly concerned with what people think.

A shame attack is an opportunity that you select to provoke yourself to feel ashamed and then to dispute the thoughts that made you ashamed. It is an opportunity to evoke and then overcome inappropriate shame. While different regions of the country have specific things that people are cautioned about doing, there probably are actions that you may be unnecessarily thinking are inappropriate even within those regions. Can you think of some of them? When we use the shame attack, it gives us an opportunity to challenge some of our personally shameful ideas. If we can successfully overcome our self-defeating shame, this will liberate us to take risks that are appropriate. Jumping off a building is an inappropriate risk. However, if you view talking to your boss about a raise as shameful, you may want to reconsider your rule book. Your shame may be inappropriate because it doesn't allow you to take an appropriate risk to get the raise that you think you deserve. Telling yourself that it would be shameful if you cursed at your elderly grandmother is appropriate shame. It's not in your best interest to curse at your elderly grandmother, even if she is unpleasant, because our culture teaches us to have scruples about behaving in that fashion.

However, is auditioning for a role you'd like to have also shameful or is that inappropriately shameful? Is raising your hand in a class where the instructor clearly says that your grade is dependent upon your participation appropriately shameful or inappropriately shameful? Even though you may have been taught never to volunteer information as a family member, being reluctant to ask questions or answer questions in a classroom gets you in trouble in that classroom.

When we ask you to do a shame attack, we are asking you to attack your inappropriate shame. You do so by risking looking silly. Many people much above the age of twelve have a horror of appearing silly to others. Indeed, many people don't even like to do something that they think might make them appear to be silly in private. As Ervin Goffmann wrote, we are performing for an imaginary public. Therefore, we won't walk around naked even in our own apartment when the shades are down and we are the only one in the apartment, for fear that we might be embarrassed.

How do you attack your inappropriate shame? You can do so by risking appearing silly or foolish in public. Take this as an opportunity to have some fun. While we will offer shame-attacking homeworks later on and throughout the book, we will introduce one now.

First, let's do one in imagination. Could you imagine yourself skipping down the main street of your town, saying like a little cartoon character, "la–la la–la," as you skip? If you could visualize yourself doing that, did you feel embarrassed? Did you feel foolish, or did you feel angry at the authors of this book for suggesting that you try something like that even in your imagination? If that is the case, then you are experiencing what we would call inappropriate shame.

Let's try this imaginary exercise again. This time imagine yourself with a three-year-old child. Imagine yourself holding the three-year-old child by the hand and skipping down the street saying, "la la–la la–la." Is it equally shameful? What's the difference? Did you give yourself permission to do something silly when you had a child with you and not give yourself permission to do something silly when you were by yourself? If you could grant yourself permission to do it with a child, the only difference in shame is in the way you perceive the two events and the conclusions you draw from doing them. We've known people who had trouble being playful parents because they believed that skipping down the street, even with their child in tow, was inappropriate for them. We're not saying that you must skip down the street, even with a real child, let alone an imaginary one. Remember the dispute: Where is it written that you should always do anything? But, if you're reluctant to skip down the street in imagination, does that in any way relate to your reluctance to speak in public, sing in public, ask for a raise, lead a workshop, or make a cold call? We believe that the thoughts that stop you from doing a shame attack in your imagination are probably the same thoughts that stop you in the real world.

Let's try a different shame attack, again in your imagination. If you are a male, can you imagine yourself going into a meeting wearing a tie that was brightly colored and had pictures of pansies on it, and saying to your boss, "Do you like my pansies?" If your answer is a horrified, "*no*," what are you saying to yourself to produce the horror? "My boss will think I'm stupid. Everyone will think that I might always wear flowered ties. I would be too embarrassed to take the risk." Stop yourself for a moment and think back. Does everyone in your company always wear solid and somber clothing? Have you ever seen people in both upper and lower management wearing something unusual and having the fun of wearing it? Have you ever felt some respect and admiration for someone who took a risk in the way they dressed because they seemed to enjoy it and therefore communicated their sense of enjoyment to others? What do you think empowered them to wear a bow tie when everyone else wears long ties, or suspenders when everyone else wears belts, or socks with a funny picture on when everyone else wears solid colors? Was it that they were gutsier than you, or did they just give themselves permission to risk appearing foolish?

Many of us learn shame about our clothing in childhood. We dress the way our parents dress us according to their pocketbook, and we go into a schoolyard, and some child laughs, "Oh, look how dumb you look, look how stupid you look, look how ugly you look." We typically don't like those comments, and as a result we may feel bad. Since we don't like those feelings, we may understandably try to avoid them. However, are you still in the schoolyard when you walk into your office and talk to someone about making a deal? Are you still walking into that schoolyard when you think about breaking in a new act? If you graduated from school, maybe it would now be a good idea to give yourself this opportunity to graduate from the schoolyard. Try a shame attack.

Listed are three shame attacks involving no personal risk, no harm, and just a little silliness.

A Child's Garden of Shame Attacks

- Try walking a banana around the block. One walks a banana by putting a banana on a rope or a leash and holding it in front of one as one walks, ignoring comments.

- Try going to the grocery with four hundred pennies, buying a half gallon of milk and a half gallon of orange juice, and paying the cashier all in pennies. Do this at a time when the cashier is not going to be too busy.

- Go into an elevatored building and announce the floors. Even if there is an elevator operator who does so already, announce it with him or her, "First floor, second floor...." Stay on the elevator. Don't stay for one stop and get off immediately. Stay on until the top floor. Take calming breaths in between and remind yourself that you're doing a silly thing and it's okay.

If these are all too difficult for you right now, let us suggest an easier one.

- Buy yourself a coloring book and crayons. Then go to a fast food restaurant and buy yourself something to drink. Take out your coloring book and crayons and color as you drink.

Some people have become so adept at doing these kinds of acts that they refer to themselves as having had a shamectomy. They have lost their inappropriate shame.

Are you willing to try to learn to dispute the thoughts that stop you from speaking or performing in public? Even thoughts that sound like they might be okay, such as, "I get embarrassed when I'm uncomfortable"? That sounds okay, and is probably true. You probably do experience some degree of embarrassment when you're uncomfortable. What you have just done is to accurately describe how you feel. But do you therefore tell yourself, "Because I feel embarrassed when I am uncomfortable, I have permission not to try to perform"? Many people, the authors included, have experienced all the dysfunctional emotions we have previously discussed. We can learn, however, not to let them stop us from accomplishing our goals.

> *The Case of Charlie A.:* Charlie was a salesman. His year-end review was very positive, causing him to be promoted. However, when he got into his new position, he found himself very unsure and unwilling to take action because he might be embarrassed if he made a mistake. His next review was therefore very poor.

What would you do if you were in Charlie's place?

If you wrote, "Take it in, but don't take it personally," you would be right. You take in what others say, both positive and negative, but you don't take it to heart. You may indeed have to take it seriously if it's a boss who says, "If you don't shape up, you're out." But by the same token, you don't want to take it personally and say, "I'm a failure, I'm a loser, I'll never be any good."

So, you're going to take it in, but you are not going to take it personally. This reminds me of a comment that was once made to me by an elderly, middle European grandmother with whom I was working. She was by no means a psycho-therapist, but she occasionally said something profound. She once said to me, when I was very excited about some good fortune that had come my way, "Sonny boy, we have a saying where I come from: You shouldn't get yourself too excited, and you shouldn't get yourself too sad. In either case you will not look where you're going when you cross the street, and you will get hit by a streetcar." The point she was making was that both extremes, the deep depression and the extraordinarily unrealistic elation, lead us to not pay attention to the surrounding environment. While she was folksy, she was right on target. There can be wisdom in folklore.

Imagine...

In a previous example, we had you imagine that you were doing a shame attack. Rational-emotive behavioral therapy uses imagination in yet another way, via rational-emotive imagery (REI). You can use REI to prepare yourself to cope with anticipated immobilizing anxiety, or any other dysfunctional emotion.

To begin with, vividly visualize yourself in a performance situation in which you usually experience some difficulty. If you need to, close your eyes and talk to yourself aloud. Using very descriptive language, describe the surroundings, what is expected of you, your physical symptoms, and your emotional response.

> *What were you telling yourself to produce those emotions?*
> *Can you identify the irrational beliefs you were endorsing?*

Can you change your dysfunctional emotion (e.g., your anxiety, self-downing, depression, or anger) to an equally intense but more functional one? Can you change your anxiety into concern, your self-downing into self-acceptance, your depression into sadness, or your anger into frustration?

Go back and once again visualize yourself in the same situation. Once again vividly recreate the scene and intensely experience the emotions that you typically associate with it. This time, try to change your dysfunctional emotions into functional ones. Try to imagine yourself in the same situation experiencing not anxiety but an appropriate level of concern. Try to imagine yourself not self-downing but accepting yourself. Try to imagine yourself feeling differently in the same situation—remember, you have options about how you can feel.

Could you change your emotions? If you could, what did you say to yourself that was different?

- Did you dispute your irrational thoughts?
- Did you reframe the situation?
- Did you try to use a more effective belief?
- Did you tell yourself to treat it as a shame attack?

If you were able to do this, you can immediately see how changing your thinking changes your emotions. If you had difficulty producing a visual image in your imagination, do not be concerned. Many people have difficulty using visualizations. The ability to use visualizations does not appear to be consistently associated with any important psychological variables, such as intelligence, creativity, or mental stability. It is only one of the many normal individual differences that we can observe among people.

If you could do the visualization, but you had real difficulty imagining yourself performing without anxiety, what were you telling yourself that made it seem likely that you were incapable of change? Are you confusing the stress reaction with anxiety? You may always experience some form of stress, but it could be converted to eustress rather than distress. Not everyone who experiences the physical symptoms of stress also experiences the emotional reaction of anxiety. So, theoretically, you could learn to experience stress and remain unanxious.

Remember, you have been learning to change your behavior your entire life. You have been adding to or modifying your emotional, cognitive, and behavioral repertoire ever since you were born. It is highly unlikely that you are totally incapable of making any change.

And Now, Class, Time for Homework

People typically do not change the way they think, feel, and act overnight. Change usually comes slowly and gradually. Even highly motivated people in therapy realize that it may take a number of weeks before they begin to experience any change, and it may take months or years before they experience and incorporate any meaningful change. They also realize that the therapeutic session is only forty-five minutes long and that there are over a hundred hours during the week when they are not in therapy. In order to effectively incorporate the useful ideas that they may get in therapy, they need to practice the more effective ways of thinking, feeling, and acting during the rest of the week.

To increase the likelihood that they will attempt to incorporate these new ideas, emotions, and behaviors into their daily life, REBT encourages people to do homework. The homework given is targeted to help clients overcome the specific problem that besets them. It has been our experience that people who diligently do their homework, or at least try to do their homework, not only are far more likely to do better in therapy but are more likely to incorporate the changes into their daily lives and as a result get better.

In the following sixteen minichapters, you will be given specific prescriptions for overcoming performance anxiety. With each prescription will be a series of specific recommendations of homework that you should try. In order to more fully experience the potential benefits of reading this book, please try to do the homework. If you have difficulty with one technique, try another. Remember, we can't be with you in person to tailor these prescriptions to fit your unique case, and so we have given you generic suggestions that have worked with many of our clients. Even if you feel uncomfortable, even if you feel initially silly or phony and believe that "this is not me," remember that most things that are new and unusual tend to feel phoney and "not me" until you've practiced them, and then, after a while, they become you. So, good luck, and remember that the way to overcome performance anxiety is the same way you get to Carnegie Hall...practice, practice, practice!

And Now, Class, Time for Homework!

Try to answer these questions whenever you find yourself feeling anxious in a performance situation. (You may Xerox these pages for your own use as often as you need to.)

1. *Take your emotional temperature.*

   - What are your emotions?
   - Are they allowing you to perform, or are they "running away with you"?
   - How strong are they? Rate them from 1 to 10, where 1 is very mild and undisturbing and 10 is incapacitating.
   - Are they functional or dysfunctional? Remember, functional emotions not only are appropriate but also help you achieve your goals and do not tend to immobilize you. Dysfunctional emotions may feel appropriate to the perceived magnitude of the situation, but they generally immobilize you and stop you from attaining your desired goals.

2. *Try to identify your irrational beliefs.*

   - What are you saying to yourself?
   - List the demands that you make of yourself, the world, and others. What are your musts and shoulds? Do you have any must-nots or should-nots?
   - How do you feel emotionally if you don't get what you demand?
   - Are you telling yourself that you "can't stand it" when you are in a problematic performance situation?
   - What is it that you can't stand: your physical symptoms, your emotional response, your being in the situation at all?
   - How do you feel emotionally if you tell yourself that you can't stand the situation that you are in?
   - Does being in a performance situation have any impact upon your worth or esteem?
   - How do you feel emotionally if you believe that your worth or esteem may be damaged by the performance situation?

3. *Try to dispute.*

   A. *Sergeant Friday to the rescue!*

      - Do you have any proof or evidence to support your belief?
      - Where is it written that you should not be in such a situation?

   B. *Is this the proper tool for the job?*

      - Are your emotions, thoughts, and behaviors effective in the performance situation, or are they only serving to increase your distress?
      - Is procrastination the proper tool for the job?
      - Is withdrawal the proper tool for the job?

- If you could use them, what would be more effective tools?
- Let Pollyanna help you build a new frame for your picture.
    Try to reframe the situation.
    Play the "glad game."
    Try to use cool words rather than hot words.
- What happens to your emotions and behaviors when you try to use more effective tools?
- Do you need to dispute your discomfort when you try to implement new procedures?

C. *What does the "old philosopher" say?*

- Try to reexamine your philosophy. Couldn't you still be somewhat happy, successful, and worthy even if you routinely found yourself in performance situations?
- Try rewriting your irrational equations to allow you to perceive that your happiness, success, worth, etc., does not hinge on only one element.

4. *Try to think more effectively.*

- Try to make a list of appropriate and rational things to say to yourself when you are confronted with performance situations.
- Try to use these more rational coping statements as often as you need to, but at least three times a day, as well as before, during, and after "awful" situations.
- Note your emotions when you use these more effective beliefs. Write them down.

5. *Please remember to breathe!*

- Practice diaphragmatic breathing—try to "pop the box."
- In a troubling performance situation, remember to take a calming/cleansing breath, dispute your disturbing thoughts, and then try to continue.

6. *How about a shame attack?*

- Try telling yourself that the performance situation is nothing more than a shame attack situation and try to act accordingly.
- Dispute your irrational beliefs that you should not be doing this "shameful" thing.
- Observe your emotions before, during, and after doing the shame attack. Did you notice that they probably were more disturbing before the shame attack than after it?

7. *Imagine—try using REI.*

- Visualize yourself in a performance situation. Vividly experience the emotions you typically experience while attempting to perform. If the emotions you experience are dysfunctional, try to change them to more functional, but equally intense, and appropriate emotions. What did you have to say to yourself to produce that change? Try using that coping sentence throughout the day.

- Visualize yourself in the performance situation. Vividly experience the emotions you typically experience while attempting to perform. Now vividly see yourself acting more effectively in the performance situation; for example, see yourself starting to avoid the dreaded awful situation and then try to see yourself effectively coping, with some effort, with the situation. What did you have to do in the visualization to behave more effectively? Try using the more effective behaviors throughout the day.

8. *Try using specific prescriptions as needed.*

Answers to the Case of John G.

What Were John's iBs?

John had a horror of delay. He hated wasting time. He despised others who made him late. He believed that lateness was a sign of weakness, and he despised being seen as weak. He also believed that he was too important to be made to deal with such trivial matters as waiting in line or other people's fallibility. He knew that when he was forced to deal with those kinds of trivial issues, he was again wasting time, and that time once wasted could never be recovered.

Encountering any hassle or lateness would so potentially undermine his comfort that he would not be able to function properly. He perceived hassles as having a cumulative effect. The discomfort associated with the first hassle would get magnified by having to experience any other hassle, and the total was bound to do him in. He was convinced that everybody was as hypervigilant and condemnatory as he was, and therefore that he deserved to be rated poorly. He had a dread and horror of losing self-worth. He tried to avoid situations in which he would encounter hassles or delays, but found that he could not. He dreaded going to work or going out to do routine chores.

What Disputes Could John Use?

Empirical

- Where is it written that you *must not* experience hassles or delays?
- What is your evidence that encountering hassles or delays undermines your self-worth?
- What proof do you have that you are too important to wait in line?
- What proof do you have that experiencing a hassle will undermine your ability to function so badly that you won't be able to recover?
- What is your evidence that you, or anyone else for that matter, shouldn't be fallible?
- What proof do you have that if others see you as weak, you become weak?

Pragmatic

- How will not going to work help you?
- What useful purpose does it serve to despise people who hassle you?
- How does being hypervigilant help you?
- What benefit do you get from dreading being hassled?

Philosophical

- Couldn't you still get some success on the job, even if you are hassled? (Maybe you wouldn't have as much success, but you could have some success.)

- Even if you feel uncomfortable, couldn't you still function despite the discomfort? (Maybe you wouldn't function as well as you would like, but you still could function.)
- Even if you always experience hassles and delays of some kind, as you undoubtedly will, couldn't you still function, be somewhat successful, and experience some happiness?

What More Effective Beliefs Could John Experiment With?

- Being delayed is a hassle, not a horror.
- I don't like being delayed, but I can tolerate it and use the time productively if I choose to.
- Even if other people think I'm weak when I am delayed or hassled, I can accept myself and not weigh myself on someone else's scale.
- While I don't like the discomfort I experience when I am hassled or delayed, I can tolerate it and continue to function and do my job.

PART 2

Sixteen Prescriptions for Overcoming Performance Anxiety

A. Physical Discomfort

B. Emotional Response

C. Behavioral Responses

D. Cognitive Responses

Prescription 1

De-stress Yourself, Don't Dis-stress Yourself!

The Case of Phyllis G.: Phyllis G. was attempting to write a book when her hard disk crashed. She thought she had made back-ups of all the chapters, but she discovered that she couldn't find the floppy disk she thought she had stored them on. Try as she might, she couldn't retrieve the missing files. The longer she experienced the frustration of failing to get the computer to function properly, the worse she felt. She became increasingly distraught as the hours wore on. She began thinking, "This is the most horrible thing that could ever happen to me. If I don't meet the deadline, I will *never* get my first book published and everyone will feel sorry for me, which is something I couldn't stand. Only a dumb incompetent would be so foolish as not to make back-ups and not to double-check that the files could be retrieved. How utterly worthless I feel. Maybe I wasn't cut out to be an author. Maybe I should quit right now rather than have to admit the shameful truth to my publishers."

Writing a book was itself a stressful situation for Phyllis. Contemplating the blank page was a never-ending torture. Even before the disk crashed, Phyllis was experiencing a great deal of stress because she never believed that she had anything important or unusual to say. She believed that only people who were erudite and sophisticated should be authors. She used the computer malfunction to prove to herself that she was neither erudite nor sophisticated.

Stress and Distress

As we saw in Chapter 3, stress comes about for many reasons. We can feel stress as a result of doing something new or doing something unexpected. We can also undergo stress as a result of real or perceived danger. No one is immune from stress—not even the authors of this book! When the stress reaction occurs, we all tend to experience it physically.

> *Physical stress.* The most basic form of stress is physical stress, which occurs when your "fight or flight" syndrome is activated in response to unexpected situations or real or perceived dangers. You may recall (from Chapter 3) the full gamut of physical reactions that occur in response to "danger."

We also tend to experience distress, however, either emotionally or behaviorally:

>*Emotional distress.* Emotional distress occurs as a result of the *way you perceive the situation you are in.* Some situations are objectively dangerous, such as coming upon a man-eating shark while you are snorkeling. Other situations are subjectively dangerous, such as being evaluated, speaking in public, or auditioning for a part in a play. As we pointed out in the previous chapters, **the degree of physical stress you experience can be ameliorated or exacerbated by your perception of the situation.**

>*Behavioral distress.* Behavioral distress occurs as a result of experiencing the other forms of stress. You show behavioral symptoms of distress when you procrastinate, perform poorly, or try to withdraw from the performance situation.

The stress reaction is normal, unavoidable, and probably necessary. You may recall that every task you do requires you to experience a certain amount of stress if you are to do the job. The mere fact that you are experiencing stress is not, in and of itself, proof of anything, except perhaps that a certain level of energy is required. You may not have much choice in the matter of whether or not you experience physical stress, but you may have a say about whether or not you experience emotional distress. You can have a variety of emotional responses to physical stress and to the settings in which you experience it.

What Are You Doing to Dis-stress Yourself?

Not everyone who experiences stress also experiences dis-stress. We have purposely chosen to misspell the word to highlight the point that some but not all stress is experienced as unpleasant. We can also experience *eustress,* or pleasant stress.

When you dis-stress yourself about performing, you are saying that the physical discomfort you experience as a result of preparing, practicing, or performing not only is uncomfortable and unpleasant, it is so intolerable that you're unwilling to go through with it. You can also dis–stress yourself about the potential consequences of either performing poorly or performing well. You can increase your physical discomfort by conscientiously reminding yourself that both your physical symptoms **and** the situation in which they occur are intolerable.

Introducing PDQ (the Personal Dis-stress Quotient)

Try this simple experiment. Right now, while you are reading this book, you are probably experiencing little or no stress. We would like you to make a note of how you feel on a scale of 1 to 5, with 1 being blissful harmony and 5 being a feeling of such awful disturbance that even if you died on the spot, you would still be a quivering mass of jelly. We will assume that your current PDQ, or personal distress quotient, is somewhat lower than 5. We now want you to imagine being asked to speak in public or to do some other performance-related activity that you typically do not like to do. Note your PDQ as you picture "having" to perform. Now, vividly imagine something going wrong as you perform and dramatically tell yourself, "I can't stand it." Repeat that last phrase over and over again, at least ten times. Again make note of your PDQ. Has your level of disturbance and stress increased? Were you successful in dis–stressing yourself? When we try this technique at the Institute for Rational-Emotive Therapy with our clients who suffer from performance anxiety, some of them report that their final PDQ breaks the scale. They feel that five points is much too low a number to do justice to the amount of dis-stress they feel.

De-Stress, Don't Dis-Stress

When you experience stress, you have options. You can respond to the stress in ways that exacerbate it and dis-stress yourself, or you can respond to it in ways that ameliorate it and thereby de-stress yourself. You can possibly also learn to reframe the stressor and perhaps turn it into eustress. When you experience eustress, you see the situation and your physical response to it as pleasant and exciting. If you experience eustress in a performance setting you may also feel a "performance high," and as a result you will look forward to your next opportunity to perform rather than dreading it.

How do people who experience performance anxiety de-stress themselves? You can de-stress yourself in two basic ways: physically and cognitively. Both can work to de-stress your dis-stress. There are a number of approaches that you can use:

- If you are most aware of your physical symptoms, but are not now experiencing any physical disturbance, you can dispute the significance of your symptoms and develop some more effective response to them. This is especially useful if you are anxiously anticipating a strong and unpleasant physical reaction when you perform, but are not currently experiencing any disturbance.

- If you are currently experiencing the symptoms of physical stress and are also dis-stressing yourself about their significance, you may want to first short-circuit the stress/anxiety/more stress/more anxiety cycle by doing some breathing or other relaxation activity *before* you dispute or use more effective thinking.

Let's take the physical exercises first. What can you do to calm down physically? Every activity that relates to calming oneself physically requires a deep calming/cleansing breath. We told you how to take that calming/cleansing breath in Chapter 5. If you don't recall how to do so, this would be a good time to reread that section. Don't dis–stress yourself by worrying about how much time it is going to take. If it will help you keep focused and feel less anxious, try using a stop watch and timing yourself. You will probably notice that a calming/cleansing breath takes less than five seconds.

Take a calming breath. You may discover that while you take that breath and are possibly preparing to take another, forty million antagonistic thoughts enter your mind. One of our clients refers to that as his "never-never" voice. This is a voice that repeats inside of his head, "You could never, never do that. This will never, never work. You will never, never be any good at this."

If you have a "never-never" voice of your own, you can tell it to wait a while, because right now you are trying to calm down. Never, never is not a calming thought. If necessary, tell that voice that you'll explore those scary self–defeating thoughts after you take your calming breath. You can always worry at a later date. If your troublesome thoughts are so important that you must pay attention to them, say to yourself, "I'll deal with them after I have taken my calming breath. Right now, I'm trying to breathe." You can then shift your focus back to your breathing.

If you have more time than five seconds, add this to your repertoire: Take a calming breath and, as you let it out slowly, begin to focus on your diaphragmatic breathing. Say to yourself as you slowly inhale, "I am inhaling…one, two." Hold your breath for a second, and then say to yourself, as you slowly exhale, "I am exhaling…one, two."

Focus on this sentence. If you find other thoughts coming in, remind yourself once again, "I can pay attention to the scary thoughts later; right now my job is my breathing." People who have done Eastern forms of meditation sometimes talk about trying to think about nothing, or "mindlessness." We have found that Westerners tend to have difficulty grasping the concept of mindlessness, which appears to mean not filling your mind with any one thing, but being aware of the flow. The closest we have been able to come to approximating the mindless state is through paying attention to the mechanics of breathing. If you are fully focused on your breathing, you may discover that it is hard to hold onto disturbing thoughts.

Another technique that we have found useful with our clients is to use the words *calm* and *relaxed*.

- Again first take a calming/cleansing diaphragmatic breath.
- Then inhale slowly, and slowly say to yourself "calm" and "relaxed" in rhythm with your breathing.
- Say "calm," and stretch out the word slowly, so that it takes about three counts: "Caaaaaaaaalm."
- When you exhale, slowly say to yourself "relaxed," and again stretch the word out slowly so that it takes about three seconds.
- Repeat the sequence to yourself: "calm" as you slowly inhale, "relaxed" as you slowly exhale. Remember to take that brief pause before you exhale.

Let's see if the technique we just described can work for you. Again, try imagining yourself getting up *in public* to do something that you normally find uncomfortable and unpleasant and are reluctant to do. Imagine doing something like auditioning for a well known director or calling an important client to whom you have never spoken before, or imagine yourself trying to make a sale to a difficult customer. Whatever it is, vividly imagine yourself doing it, or trying to do it. How do you feel right now?

Can you visualize yourself getting up and trying to do the thing that you find uncomfortable and perhaps unpleasant? Is your mouth getting dry? Is your stomach beginning to churn? Are you perhaps feeling fearful? Take your emotional temperature. If you need to, note it down in the margin of the book. Make a note of your PDQ. We now have an indication of how bad you feel.

Now try a calm breathing exercise. Take a cleansing breath and then begin. Slowly tell yourself, "It's all right; I can cope." Focus on your breathing, using either the inhale/exhale script, "I'm breathing in, I'm breathing out," or the calm/relaxed script. You might also like a technique that one of my clients calls "aces high." He visualizes an ace floating in the air. He watches the ace drift to the top of the ceiling, stay suspended for a second and then slowly drift downward to the floor. He finds that paying attention to the drifting ace as he breathes works for him. Another client prefers a spiral ice cream cone. As she visualizes the ice cream's spiral and follows it through the various soft swirls, she finds herself becoming more and more relaxed. You may want to find a visual image that works for you as you're breathing.

Repeat whichever you prefer for about five minutes and then take your PDQ. How do you feel now? Do you feel less unpleasant, slightly more relaxed? Do you feel very much better? It's been our experience that many people who try this technique for even a small amount of time get some relief almost immediately. You will need to practice this many times in order to get the full benefit of it. But practice it until you can break the cycle of stress.

Pavlov and You

Some of our clients have gotten so proficient at this technique that just by slowly thinking the word *calm*, they begin to feel more relaxed. It is like the story of Pavlov's dog. Pavlov trained a dog to salivate at the sound of a bell by teaching it that the bell signaled the arrival of food. The dog got so accustomed to the bell's significance that it started to salivate even when no food was present. You can train yourself to calm down to the sound of your thoughts saying "calm" or some other word, such as "gently." You begin by associating the breathing technique that we have just practiced with a key word or phrase. After a while you may discover that since the word or phrase signals the arrival of a relaxation exercise, you will begin to feel relaxed when you just say or think the word.

Cold Hands, Hot Thoughts

You may have discovered that you have cold hands or cold feet when you perform or when you think about performing. You may also have discovered that the more you endorse irrational beliefs about yourself, others, and the world you are in, the more likely it is that you will feel stress, dis–stress, and (if you have the tendency to them) cold extremities. Many people find that cold hands are a particularly distressing symptom because they then have trouble holding on to their notes. One of the benefits of diaphragmatic breathing is that our extremities warm up when we breathe properly. We can use other warm up techniques, as well, to help us de-stress before we perform.

Always Warm Up before Public Speaking or Other Vigorous Activity

Another way to interrupt the cycle of stress is to relax your tight muscles, either by muscle isolation and rotation or by systematic muscle tension and relaxation. Many professional performers use some form of muscle relaxation before they perform in order to warm up. These techniques may take a little longer to do than the breathing exercises, but they can be done as you are waiting to go on. They can be practiced at any time and can be added to your set of useful tools to be called on when needed.

One useful isolation is a shoulder isolation and rotation.

- Stand or sit with your arms and hands held limply by your sides.

- Lift your shoulders and bring your arms and hands with you as you lift.
- Now, slowly, moving only your shoulders, lift your shoulders and bring them forward, around, down, and back.
- You will appear to be rowing a boat with your shoulders.
- Repeat this isolation slowly for three to five minutes.

Another method for breaking the cycle of physical tension is to systematically tense and then relax each muscle in your body, starting from the top of your head (you may be surprised to discover that you can even make the muscles surrounding your scalp contract). Arnold Lazarus instructs his listeners to make the muscle very tight, until they can feel that part of their body tremble.

As you constrict each muscle group, from the top of your head straight down your neck to your shoulders, make the muscle very tense until it trembles, then let it go. And then let it go a little more, and then still a little more.

When you first practice this, practice it before bedtime. You may find that you become very relaxed and get very drowsy and wish to sleep. Remind yourself that no matter how tense you are, you can always gain a little relaxation. Compare the experience of tensing the muscle with that of letting the muscle go. Practice it for each of the muscle groupings in your body, but focus on those muscles that you tend to somaticize when you are nervous.

If you tend to tell yourself, "Everything happens in the pit of my stomach," learn to contract those muscles and relax those muscles. If you say to yourself, "The back of my neck is always bothering me," learn to constrict and relax those muscles. You can practice these techniques well before you need them. Then, when you are in a performance setting and you suddenly feel the tension in some part of your body, you will know what it feels like when you are relaxed. You can train yourself to be aware of how your muscles feel when they are purposely overstressed and then when they are relaxed. You can remind yourself that not only do you know how to tense your muscles, you also know how to relax them.

You can do relaxation exercises backstage and no one will know. We will assume you have already reviewed your notes or are sufficiently rehearsed and therefore don't need to quickly ruffle through your notes or study your lines right that very second before you go on. (We are assuming a lot, but we'll talk about preparation in the next two chapters. If you are habitually underprepared and overstressed, maybe you should read those next two chapters now.) While you're standing there, waiting to go on, you can make a muscle tremble and then let it go. It's a good way of calming down. If you can, once again remind yourself that you are in charge. You made it worse; you have some power to make it better. Once you discover what the difference feels like, you are well on your way to being able to recreate a relaxed feeling from memory.

Try to Challenge Your Dis-stressing Thoughts

In this chapter we have focused on physical exercises to help you de-stress yourself. You can also de-stress yourself cognitively by disputing those irrational thoughts that change stress into distress. You can dispute how awful it would be if you were uncomfortable. You can remind yourself that even if you are uncomfortable, there is no rule that says you should not be. You can dispute your self-rating that declares that you are totally worthless when you are imperfect. You can remind yourself that it is human to be fallible. You can use "It's bad enough...." Remind yourself that

> "It's bad enough that I did badly. It's bad enough that I didn't get exactly what I wanted. It's bad enough that I may be trembling right now as I'm trying to speak, **but it's not awful, it is not the end of the world; it is** *merely* **bad."**

What else can you do to de-stress yourself? What other thoughts can you think? You can think, "I can take it." Think about the situation in which you experience performance anxiety, and imagine yourself saying, "I can't take it." What does it truly mean when you say, "I can't take it"? If you can't take something, it means you are about to die, because whatever it is, is going to do you in. While you may feel very uncomfortable when you get up to speak, when you get up to perform, or when you meet a new person, you are not about to die, even though it may feel that way. In fact, many people with extreme panic have gone into the emergency wards of their local hospitals, only to be sent home because they were diagnosed as having hypochondriacal symptoms.

Throw Away Your Crystal Ball, Grandma; It Only Tells You Lies

We don't know if there is a country-and-western song with the above title, but there should be. It has been our experience that many people creatively turn their stress to dis-stress by engaging in magical predictions regarding the future, their ability to know unequivocally what other people are "really" thinking or feeling, or their imagined ability to control people's thoughts, emotions, and behaviors.

You engage in magical thinking about the future when you tell yourself:

- I know I will never be able to perform well.
- I know that since I have had so much difficulty with speaking in public (or auditioning, or meeting new people) in the past, I will never be able to do so in the future.
- I know that I will always be _____ (fill in the blank using any level of status or ability).

When you engage in magical thinking about the future, you, like the client we wrote about previously, visit "never-never land" or its equally unrealistic, sister state, "the land of always-always." Never-never land and the land of always-always are both states of mind in which you magically believe that you can *unequivocally* predict that something in your future or someone else's future will not change from the way it is now or the way it has been in the past. Statisticians do indeed tell us that the best prediction for tomorrow is that it will be no different from today, because they assume that there will be no countervailing force to upset things. When you read a self-help book, go into therapy, or ask for someone's advice to help you solve a problem, you set in motion countervailing forces that increase the likelihood that **tomorrow could be different from today!** Therefore, you have no real evidence that the future must be bleak, even though the past may very well have been dismal. This form of magical thinking is a broken tool in your tool kit, and like other broken tools, is best discarded. The only purpose it serves is getting you upset and immobilized. Therefore you may want to remind yourself, ***Don't write your obituary before you are dead!***

Another form of magical thinking is the belief that you *know* what people are thinking. We call this form of thinking, *mind reading*. You are mind reading when you say to yourself:

- I know that when I dropped my notes, everyone in the audience thought I was very dumb.

- I know you really think I did poorly. You are only saying I did well to be nice.

- I know you don't really mean it when you say that you are angry with me (or when you say that our romance is over).

- I know you didn't like the way I sang that song.

No matter how well you think you know somebody, you cannot get into that person's mind and unequivocally determine what he or she is really thinking or feeling. This "skill" is generally unavailable to you even if you have raised the other person, are living with the other person, or are in love with the other person. Mind reading is especially unavailable to you when dealing with strangers. We constantly remind our clients that mind reading is not on the curriculum of any college, and as a result we have not learned this skill either, even though it might be a useful one for a therapist to have.

It has been our experience that when people use this magical power, they generally sabotage themselves. The thoughts and feelings that they "uncover" are typically in aid of either some self-defeating self-fulfilling prophecy or some unrealistic self-aggrandizing prophecy. Neither form of prophecy tends to be helpful. When you use either of these prophecies, you stop yourself from paying attention to information that can be useful, and that can immobilize you. You might want to remind yourself, ***when you try to look into someone's mind, you may only see a mirror.***

Magical thinking also includes the belief that you can *control* other people's thoughts, emotions, and behaviors. No one doubts that we all have the ability to influence others. The greatest impact you may have, however, is as a catalyst for their thinking. Your actions may provoke them to *think*, but your actions *don't* make them think in a specific and predictable way.

I once had a client who was dating a woman whom he loved, and who had said that she loved him, too. One evening, as a treat for her, he decided to cook her a special dinner. He went to the trouble and expense of buying her favorite foods and wines, set an elegant table, and assumed that when she saw it, her feelings of affection for him would increase. However, much to his dismay, when she saw it, she picked up the food and threw it at him, saying, "You make me so angry. No man treats me like this. How dare you try to take care of me."

Everything you do has *some* impact on the people around you, but not always in the hoped-for direction. Your belief becomes magical when you tell yourself:

- I know you don't love me now, but I'll make you love me.

- I will give such a powerful performance that the critics won't have any choice but to sit up and take notice.

- Since I gave such a lousy performance, my boss can only give me a poor rating.

This form of magical thinking, which we will call thought projection, assumes that people have no independent will of their own, and that therefore your actions will cause them to think, feel, or act in a certain way. Just as no can one can *make* you feel, think, or act the way you do because you are the ultimate authority over your own emotions, thoughts, and behavior, you cannot *make* someone else feel, think, or act the way you want them to. They too have the ultimate authority over their own emotions, thoughts, and behavior.

It is foolhardy to assume that just because you worked hard, you will always be seen in a favorable light. It is equally foolhardy to assume that just because you know you did a bad job, everyone else will see it as negatively as you do. We once had a participant in a workshop on dealing with difficult people who was complaining about a boss who could charitably be described as ineffective. The participant described the number of times this boss had been unpleasant, demanding, and unreasonable. The participant then said, "I worked so hard, I thought that this time my boss would surely see how hard I worked and would treat me more pleasantly." We pointed out that while working hard may generally help you reap rewards, it doesn't always do so. We also pointed out that no matter how much you may try to control another person's thoughts, emotions, and behaviors, you cannot take away the other person's right to see things the way he or she chooses to see them. In this particular case, we reminded the participant that no one could take away the boss's right to be stupid and demanding (or a fit subject for proctological examination). You might do well to remind yourself of the same thing—*people will act as they want to, not as you want them to.*

The remaining chapters in this book all focus on specific irrational beliefs that defeat you in performance situations. Each chapter addresses specific strategies for recognizing and challenging the irrational beliefs that turn your performance stress into performance distress. Read on and learn how to recognize and dispute your irrational beliefs and replace them with more effective alternatives so that you can conquer your performance anxiety. We also hope that as you challenge your irrational beliefs, you can turn your performance you-stress into performance eustress.

When we wrote that there was no specific country-and-western song that addressed the problem of magical thinking, Mitch Robin's alter ego Dr. Mitchagoss* got to work and wrote one. It needs some sort of accompaniment and a nasal twang. Why not make up your own melody and try it as a shame attack at your next party?

Throw Away Your Crystal Ball, Grandma; It Only Tells You Lies
Lyrics by *Dr. Mitchagoss*, Music by Gum
April 15, 1994

Chorus
Throw away your crystal ball, grandma; it only tells you lies.
The future's in the future,
And it's all a big surprise.
When you tell yourself you're failing,
It only makes you cry.
Throw away your crystal ball, grandma; it only tells you lies.

You tell me what I really feel, and you know I feel regret,
But my brain and my emotions are not on cable yet.
If you'd make a bet on what I think, you might just up and die.
Throw away your crystal ball, grandma; it only tells you lies.

Chorus

When you predict the future, you never seem to win.
All your crystal gazin' only does you in.
When you foretell my distant fate,
You just awfulize.
Throw away your crystal ball, grandma; it only tells you lies.

Chorus

You think that you can make me different than I am,
And that if you tried real hard that I would give a damn.
I am the way I want to be, so open up your eyes and,
Throw away your crystal ball, grandma; it only tells you lies.

Chorus

---

*Mitchell W. Robin, Ph.D., mild-mannered psychotherapist, was turned into Dr. Mitchagoss one steamy July afternoon at the Institute for Rational-Emotive Therapy. He was sharing a parody of a popular song with some of his colleagues when he was christened Dr. Mitchagoss, in honor of his *mishagoss*. *Mishagoss* is a Yiddish expression that means one's own unique brand of craziness.

And Now, Class, Time for Homework!

De-stress Yourself, Don't Dis-stress Yourself

Try to use the specific recommendations of this prescription whenever you find yourself beginning to feel dis–stress in a performance situation. You may also want to use the homework suggestions at the end of Chapter 5.)

1. Take your emotional temperature as you are doing an ordinary task that you do not typically associate with stress. Compare your emotional temperature during the nonstressful task with your emotional temperature when you are in a performance situation. What is the difference? Is it the situation, or is it the things you are telling yourself? What more effective things could you tell yourself to de-stress yourself?

2. Practice taking calming/cleansing breaths throughout the day. Using the P.D.Q., compare your level of stress on days when you have been taking calming/cleansing breaths and on days when you haven't.

3. Practice muscle relaxation exercises. Try using them whenever you expect to encounter a stressful situation. Using the P.D.Q., compare your level of dis-stress when you use the muscle relaxation exercises to that when you don't.

4. As you imagine yourself in a performance situation, take your emotional temperature and your P.D.Q. Try calming it down by first taking a calming/cleansing breath and then using either a breathing exercise or a muscle relaxation exercise.

5. Practice both the breathing exercises and the muscle relaxation exercises until you can do them on demand. Try to use them when you are in situations that might be stressful.

6. Try to challenge your magical thinking. Develop disputes that will help challenge self–defeating magical beliefs.

Prescription 2

Rehearse a Skill,
Not a Symptom

The Case of Lilly: Lilly, an experienced character actress, was called to audition for a part in a drama being revived by a famous director. Lilly had wanted to work with this particular director for many years and had dreamed of getting a role like the one she was scheduled to audition for. Lilly stayed up nights pacing the floor and worrying about her audition. She repeatedly asked herself, "How will I look to him? Will I look the part? Will I be able to master the southern accent necessary to do this role? How will I ever learn the lines or the staging? I'll never be able to do this."

Lilly further upset herself by persistently reminding herself about her anxiety. "I can't stand to be this nervous. Look how upset I am. I am trembling, my heart is racing. I am having trouble breathing. I shouldn't be this nervous.... It's only a part. I've gotten parts before. If I keep this up, I will be a basket case...I feel wretched and nauseous."

Night after night, Lilly paced and upset herself more and more. When the time came for her to audition, she called her agent and asked for a postponement, citing the onset of a sudden illness, characterized by nausea, vomiting, and a racing pulse. She asked that her excuses be made to the director, and if possible, another time be chosen when she was feeling better. As soon as Lilly made this call, she found that she made a miraculous recovery, which she had difficulty understanding.

What was Lilly really experiencing? Lilly didn't have a virus. She was experiencing performance anxiety. By pacing the floor night after night, she had rehearsed her anxiety so well that she had really increased her nervousness, without ever practicing her lines or her accent. Lilly was rehearsing her symptoms, but alas, not her skills.

Do you fret and stew like Lilly when a deadline approaches?

*Do you work very hard on your symptoms,
without ever practicing the material you need for whatever
type of presentation you need to make?*

What Is a Rehearsal?

When we need to perform a task, we often need to rehearse our skills in order to do the task justice. What is rehearsal? Rehearsal is another name for practice. Do only people who are rusty or inexperienced need to rehearse or practice? The answer to this question is *no*, not at all. Everyone who is performing in any way needs to rehearse. Pavarotti warms up every day, as do most singers and musicians. Major leaguers both go to training camp in the spring and practice before a game.

If you are a public speaker, you may rehearse by preparing your notes, going over your material, and even doing a trial run of your presentation, both for timing and for emphasis. You may make notes to yourself, or you may review other supportive materials you are using, such as overhead transparencies or computer slide shows, or you may discover that you have to make changes. You just don't walk out and say, "OK, I have my skills. I'm a great speaker; I can do it cold." You probably could, but not as well as you'd like to. Remember, the purpose of rehearsal is to maintain your skills as well as to improve them.

Why do some of you go to health clubs and gyms on a regular basis? You probably go because you want to improve your muscle tone and your general condition. You probably want to keep in shape, and you probably want to stay healthy. When you stop going to the health club for a while, what happens to your muscle tone, and what happens to your stamina? You will probably find that your muscles, like your skills, need maintenance. When you stop exercising, you may lose both strength and tone. You are no longer giving your muscles the exercise they have become accustomed to getting.

Doesn't a similar thing happen to your skills when you stop rehearsing? Don't your skills get rusty? If you are a singer, and you stop vocalizing daily, you may find that your voice becomes stiff and inflexible. Your vocal apparatus probably will not respond as quickly or as easily as it would if you were practicing daily. If you are a musician and you do not play for a while, your technique will probably become rusty and you will have a difficult time regaining the ease with which you played previously. If you've ever played the guitar, even as a hobby, you know from experience that if you don't play for a few months, your fingers will no longer be strong enough or calloused enough not to hurt when you try to hold down the strings to play chords. If you are a teacher, you don't want to use twenty-year-old lesson plans to teach history.

Whether you are a speaker, a singer, or a teacher, you need to rehearse. Everybody rehearses. Rehearsal is an essential. Choosing the right thing to rehearse is also essential. You want to rehearse to improve your *skills* in your area of specialization, whether it be singing, dancing, acting, teaching, speaking, selling, training, or defending a client in court. What happens when you rehearse a symptom instead of a skill? Remember Lilly? Lilly did a thorough job of rehearsing her performance anxiety rather than her acting. Her acting ability did not improve at all, and she didn't learn the material that she needed to learn. She did, however, practice her anxiety-related behaviors, and as she did, these became stronger and stronger. Remember, practice increases or strengthens the thing that you are practicing. If this thing is a symptom, the symptom will get stronger.

Can you rehearse a skill when you are experiencing strong symptoms, especially those related to performance anxiety? Happily, the answer to this question is *yes, you can*. How many people do you know who perform with sweaty palms or trembling hands? If they are performing, they obviously are not letting their symptoms stop them. These performers probably experience some of the symptoms we just mentioned even when they are rehearsing. The symptoms they experience during rehearsal may not be as strong as those experienced during performance, but they are still there.

Do you experience the symptoms related to performance anxiety when you rehearse? Let's say that your hands are trembling and your knees are shaking as you try to rehearse your acting skills and learn your lines. What can you tell yourself to allow you to achieve your goal? You could tell yourself, " I can rehearse despite my trembling and shaking. I don't need to concentrate on my symptoms, but I do need to focus on my acting skills."

By using this coping statement, you are acknowledging your symptoms and saying that *you can tolerate them and perform or rehearse in spite of them.* Once you realize that you are able to work despite your symptoms, you are probably going to be able to stop focusing on the symptoms as much and start focusing more on the task at hand, which is learning your lines, practicing your acting skills, preparing your lecture, or practicing your brief.

"Boy, Am I Thirsty"

Some of you may still be doubting what we are saying regarding what happens when you practice a symptom. Therefore, try this experiment by yourself before proceeding with this chapter. Stand in front of a mirror and note the way you look before you do this exercise. Now, start with the sentence, "Boy, am I tense!" Repeat it twenty times, saying it faster and faster and louder and louder until you are shrieking it at the top of your voice. If you don't want to shriek, try repeating it more quietly, while each time thinking to yourself, "Something bad is about to happen." How do you feel right now as compared with how you felt before you began this exercise? We would guess that even if you were not tense to begin with, you probably don't feel so well right at this moment. What you feel is the result of practicing the symptom of tension. Now look in the mirror. Do you look more tense than you did at the beginning of the exercise?

People who rehearse their physical symptoms are like the actor in the old vaudeville blackout sketch who comes on stage and announces, "Boy, am I thirsty. Boy, *am* I thirsty. *Boy, am I Thirsty!*" He is joined on stage by an actress dressed as a waitress, who asks, "What seems to be your problem, sir?" He responds, **"Boy, am I thirsty. *Boy, am I Thirsty.*"** She hurries off and gets him a large glass of water, which he proceeds to drink in one gulp. She looks at him expectantly, and he says, "Boy, am I thirsty." "But, sir," she replies, "I just gave you a large glass of water." "Oh, yes, that's right! ...Boy, *was* I thirsty...."

The better, and less laughable, approach would be to develop more appropriate coping skills. What kinds of coping statements are there that could help you to focus on your skills and not your symptoms? What kind of coping statement could Lilly have used to help her focus on the part she was to audition for? Lilly could have told herself, "I know that I am nervous about auditioning for this part in front of this director, but I can stand the discomfort of being anxious, and still rehearse my part. I can rehearse my lines and my accent even though I feel tense and nervous." If Lilly had used this coping statement, she would have been able to put her focus where it belonged, on working on her acting skills.

What are some other coping statements that you can use to help you focus on your performance or rehearsal rather than on your symptoms? You could tell yourself the following:

1. "I can still perform even though I am a little (greatly) worried about the outcome."

2. "I can still rehearse (perform) even though I am uncomfortable. I can stand the discomfort, and I can concentrate on what I need to do."

3. "I can still act, teach, sing, lecture, dance, paint, even though I am experiencing this symptom (trembling, shaking, nausea, dizziness, shortness of breath, etc.). I am not going to let the symptom get between me and my goal."

The Case of Ralph: Ralph, an executive with an advertising agency, was a good 'idea man'. He was not, however, very good at client presentations where he had to sell his ideas and strategies, no matter how brilliant they were. He relied on the rest of his team to put his work across to the client while he stood by, nervously awaiting the outcome. Ralph's immediate supervisor approached him and told him that his ideas would be better received if he were to do the presentations himself, because he, the idea man, would be able to answer all of the clients' questions.

As the date for his first solo presentation approached, Ralph found himself getting more and more anxious. He looked at his trembling hands and told himself over and over again, "Look how badly I am shaking. I must be terribly frightened. My voice is even beginning to quiver. How can I ever present my ideas fairly with a quivering voice? It must mean that I am terribly anxious. I would not be able to stand it if the client ever saw how nervous I am. This is terrible. I will never be able to do the presentation the way I feel."

It took a lot of prodding from his supervisor and coaching from his coworkers for Ralph to rehearse his presentation. He was able to get through it because one of his fellow workers taught him to substitute a coping statement for his ruminations. The coping statement, simply stated, was, "I can practice presenting my ideas even though I am trembling and my voice is quivering. My shaking and quivering are not related to my ideas, and I can tolerate the discomfort of the symptoms while I rehearse my presentation and as I sell to the clients." Using this coping statement, Ralph was able to prevent himself from rehearsing his symptoms and as a result was able to concentrate on rehearsing his presentation. As you will note, Ralph was making himself needlessly miserable by concentrating on his symptoms rather than his material. He was, however, able to learn how to get through the necessary work even though he was uncomfortable.

You can do this as well, or you can try to intervene before the ruminations take over. When you first notice your symptoms, you can tell yourself, "My presenting my ideas to the client is my focus. Even though my symptoms are uncomfortable, I do not have to focus on them." If you take the focus off your symptoms, you probably will not intensify them, and you can then concentrate on your skills.

You can rehearse your skills despite your symptoms of performance anxiety. You can also rehearse *with* your symptoms. Let's say that you are going to give a training lecture and you have a severe allergy that sounds like a head cold. If you tell yourself, "I can't rehearse or perform when I sound this terrible," you may never get the opportunity you want. Instead, you might try using a coping statement that has worked for some of our clients: "I can perform despite sounding nasal and congested."

You could use the old philosopher's suggestion: You could tell yourself, "I have an allergic condition that causes me to sound nasal, congested, as if I have a constant head cold. For now, at least, that is part of me. I can rehearse with these uncomfortable symptoms, and I can give my training lecture with them." If you approach the problem this way, rather than fighting the symptoms, you are really saying, "Conditions are not the way I want them to be, but I can handle things the way they are." This is a more inclusive and elegant solution. What if you are a performer in an ongoing stage presentation and you develop this same allergy? Do you have to give up your part? Could you as well rehearse your part with your symptoms and say to yourself, "Isn't it disappointing that tonight my character is going to sound like he or she has a head cold? I can still rehearse and perform even though I sound this way. I would have preferred it if my character did not sound this way, but it does and it will, at least for now."

> ***The Case of Deidre:*** Deidre was a beginning lawyer. She had just passed the bar exam in her state of practice and was about to present her first court brief. Deidre, who had always done well in moot court presentations during law school, now found that she was a bundle of nerves. She kept telling herself, "I shouldn't be feeling this way. I shouldn't be so nervous and scared. Real lawyers should be able to present a brief without feeling light-headed and without trembling hands."
>
> Deidre practiced and practiced. She imagined standing in front of the judge and presenting her material, but each time she found herself fearing her symptoms and comparing herself to the senior partners in the firm. She was almost too frightened to present until one of the senior partners saw her distress and sat her down for a chat. The senior partner told her that he too had had the type of reaction that she was having the first few times he went to court.
>
> The lesson that Deidre learned was that when you practice your skills and try to work with your symptoms, it is really in your best interest to take your level of expertise and experience into account. If you are a beginner, like Deidre, it is unrealistic to expect yourself to act and feel like a senior partner who has done this hundreds of times. The senior partner told Deidre that when she rehearsed her presentation, she would feel better if she told herself, "Given my current level of ability and experience, it is not unusual to feel the way I do. I can still work on the material that I need to present, despite the way I feel. I cannot yet expect to rehearse or present in court with the ease of someone who has had many years of experience at doing this."

No matter what you do or what skills you practice, it is best to tell yourself, "I will do what I need to do and practice the skills I need to practice, despite my symptoms, within the constraints of my current level of ability and experience." If you are a singer performing in *La Traviata* for the first time, you are probably not going to feel as much at ease with the material you need to rehearse as an experienced performer who has done the role many times before. If you are an actress playing in *Medea* for the first time, you are not going to feel as at ease rehearsing the material as an experienced performer who specializes in the classics. Remember, it is in your best interest, especially if you are fairly inexperienced or new in the field, to tell yourself, **"Given my current level of ability and experience, I can rehearse my skills, despite my symptoms."**

And Now, Class, Time for Homework!

Rehearse a Skill, Not a Symptom

Try to use the specific recommendations of this prescription whenever you find yourself beginning to rehearse your physical or emotional symptoms of performance anxiety. (You may also want to use the homework suggestions at the end of Chapter 5.)

1. Remind yourself that "Boy, Am I Thirsty" may be amusing in a theater, but when **you** rehearse a symptom, **your symptoms intensify, and that's no joke!**

2. Write out a list of coping statements to help you stay focused on your skills and not on your symptoms. Use them when you begin to notice that you are ruminating about how bad or anxious you feel.

3. Write out a list of coping statements to help you rehearse/perform despite your symptoms. Use them as needed.

Prescription 3

Don't Confuse Anxiety with Effort

The Case of Hank P.: Hank was a student who was preparing to take a final exam in one of his core courses. He knew that the exam was two weeks away, and he was determined to study in a timely fashion. Each night, he would diligently take out his textbooks and class notes, find a comfy chair, put on a good reading lamp, and promptly panic. He would begin to worry about whether he had taken enough notes. He then would review all the "dumb" things he had said in class. He constantly reminded himself that if he didn't pass the test, he would probably fail the course, and would never be allowed to go on into his major subject. He would then bring to mind how disappointed his family would be if he did poorly in college. After this thorough review, Hank would fall into an exhausted sleep.

Hank continued this pattern of "preparation" every night. Whenever his classmates questioned him about his progress, he would reply, "I was up all night." When the exam grades were posted, Hank discovered that he had done very poorly. He would probably have to repeat the course unless he could convince the instructor not to give the final exam grade much weight. He was dismayed with his grade. He could not believe that someone who was up every night for two weeks preparing for the final could do as poorly as he had done. "After all," he reasoned, "I worried a lot about my grade. No one was as concerned about the test as I was. I prepared for the exam every night for two weeks. I am amazed that all my hard work was not rewarded. I *deserve* a better grade!"

A hundred minutes of anxiety is not equal to one minute of preparation!

Hank, like a lot of people, confused anxiety with preparation and effort, and therefore assumed that he deserved the rewards that are usually associated with hard work. People make this mistake because they experience a certain amount of discomfort when they prepare, work hard, or feel anxious emotionally. Hank assumed that just because he worried very hard for the two weeks before the final exam, he was preparing as completely as the other students in the class. When you, like Hank, confuse anxiety with effort, you set yourself up to fail. If you spend your preparation, study, or rehearsal time in endless ruminations cycling through all your "what ifs," you will certainly feel tired from the effort expended in worrying, but you typically will not accomplish your goal.

Many teachers, trainers, and coaches have had students like Hank. They have spoken to their students or trainees in an attempt to help them do better. These students make an interesting and very common error in logic. They assume that the amount of time they spend in worrying or anxiously procrastinating is somehow equivalent to the amount of time that another person spends in preparation or rehearsal. Unfortunately, while it's certainly the same amount of time (four hours is four hours is four hours), it generally doesn't produce the same results. Four hours of rehearsing your own misery and stewing in it generally makes you more miserable, or at least contributes to further misery. It certainly doesn't help you master a new skill or maintain an old one.

Both maintenance and mastery require a certain amount of effort on your part. Unfortunately, if you suffer from performance anxiety, making an effort to prepare, practice, or perform usually means that you will have to overcome LFT, or low frustration tolerance.

Imagine yourself being asked to speak before the board of an organization that you belong to or a board that you are working for. You're given two weeks' notice that this meeting is coming up and that you will be asked to say a few words about something you know reasonably well, but you are not perfect at. If you have spoken in public before and are reasonably assured of your skills, you may not have a problem. This may not be an occasion for you to get anxious and stew. If, however, you have had little occasion to speak in public, or if this is something that you do routinely, but are afraid of doing, how would you respond? The decision you make in the next few seconds is a relatively important one. Are you going to reflexively decide, "This is too much. I can't do it. I hate speaking in public. Why do they always pick on me?" and therefore delay and procrastinate until the last second? Are you going to say to yourself, "I really don't like these chores that they give me, but I can cope with it. I will at least start to prepare and see what happens." Or are you, like Hank, going to start preparing and then go into a tailspin thinking about all the things you need to do to prepare and anxiously wondering about all the possible things that *could* go wrong (getting a bad microphone, forgetting your notes, dropping your notes, etc., etc., etc.)?

When you use "what if," you throw the switch on your anxiety response. Remember what we told you in Chapter 3: When you ask yourself "what if," you can answer it in two ways, rationally and irrationally. The rational answer to the "what-if" question is one that is logical and factual, helps you think of effective strategies, and typically does not result in self-defeating emotions. The irrational answer usually leads to anxiety, or some other dysfunctional emotion, and immobilization.

When you turn the anxiety switch on, you may open yourself up to even greater anxiety and panic, especially if your answers provide you with sources for additional "what ifs."

> "What if something bad happens? I won't be able to cope. I'd better figure out a way to cope. Isn't it terrible and awful that I can't cope?"

As time goes by, you may look at the clock and discover that you spent more time stewing than you did preparing. You are probably far more nervous than you were when you first got the assignment, but you haven't done anything productive to either prepare for the task at hand or to reduce your anxiety. Both preparation and anxiety reduction are more likely to help you to improve your performance in the future. What would be a more effective response? What do you need to do to implement that more effective response?

Let's reexamine the "what ifs" that we previously listed. We will list the horrible consequences that Hank, or someone like him, might predict. We want you to write down a more rational response next to each, or on a separate piece of paper. (You may want to review Chapters 4 and 5 before you begin.) You can check your answers at the end of the chapter.

Shutting Off the Anxiety Switch

What If...	Irrational Response	Rational Response
I didn't take enough notes?	It would prove how worthless and ineffective I am.	a)
I asked too many "dumb" questions?	The people around me could never respect me, and I would be humiliated.	b)
Something bad happens?	I would be immobilized.	c)
I fail?	It would be the end of the world.	d)
I feel *very* physically upset?	I would never be able to continue performing.	e)

One possible rational response to "What if I drop my notes?" is to reply, "So I drop them. Too bad, it's not the end of the world. I can always unashamedly pick them up, reorganize them, and return to my speech." While this might be a marvelous opportunity to self-down, you can stubbornly refuse to do so. When you say to yourself, "How stupid I am. How embarrassed I am. This is more proof of my irremediable worthlessness," all you do is immobilize yourself, make yourself feel bad, and reduce your chances of wanting to speak in public in the future.

When you make a mistake, it *undoubtedly* proves that **you are fallible, and therefore human.** You made a mistake, too bad. You are, however, capable of learning to improve, even if it takes effort. In the future, you can remind yourself to number your note cards, so that if you drop them, you can pick them up more easily. I learned the trick of numbering my note cards when I too dropped my notes. It's a common human error. It's not much fun, but it proves nothing except that you're human.

Picture yourself in your performance situation. If you're a professional performer, picture yourself on stage. If you're a lecturer, picture yourself in front of an audience or a classroom. Vividly picture yourself in the performance situation. Write down a list of *your* "what-if" questions when you are in a performance situation. Now that you have your "what ifs" in front of you, write down the beliefs that you have that tend to help you feel anxious. Can you effectively dispute your own "what ifs?"

You may notice that when you begin to practice thinking straight, even in this brief example, you may experience a reduction in your discomfort. You may begin the process of mastering a skill that is useful for combatting performance anxiety by completing this assignment. One problem you may encounter in doing this exercise, either now or in the future, is that **it,** like preparation, practice, and performance, requires some effort, and therefore may set you off on yet another round of self-defeating "what-ifs." You may tell yourself that it pays to be careful when encountering situations that you associate with anxiety and therefore discomfort.

What gets in the way of taking the time or making the effort to do something? Many of you who experience performance anxiety or stage fright realize, at least intellectually, that it would probably be a good idea to stop stewing and start doing something useful. You realize that it would be helpful to work on combatting your discomfort, even though it feels very strong. You realize that it would be a good idea to prepare, practice, or perform. You probably also realize that it would be a good idea to go to the library to check your sources or to research your presentation. You realize all these things, yet you may feel uncomfortable, distracted, or distractible when you see these opportunities arise.

Leave Stewing to the Chefs

You may recall from our earlier chapters that anything that's new and unusual is accompanied by symptoms of stress. Anything that we have taught ourselves to perceive as dangerous to us is also accompanied by symptoms of stress. You probably don't wish to have those symptoms, and you may choose the magical solution of self-medication. However, if you are going to effectively master an appropriate skill, you don't want to self–medicate. Self-medication won't help you prepare, practice, or perform, nor will it help you learn how to combat your performance anxiety.

When we address this issue with our clients, many begin by saying, "Yeah, I know I am supposed to tell to you now that I will work a little harder. But performing is too hard. It's too unpleasant and uncomfortable for me. I don't like the way I feel when I try to perform." Their initial solution to their discomfort is to stew about it, delay taking effective action, and then stew about the consequences of their delay. They spend more time in stewing and procrastinating than they do in preparing, practicing, and performing, yet they expect the benefits that the latter activities bring.

I Can Tolerate Anything, Except Frustration

Whether you're spending time stewing or you're spending time delaying, it typically doesn't get you what you want and is therefore dysfunctional. Stewing doesn't work for you, unless you are a chef. A more appropriate response would be to combat your discomfort by disputing your LFT (low frustration tolerance).

Low frustration tolerance, or "I-can't-stand-it-itis," as one of our colleagues calls it, is the belief that you cannot stand the discomfort that you are experiencing, be it physical or social. When you tell yourself that you can't stand something, you probably sensibly wish to avoid it, because you have convinced yourself that you will die if you encounter it. What you may want to do as a result is stew, avoid, or procrastinate, since placing yourself at deadly risk doesn't sound too smart. Avoidance and procrastination may initially seem like good fixes. Unfortunately, they are only quick fixes. The quick, and deceptively good, fix is to delay; unfortunately, the solution has severe drawbacks.

Why would you, or anyone, see delay as a solution? It initially feels good to delay. If you procrastinate, you make an interesting, self-reinforcing, and unfortunately self-defeating discovery: Delaying feels good physically. When you are faced with an unpleasant task or chore, you probably, if you are like our clients, feel an increase in physical stress, an increase in negative emotion, and possibly an increase in self-damning dysfunctional thoughts. You may say to yourself, "It's awful that I feel this way. I can't stand it when I am placed in this position. If this continues, I will really be royally screwed."

When you choose to procrastinate, then magical things begin to happen *temporarily:* Your physical stress temporarily diminishes, your negative emotions temporarily improve, and you temporarily start thinking in a more positive way. When you procrastinate, you get an immediate pay off.

To repeat: As you approach doing a difficult or problematic task, you feel your discomfort increase. If you choose the quick fix, the discomfort goes away and you learn to delay in the future. You may learn to confuse your diminished discomfort with accomplishing a goal. Just as some people confuse anxiety with effort, procrastinators confuse comfort with goal accomplishment.

Don't Confuse Comfort with Achievement.

When you confuse comfort with achievement, you are telling yourself that since you are no longer feeling dis-stressed, you have accomplished the task that inspired the stress in the first place. When we recommend that you de–stress yourself, we see that as a preliminary step toward helping you behave more functionally, in line with your long-range best interests and goals. When you are dis-stressed, the goal for now is comfort; but the goal for later can be achievement. When you de-stress yourself, you've achieved one goal, that of no longer scaring yourself. When you achieve comfort using the broken tool of procrastination, you are again like the brain surgeon we described in Chapter 5 who used only ineffective means.

When you procrastinate, you initially feel better; however, as the deadline approaches, the opportunity for effective preparation decreases. You are suddenly confronted with a missed deadline, or more commonly a series of missed deadlines, a diminishing achievement record, and possibly an increase in the number of things that should have been done, but weren't done.

If you habitually procrastinate, you probably tend to procrastinate in many areas of your life. You may now be in the unenviable position of looking at a longer list of stressors than you initially started out with. You may be saying to yourself, "Not only did I miss the opportunity to prepare for my speech, but I didn't do my taxes, I didn't clean up my room, I didn't get to work on time, etc., etc., etc." If you sabotage yourself in this way, you may also discover that you add insult to injury by putting yourself down. While it is true that you may not have accomplished your long-range goals, putting yourself down is probably not going to motivate you. Self-downing will depress and immobilize you. If you have a tendency to rate yourself negatively as a result of missed opportunities, poor performance, or other "shameful" or "awful" behavior, you may want to consult Prescriptions 13 to 16.

The Long and Short of Hedonism

When you procrastinate, you go for the comfortable solution, you choose pleasure over dis–stress. This is a very human tendency. You make the hedonistic choice. You opt for pleasure. Hedonists maintain that achieving personal pleasure is the greatest good. When you choose short-term or immediate pleasure, you agree with Garfield, the cartoon cat, that "Life is uncertain; eat dessert first." There may be times when short-term hedonism may be preferable; however, when you continually choose immediate pleasure, as when you procrastinate, you often trade short-term pleasure for long-term pain (as you will also see in Prescription 4). The more effective response would be to teach yourself HFT (high frustration tolerance) or SFT (sufficient frustration tolerance). Both HFT and SFT lead to long-term hedonism, that is a longer lasting feeling of pleasure and a greater likelihood of success in achieving your goals.

HFT and SFT

We sometimes joke that people who avoid stressful activities have NFT, or no frustration tolerance. We try to teach them to have HFT, or at least SFT. High frustration tolerance occurs when you steadfastly refuse to avoid stressful situations and resolutely stay calm rather than distress yourself in the face of them. You can achieve HFT by reminding yourself that life's hassles are tolerable, and that you *can* learn to tolerate them. You begin to help yourself develop "I–*can*-stand-it-itis," rather than telling yourself that life's hassles are toxic or deadly.

If you know that you are not a habitual procrastinator but rather a selective procrastinator, you might want to try teaching yourself to develop SFT, or sufficient frustration tolerance. Many people do not have SFT for specific situations. When you don't have SFT, it may be because you have set your ceiling for frustration too low.

Try a Frustration Unit Evaluation, or FUE (Pronounced Phooey)

When you are about to attempt a stressful activity, you may be prepared to encounter frustration, but you may be willing to encounter only a limited amount. You may be telling yourself that a particular activity entails "50 units" of frustration. You are prepared for those 50 units of frustration, and you might even have the good grace to tolerate slightly more than 50 FUEs. But what if the job seems to need 70 FUEs or 100 FUEs? You may get stressed out, angry, fearful, or avoidant, stubbornly refusing to accept the increased level of frustration.

Many people who experience performance anxiety are setting their FUE level too low and therefore experience performance dis-stress rather than performance eustress. Once the situation they are in seems to require more stress or frustration than they are willing to bear, they become angry because the situation is too hard or requires too much effort. In reality, they have unrealistically set their FUE ceiling too low. One way of conquering this problem is to assume that stressful activities are generally more frustrating than you care for them to be and to set your frustration ceiling higher for them. You can remind yourself that if the stressful anxiety evoking situation was supposed to be easy, it would have been easy. You can also remind yourself that you have successfully coped with frustration in the past and that stewing, delaying, and avoiding are not effective coping strategies. When you practice SFT, you develop realistic expectations and are therefore less likely to be disappointed or overstressed. When you develop SFT, you are more likely to be prepared to exert the amount of effort necessary for the task at hand.

And Now, Class, Time for Homework!

Don't Confuse Anxiety With Effort

Try to use the specific recommendations of this prescription whenever you find yourself beginning to ruminate and stew about the performance situation and your behavior within it. (You may also want to use the homework suggestions at the end of Chapter 5.)

1. Try to remind yourself that 100 minutes of anxiety are not equal to 1 minute of preparation. Then, turn off your stew pot. Try to develop rational coping statements that will help you to see things in their proper perspective.

2. Try to develop a series of rational answers to your "what-if" questions. Repeat them to yourself rather than stewing, then return to the task at hand, whether it be preparing, practicing, or performing.

3. Dispute your desire to procrastinate. Try starting the activity, rather than putting it off. Then celebrate your victory over eating dessert first.

4. When you are confronted with a stressful situation that you might be tempted to avoid, try saying "FUE" (phooey) and raising your ceiling for frustration.

5. Try to remind yourself that when you avoid performance, you may be comfortable, but then ask yourself whether you are trading the possibility of success for the guarantee of comfort?

Answers to "Shutting Off the Anxiety Switch"

We have provided you with one set of rational alternatives. There are hundreds of others.

a. If there is something missing in my notes I can always ask for help.

b. The only "dumb" question may be the one I don't ask. I can't control how others view my questions.

c. Nothing is so bad that I can't cope with it in some fashion.

d. Failure would be unfortunate but not the end of the world. Besides, even if I fail at a task it doesn't mean I will fail in life.

e. My physical upset is proof that I am alive and involved with this activity. It doesn't require that I stop myself from performing, although I would much prefer to be able to perform in a calm manner.

Prescription 4

Don't Self-Medicate

The Case of Karla: Karla, a college professor and occasional public speaker, found that while she had no difficulty in teaching small groups, she always froze in front of larger groups. Whenever she had to lecture in a large lecture hall or at the local auditorium, she stuttered and found that she had to frequently refer to her notes. One of Karla's friends suggested that she try having a beer or two before lecturing to "relax her." Karla tried it a few times and found that it worked fairly well. She then reasoned, "If a mild beer or two helps me this much, wouldn't a shot or two help me even more?" As time went by, her tolerance increased and "one or two" became four. Karla also found that she usually felt depressed the day after one of these large lectures. She assumed it was because "I never can perform in front of crowds." After a few months, she also found that her students were becoming less and less attentive. The situation deteriorated, and she was soon replaced as a general lecturer in her department.

What happened to Karla is all too common. She assumed that she needed magical help to get through her lectures and never realized that her adopted "helper," alcohol, was helping to defeat her.

"I saw the best minds of my generation destroyed..." Ginsberg
The United States has become a nation of people looking for a quick and easy fix. It is easier to take a pill or swallow a substance than to work on a problem. The belief is that since life *should be easy,* if one takes a drink or pops a pill or two, problems will magically disappear without any further effort or inconvenience.

We're certain that you've heard people say that they must have a drink before they go on stage to perform, or before they meet new clients, or before any business presentation. Those who "need a drink" claim that it steadies their nerves. Does drinking really accomplish this goal? Research has shown that alcohol does not act the way most people expect it to act. Alcohol has some very interesting effects.

At first, it may act as a stimulant through both the increased caloric energy it releases and some disinhibitory actions; however, it later inhibits and becomes a depressant. What does alcohol really do for your judgment and your presentation? The literature agrees that when someone is using alcohol, his or her judgment is impaired, estimates of performance are usually blown way out of proportion, and the individual is unable to monitor (with any type of accuracy) what is occurring in the environment.

Have you ever been in the audience when a speaker slurs and stops making coherent sense or when a lecturer seems disoriented and cannot seem to grasp even a simple question? Have you ever attended a performance where the actor or actress, although vibrant, seems to be ahead of the others or lost to the emotional reality of the character and therefore is not in harmony with the other actors or the story? If you have experienced any of these as a member of the audience, you may very well have been witnessing the negative effects of substance use or abuse.

Have you ever been offered a drink to calm you or steady your nerves? Do you believe that taking a drink will enhance your performance? Recent accounts of a famous singer's stage drinking habits were very revealing regarding how alcohol impedes performance. The disinhibitory effects of alcohol may also lead to an embarrassing performance, be it on stage or in business, because you, like the aforementioned singer, may lose control of your behavior and act in inappropriate ways. There is no magical blessing conferred by alcohol use, and its use may become a curse!

*Have you ever used some "magical assistance" to help you
get through a performance?*

What did you tell yourself about your need for help?

Karla told herself that she couldn't face a large group of people without help and that alcohol was the helping agent. When she experienced the negative after-effects of her drinking, she again related her reactions to the situation of not liking crowds. She didn't seem to realize that the only long-term assistance her "helper" was providing was to help her feel bad and perform poorly.

Let's look at some of the beliefs connected with the use of alcohol:

1. Alcohol is a relaxant. It will loosen me up so that I can perform more naturally.

2. Alcohol is good for you...after all, some health studies have said it won't be harmful if used in moderation, so why shouldn't I use it to help my performance?

3. Alcohol is disinhibitory. I couldn't be appropriately social without it. It was invented for people who are shy. It helps me loosen up. I couldn't be appropriately social without it.

4. Nobody will notice if I've had a couple of drinks.

5. I've always been able to control my drinking. Doesn't everybody drink when under stress? I can stop, at will, when the stress is over.

6. Only uptight people don't drink.

7. Alcohol can only enhance my performance. There is no way that it will detract from my performance.

As you can see, these are all fallacies concerning alcohol use. Many of these fallacies can lead to alcohol abuse. Others will lead to other substance abuse and possibly to a poor health picture. Karla endorsed the belief that alcohol could only enhance her performance. She denied that it could detract from it. She also endorsed all the other beliefs about how alcohol is used. This type of denial is quite common in substance abuse. When the abuser is "under the influence," he or she is unaware of how he or she appears to others. Alcohol also has effects on short-term memory. After enough use, the user becomes unaware of what occurred during the use. Karla was unaware that her students' disinterest was a function of her not adequately being able to handle her lecture material while under the influence of alcohol. She therefore suffered the long-term consequence of losing her lecturing position.

Is alcohol the only magical drug used to help performance anxiety? Many other magical cures besides alcohol are used to help relieve anxiety and supposedly enhance performance.

> *The Case of Phil:* Phil, a jazz musician, earned his living playing with a number of different combos in a series of jazz clubs. Phil liked his work, but found that to decrease his anxiety, evidenced by his "nervous, twitchy hands," it helped to use a few drugs before going on. He felt he was lucky because one of the drummers on a previous gig had let him in on the secret of which pills would accomplish this most easily. Each night, before Phil left for work, he mixed himself a "pill cocktail," which he named the Ricky Special in honor of the drummer who had originated it. By the time he arrived at whatever club he was playing at, he would have a mild buzz on, but his hands no longer twitched.
>
> None of his fellow musicians seemed to notice Phil's buzz because they too "used." It seemed to be a given that their kind of musicians would use drugs to help them be "mellow and cool." Phil didn't see his preperformance jitters as a problem, nor did he notice when his playing became erratic, until one of the club managers told him to "get with it or get out."

Has anyone ever told you that pills or marijuana enhance performance, creativity, and well-being? Have others, especially in the performing and creative arts, ever told you that hallucinogenics such as LSD add to their creativity and inspire their performances? Phil thought that his Ricky Special was making him a better musician. It was not until the club manager pointed out that he had problems that he began to realize that his drug use was impeding and not enhancing his performance.

As a culture, we tend to hang onto the belief that Wonderland really exists and that we, like Alice, can find a magical potion or biscuit that can help us do wonderful things without effort. Alice, however, was more aware of reality than some of those who emulate her. She knew that "if you drink much from a bottle marked 'poison,' it is almost certain to disagree with you, sooner or later."

Give Me Librium or Give Me Meth!

Many people use agents other than alcohol or recreational drugs to calm themselves or to give themselves a sense of well-being. We have become a society that takes pills to cure everything from the common cold to psychosis. How many people do you know who cannot face a stressful situation without taking a tranquilizer? In the 1960s and 1970s, Valium was the drug of choice, and it is still used by many to calm down. You will often hear someone who has to engage in what he or she considers a stressful act talk about popping a Valium so that he or she "can get through and survive."

How do tranquilizers act? Do they really calm you down? Do they add to your performance, or do they take the exciting edge off your performance? Let's talk about tranquilizers and sedatives. Tranquilizers and sedatives are prescribed in order to relieve symptoms related to extreme anxiety. The *Physician's Desk Reference* (1994), however, states that "Anxiety or tensions associated with the stress of everyday life usually do *not* require treatment with an anxiolytic." This is repeated in the "Indications" section under each tranquilizing agent. There are many types of antianxiety or anxiolytic medications. There are sedatives, and there are barbiturates. All of the agents work on areas of the brain and have central nervous system side effects. Most, especially the barbiturates, warn the user not to engage in any hazardous activity, such as driving a car, while on the medication. Almost all of the tranquilizing agents share the side effects of dizziness, confusion, and problems with judgment. Many warn of even worse side effects, including depression. Almost all carry the added hazard of possible physical and/or psychological dependency.

If you think about how the sedatives, hypnotics, and barbiturates affect you and how their side effects may affect you, do you want to take the risk of further impeding your performance just to have their calming effect?

Our cultural belief, which is also endorsed by many in the media and popular press, tends to be that there is a magical cure for everything, and that if you just find that certain magic pill for you, you will never have to do the hard work associated with overcoming your problems, be they dietary, mood, or performance-related.

Sadly, this is not a belief that will work for you. The pills that you hope will magically dispel your anxiety are much more likely to impede your performance or to keep you from improving your performance than to help you perform. You will also discover that when you stop the magic pills and go back to the status quo, the problems that you began with are still there and are as frightening as they ever were.

Trading New Problems for Old

Many people who self-medicate do so in an attempt to effectively deal with their problems. They don't like the discomfort they feel when they try to prepare, practice, or perform or even think about doing these things. They seem to irrationally believe

1. I shouldn't feel any discomfort associated with performing.
2. If I feel any discomfort, it is proof that there is something wrong with me.
3. I *must* have instant relief!

It is understandable to want to avoid or minimize discomfort, but when you habitually self-medicate to do so, you inevitably trade one problem for a series of larger problems. You trade the relatively small problem of discomfort or distress for the potentially larger ones of impaired performance, impaired judgment, loss of reputation, loss of job or position, and possible dependency or addiction. We are not, in the great tradition of *Reefer Madness*, trying to scare you or to shame you. We are merely trying to help you think consequentially.

Many people who begin self-medicating are dismayed to find that it has become habitual. They start out with a benign desire to feel better. In order to feel good, they may take a drink or two or use a small amount of recreational drugs. They may find, like Karla, that they quickly become habituated to the amount they are taking. As time goes by, they find that they need larger amounts to help them feel good. If this pattern continues, they will become habituated to even larger amounts and will unfortunately discover that even these amounts do not help them get that "at ease" feeling. These individuals then may find that they need ever-increasing amounts of whatever they are taking just to avoid feeling bad. This pattern is known to psychologists as an "opponent process." Researchers have discovered that when people become addicted, the primary process (seeking pleasure or comfort) is eventually superseded by an even stronger secondary process (avoiding pain). The irony is that those individuals who get hooked were trying to avoid pain in the first place and now wind up with even greater pain.

How do you determine whether your use impedes your performance? You can start by asking yourself these questions:

1. Do I tell myself that I need the drink or pills and that I could not perform without them?
2. Do I wait to perform until I have a pleasant feeling from the substance?
3. Do I need increasing amounts of the substance before I feel ready?
4. Do others tell me that I am using too much, and do I either ignore them or put them down for their comments?
5. What types of critical comments am I getting from others about my performance, and do I take them seriously?

These questions are the beginnings of a technique we can call *consequential thinking*. We hope to teach you to ask yourself what both the long- and the short-term consequences of your actions might be. We are also suggesting that you at least listen to those who give you feedback. One of the consequences of substance use is not being able to fairly judge a situation, because your judgment will be impaired. A major country singer, in his recently issued biography, talks about how his audiences were giving him more and more negative feedback, but he was using cocaine and couldn't understand why he was being booed, heckled, and not earning his usual applause.

If your responses to at least three of the preceding questions were yes, you might want to consider getting help. You might want to join a self–help support group such as Rational Recovery* which uses the techniques described in this book. There are also other groups that help people with their substance abuse problems. We have found that disputing and the other techniques of REBT offer a much cheaper, more effective, and more readily available solution to your performance anxiety than self-medication.

You could first take a calming/cleansing breath and then, using the pragmatic (toolbox) dispute, ask yourself, "Is using a substance to calm myself really

---

*Rational Recovery is a self-help program that was developed as an alternative to AA and other "twelve-step" programs. Many people prefer RR to AA. There are many RR groups in the United States. You can locate the one nearest you by calling the Institute for Rational-Emotive Therapy, (212) 535-0822.

beneficial to me?" You could also ask, "Is my belief in magical solutions helping me to prepare, practice, and perform?"

You might want to use the empirical dispute (the Dragnet dispute) to ask yourself where the evidence is that increased use will improve performance. If you don't know where to get this evidence, go both to the literature on substance use and to the biographies of some of the people who have been through programs like the Betty Ford Clinic and have written about what substance use did to them.

The old philosopher might get you to examine your irrational equations. You might be surprised to learn that you believe that

> Relaxation = drinking/drugging
> Worthiness = zero performance stress
> Good Performance = mellow drug-mediated performance

If these equations are the ones you espouse, you may well benefit from re-reading this chapter, especially the parts concerning how drug mediation impairs rather than enhances performance. You may also wish to reread the first prescription, "De-stress Yourself, Don't Dis-stress Yourself."

The disputes and other techniques contained in this book will not impair judgment, cloud memory, or negatively affect your physical health, as using medications of the type described will.

One last word of caution. There are times when prescription medications are useful. Some people become so anxious that they may need some type of medication for their anxiety. If this is true for you, *do not self-prescribe or self-medicate!* Instead of panicking or self-medicating, take a calming/cleansing breath and call your doctor. Only your physician can make the determination as to whether or not you *really* need medication and what medication would be best for you. Currently, a physician is the only one who can monitor the effects of the medication. Many prescribed medications do have side effects, which may need to be monitored through blood tests.

Remember: The person who prescribes alcohol, barbiturates, sedatives, hallucinogenics, and marijuana for himself or herself almost definitely has a fool for a physician.

And Now, Class, Time for Homework!

Don't Self-Medicate

Try to use the specific recommendations of this prescription whenever you either are self–medicating or are tempted to do so in an attempt to magically cure your performance anxiety. (You may also want to use the homework suggestions at the end of Chapter 5.)

1. If you think that your physical symptoms are abnormally intense and require medication, consult your physician to see if you are right.
2. If you are self-medicating or thinking about doing so, what are you telling yourself about the performance situation and your discomfort in it? Write down your thoughts on a piece of paper.
3. How do you feel emotionally when you tell yourself those things? Take your emotional temperature.
4. Try identifying your irrational beliefs and disputing them.
5. Is self-medicating worth the risk of trading one problem for many larger ones?
6. Where is it written that "dummies," lower-class or poorly educated people, are the *only ones who get hooked?*

Prescription 5

Concretize, Don't Awfulize

Many activities, situations, and outcomes are important in all of our lives. (We will discuss important people in the next prescription.) Activities, situations, and outcomes are important to us both because of the significance they have and because of the significance we attach to them. Many students, for example, have discovered that getting good grades is important for both objective and subjective reasons.

Objectively, good grades in a course are generally an indication of how well you have mastered the material. When you get good grades, you may also be provided with the opportunity to take more interesting courses or be offered scholarships or other rewards. You may also discover that when you get good grades, you typically gain the approbation of your instructors, and possibly that of your parents as well. Their approbation may also provide you with additional rewards, both tangible and intangible.

Subjectively, when you get good grades, you may experience heightened pleasure and the personal satisfaction of a job well done. You may also be pleased about the potential increase in opportunities, rewards, and approbation.

In fact, you do not need to provide any reason, to others or to yourself, why you believe an activity or a situation is important to you. It is important to you because it is important to you. No one will ask you to dispute why you evaluate something as important. However, we will ask you to consider the consequences of telling yourselves that certain activities, situations, and outcomes are so important that it would be awful, terrible, horrible, or the end of the world if they occurred.

> *The Case of David W.* David W., age thirty-six, was an artist who had been compiling a portfolio of work and was beginning to feel very anxious. He had been invited to bring his portfolio to a major gallery to have it evaluated for a possible group showing. David was delighted, but amazed, that "such a prestigious gallery would even consider looking at my work." He began to have trouble picking out the slides and samples that he wanted to show them. He began dreading the moment that he would have to appear in the gallery. "They probably won't really want to show a little hick nobody like me. I won't know how to talk to these people. Its awful to be in this predicament. Maybe I shouldn't go." When he began to think of not going, he realized that he might miss a good opportunity to be seen and therefore might never get the exhibition he had dreamed of. "It would be awful," he thought, "to not be accepted for an exhibition. It would be unbearable to never have my work seen. I couldn't take it if that happened." Whenever David

thought these things, he became increasingly upset and anxious. Whenever he told his friends about his concerns, many of them, unfortunately, agreed with him. They too thought that if they couldn't get accepted for a gallery exhibition or be hung in a museum, it would be, at the very least a catastrophe of major proportions. David's anxiety began to immobilize him. Whenever he looked at a canvas, he began to worry that his work might not be good enough to be seen by a major gallery. He began to postpone starting new canvases because he might not have anything "worthwhile," that is, worthy of hanging in a gallery or museum, to show.

David was in the process of doing himself in because he was perceiving an activity and a potential outcome as awful. When you, like David, consider some situation or outcome so terrifying or so impossibly hard to cope with that it's awful, you do more than say that it is important to you. You make a prediction that you could not cope and would be overpowered if the situation or outcome materialized. You tell yourself that the only appropriate response to the situation is immobilization or retreat.

When you see something as potentially horrible or awful, you sensibly wish to avoid it. No one says, "I am going to do something that causes a nuclear war, and I am going to put myself at ground zero." However, is it ground zero when you walk into the auditorium or into the lecture hall? Is it ground zero when you raise your hand to speak? Is it ground zero when you go for an interview for a job?

I Can't Take It...Its Awe-full!

To acknowledge the power and importance that many of us give these situations, we would like to suggest that rather than spelling the word as A–W–F–U–L, you respell it, for a moment, as A–W–E F–U–L–L. In other words, remind yourself that sometimes you allow activities, situations, and outcomes to fill you with dread and awe.

The awed response to a situation usually suggests that this is the worst imaginable situation in the world. Are there any situations in your life that would be so intensely horrible that it would be useful to be struck dumb in the face of them? If so, then becoming immobilized would be appropriate in that situation. However, in the case history above, we described an individual who was contemplating an invitation to show his work and then was immobilized by the wonder of it all. He was equally immobilized by the possibility that he would not be accepted for a gallery show. That possibility resulted in his suddenly becoming frozen—struck with the terror of it all.

If you also have the tendency to think that certain situations are appropriately awful, try this technique: use the phrase "struck dumb" instead of awful.

For example:

- "It would strike me dumb if I had to get some place on time."
- "It would strike me dumb if I had to go quickly to an audition without six months of preparation."
- "It would strike me dumb if I had to listen to criticism."
- "It would strike me dumb if anything bad happened to me in my life."

Now write down a few of your own personal favorites.

Remember to substitute the phrase, "It would strike me dumb,"
for the phrase, "It would be awful."

Is being struck dumb an appropriate response to the above situations or to the personal ones that you listed? Do you have evidence that immobilization is required? Is immobilization a useful tool? Even if the outcome is very dire indeed, couldn't you still experience some happiness or success in life despite that outcome?

In our workshops we have worked with people who ostensibly had the goals of increasing the fun they had out of life by widening their circle of friends and having more fun at parties. When it was suggested that they might start by talking to people or accepting offers to dance when asked, they recoiled in horror. They couldn't even *contemplate* doing something new or unusual for them, like speaking to a stranger in public or getting up at a party and dancing, let alone actually doing it. They thought, "I cannot do that. If I did, it would be terrible, awful. (I would be struck dumb with the horror and the wonder of it all.) What would happen if I took a misstep and stepped on my partner's toes, or said something stupid? Wouldn't *that* be awful?" Struck dumb with the wonder of those thoughts, they stopped themselves from trying to dance or meet new people and therefore stopped themselves from accomplishing their goals.

Get Out the Anchor

Is this the only response you can have to important or unusual activities, situations, and outcomes? What else could you do? One technique that we have used successfully with our clients at the Institute for Rational-Emotive Therapy is to have them develop a concrete anchor. An anchor is a model for the worst-case scenario.

What is the worst, most awful thing you can think of? Many of our clients come up with nuclear holocaust as a generically awful thing. Other clients have used the anchor of having everyone in the world die of cancer. They judged that as being a particularly awful thing. Still others have used the notion of being in a concentration camp, or genocide more specifically, as being a pretty awful thing. Probably no one would dispute that those outcomes are very, very bad indeed.

For our purposes, let's establish genocide as an anchor. We are all going to agree that killing off an entire population is pretty bad, maybe as bad as it gets. We will establish genocide as the worst imaginable thing in the world. On a hundred-point scale of worst possible things, we will give it the highest score.

Let us also establish the other anchor. What is the least awful thing you can imagine? What activity, situation, or outcome should have the distinction of being awarded only one point on our awfulness scale? Many of our clients have chosen such things as sneezing in public without a handkerchief, getting a spot on their tie before an important meeting, or discovering that they had a run in their stocking. This low score does not ignore the fact that these outcomes are undesirable, but rather acknowledges that they pale in comparison to genocide or nuclear holocaust. For our purposes, let us choose a spot on the tie to occupy the least awful position on our awfulness scale.

We can now use these two anchor points to get a better understanding of other undesirable outcomes. How does showing your portfolio compare to getting a spot on your tie? How does it compare to genocide? How do either compare with getting rejected or with taking an exam?

The Awfulness Scale

(Spot on tie) 1 _____ 50 _____ 100 (Genocide)

Fill in the above scale. Do you need to have the same level of emotional or behavioral response to the possibility of showing a portfolio, getting rejected, or taking an exam as you do to possibility of the death of an entire population? How does making a cold call compare with genocide? How does stuttering when you speak compare with genocide?

We would all agree that many of the activities listed above can be unpleasant for you. In fact, some of you may find them very unpleasant. We are not suggesting that you shouldn't find them unpleasant. Rather, we want to help you put things into proper perspective. We are not trying to deny the importance to you of doing well; rather, we are trying to help you take the onus out of doing badly. We are not recommending that if you are concerned about doing poorly in front of a powerful director, the appropriate response is to say to yourself, "Oh, boy, I am going to fail in front of the director. I really want to do that. Thank you, give me a double helping of failure in front of this powerful director."

This approach does not require that you like a thing you dislike, or that you not be displeased by unpleasant outcomes; rather, it requires that you not scare yourself with unimaginably dire consequences when bad things happen to you. If you unrealistically tell yourself that some activity, situation, or outcome is the worst thing in the world, you inevitably send a message to your body to produce the amount of energy (stress) needed to cope with a dire emergency. The body ups the volume of your stress reaction, and the net result is that you dis-stress and immobilize yourself, since you are now preparing to put out a forest fire rather than roast marshmallows over a campfire. If you have a tendency to see many situations as potentially threatening, then you will quickly become exhausted and not be able to cope.

By placing things in proper perspective, you also allow yourself the luxury of a wider range of emotional reactions to a wider range of situations. Let us imagine that you have been telling yourself that performing in public is awful and that you have just been asked to give an impromptu talk at a business meeting. You will begin to experience a level of stress appropriate to the task of dealing with awful things. Let us also imagine that you have just received word that your child, or some other significant person in your life, has just had a serious accident. How much more additional energy both physical and emotional, do you need to cope with this rapidly developing situation? Let us further suppose that the bank has called to tell you that you don't have sufficient funds to cover a check.

All of these situations can be, and have been, viewed as awful by many people. Are they equally awful to you? If you are suddenly confronted with a barrage of awful events, do you cope effectively? Would it be easier to cope if you could reframe the various outcomes? Would you have different, though still negative, emotions? Would you still be overwhelmed, or would you be able to say to yourself, "Boy, when it rains it pours, but it could be worse"?

By reminding yourself that "it could be worse," you may discover that you are less likely to be overwhelmed by negative outcomes. If you fail a test—it could be worse. If you miss an appointment—it could be worse. This philosophical shift does not require that you give up your desire to do well or succeed. You still want to do well. You still don't want to do badly, and you can still work hard not to do badly. But, if you did badly, if you used both the concrete anchor and "it could be worse," it might help you to see that certain situations and outcomes are unpleasant, unfortunate, and disappointing, but not terrible, horrible, or awful.

So, What Is the Worst that Could Happen?

It's bad enough that the situation is disappointing, unpleasant, and unfortunate for you. But if you tell yourself that the situation is truly awful, you may also be saying that you have convinced yourself that after this unpleasant situation, there can be no next time for you. After a nuclear holocaust, there is no next time. After genocide, there is no next time. But if you fail at an audition or at some other equally important activity, there can always be a next time. There are always other auditions. There are always other interviews. There are always other parties. There are always other chances to make a presentation.

Certainly, doing well at a business presentation in front of the group you most desperately want to impress is important to you. In fact, it may be 100 percent important. But telling yourself that not doing well is awful probably doesn't serve any useful purpose. It has been our experience that contemplation of the awe–full does not spur the creative juices. It spurs the creation of flop sweat instead. It spurs the development of anxiety that stops you from functioning.

When you use a concrete anchor, you can use it as a prelude to reminding yourself not to editorialize, or as a prelude to calling on Sergeant Friday and getting at the facts in an empirical dispute.

Yes, it is true that if you do badly, you might not get the job. Yes, it is true that if you perform badly, you might get a bad review. Yes, it is true that you *might*. The probability might even be high. If you did poorly on a promotion interview, for example, you could rationally say to yourself, "Well, I really didn't do well on my promotion interview. I'm probably not going to be promoted today." Indeed, your employer may make a note on a card that goes into a central file somewhere that says, "X is capable of messing up an interview." That would not be very nice, but it doesn't mean that you will never get a promotion, or that you will never have a happy and successful life. When you irrationally turn that moment into an awful moment by saying, "It is awful that I have done poorly on that interview, and it is a catastrophe that now I won't get promoted," you are saying that not only is the situation worse than bad, but you cannot recover.

What is really the worst that could happen as a result of a missed opportunity, a botched interview, a failed test, or a bad review? Objectively, what is really the worst that could happen to you as a result of these undesirable outcomes? You would certainly feel unhappy. You *might* have to work harder. You *might* want to reconsider your priorities and strategies. But, would you have to be destroyed? Is it objectively true that you have been eradicated? Even after a bad review, you are still here. Even if you don't get promoted, you are still here, and you have not lost your ability, knowledge, and experience, all of which could be used on other jobs—or on the same one if you can dispute your irrational belief that when something goes wrong, it is horrible or awful.

It is undesirable if you don't do well or do badly, but you could say to yourself:

- "I didn't do well. That's too bad, but it's not the end of the world."
- "It is bad, but I can cope with it. I am not going to die as a result of having this bad thing occur, and my future is not damaged beyond belief, even though I may have to cope with the unpleasantness of the present."
- "It would be highly unpleasant, in the present, to fail to get the job (to perform badly, to get a negative evaluation). That's all—*highly* unpleasant. It's not terrible, nor is it the worst thing imaginable, even though it is not pleasant."
- There are many more imaginably or even unimaginably worse things than doing badly at a job or doing badly at an audition."

You Can't Always Say, "Hold the Onions!"

Many activities, situations, and outcomes are *un*wanted, *un*pleasant, and *incon*venient. To help you remember these three cool words, we are going to call these situations "onions," because they often smell, and they are routinely associated with tears. Could you imagine yourself having an unwanted, unpleasant, and inconvenient "onion" experience? What would your response be? What could you say to yourself?

A Bunch of Onions for the Speaker

- You are speaking in public, and you discover that you are two pages ahead of yourself and you didn't even notice. You went from one sentence to another, and they did not connect.
- You are speaking in public and, like a former vice president, you spell a word wrong, or you make a misstatement of fact.
- You are about to speak or perform, and you realize that you are sweating uncontrollably.

What could you do, or say to yourself, that would reduce your stress?

You could take a calming/cleansing breath and continue. You could remind yourself that even highly experienced public speakers have had this happen to them and have survived. You could dispute your irrational belief that you must be perfect. You could dispute your belief that human error is awful.

Is there anything that you can do that *guarantees* you will never experience these "onions?" Unfortunately, in all our years of experience, we have found no effective means of helping clients say, "Hold the 'onions' on my hamburger of life." We have helped them see the "onions" for what they were—situations that stank, that they might cry over for a time, but that were merely "onions" and not awful tragedies. We have also helped them realize that "onions" may be useful. When you do something and get an undesirable outcome, you have the opportunity to learn what to avoid doing in the future. You can also learn how to behave in more appropriate ways that not only reduce the chances of undesirable outcomes but also improve the quality of your performance in doing so.

To demand that you not be handed an "onion" is to deny reality—you have just been handed one. To demand that the "onion" situation not stink is to deny reality as well—"onions" are supposed to stink. Many people view the request to deliver a speech as rather more than *un*wanted, *un*pleasant, and *in*convenient. They perceive it as an opportunity to fail or appear foolish, which it may be if things do not go as well as they would like. No one truly wants to appear foolish in the eyes of others. But sometimes you can't help yourself. Sometimes you are foolish unwittingly. Sometimes your audience, for reasons of its own, chooses to see you as foolish, even though you are performing well. It might even have the poor manners to say to you, "Why are you wasting my time?" No one likes to hear that, and it would certainly be unfortunate if a member of the audience said this, but would it be terrible? Many people who dread this very possibility refuse to accept opportunities to speak or perform rather take the risk of being handed an "onion."

However, *worrying* that you might be seen as foolish or that you might make a mistake won't stop others from thinking as they choose to, nor will it stop you from making a mistake. Quite the contrary, over-stressing yourself increases the probability of errors. Avoiding performance situations may seem like a good idea initially because you avoid the possibility of speaking and therefore the possibility of appearing foolish or making a mistake in public, but as a result you rarely get the chance to improve your skills, and you therefore perpetuate both your lack of ability and the emotionally scary quality of the situation.

The better, more effective, response would be:

- To accept that it could happen
- To develop coping strategies to deal with it if it does happen
- To remind yourself that even if it does happen, it is not the end of the world, but rather one of those darned, unavoidable "onions"

And Now, Class, Time for Homework!

Concretize, Don't Awfulize

Try to use the specific recommendations of this prescription whenever you find yourself beginning to awfulize about the performance situation. (You also want to use the homework suggestions at the end of Chapter 5.)

1. How awe-full is it? Make out an awfulness scale.

The Awfulness Scale

(Spot on tie) 1 _____ **50** _____ **100 (Genocide)**

2. Does this situation *really* require that you be struck dumb in the face of it, or is it an **onion?**
3. Try to dispute your awfulizing thoughts.
4. When you use more effective thinking, does it reduce the "awful" quality of the situation?
5. Can you use cooler language?
6. What is the worst that could really happen? What coping strategies do you have to cope with this outcome?
7. Do you need to learn better strategies? Make a list of resources where you can learn to cope if you need to.
8. Reread the coping sentences on page 110.

Prescription 6

De-sacredize, Don't Idolize

Contemplating the Sacred

Throughout this prescription, we will encourage you to examine your "private religion," those sacred ideals that may not appear in any Bible, but that you believe in nonetheless. Many nonreligious people are surprised to discover that they have religiously held sacred ideals. Many devoutly religious people are equally surprised to discover that they have created their own personal gospel that may have more power over their lives than the Old and New Testaments combined.

These beliefs take the form of demands or commandments about appropriate behavior in specific settings or toward specific people. These beliefs may also include demands or expectations about how people "should" or "should not" behave toward them. We call these beliefs *sacred ideals* because they are so tenaciously held, so rarely challenged, and so frequently defended.

People who maintain these sacred ideals tend to have the same awe-full response as those we wrote about in the previous prescription. They have the awestruck response and certain physical symptoms as well, when they contemplate certain people. Many even treat their own performance as sacred. They have developed "religious rituals" as preliminary to their performance in the hopes of ensuring a benevolent response.

De-sacredize People

The Case of Sigmund L.: Sigmund L. was about to audition for his first big part. He knew that both a famous casting agent and a famous director would be watching his audition. As he began to contemplate this exciting possibility, a possibility that he had worked hard all his life to make happen, he began to worry. "What if they don't like me? What if they think I am not physically right for the part? What if they think I have no talent? They have been in the business for years, and I am not worthy to be in their presence. Maybe I am not ready to audition before these big shots. If they don't like me, maybe I should just pack it in. Maybe I should just pack it in anyway. I hate this feeling."

All of us have people we love, respect, and admire. Some of them may be parents, coaches, teachers, or employers. They are people who have had an impact on our lives in both positive and negative ways. Some of these people have legitimate authority over us because they have been given it by either the cultural or the legal system. They are allowed to control some element of our lives, or at least to very strongly influence some *element* of our lives. They may be allowed to fire us or hire us. They may be able to give us rewards and various other kinds of goodies. We may also choose to give other people, who don't have this legitimate authority, some degree of power over our lives. In either case, an appropriate response to them is to be *concerned* about how well you are doing in relation to them.

Don't Build Any Idols, False or Otherwise

In Chapter 3 we discussed the difference between anxiety and appropriate concern. When concern turns to anxiety in front of these significant and very important people, we call that idolizing them. When you turn concern into anxiety, it is as if you were bowing down before an idol or an all-powerful deity. While that might be very nice to do if the person is a king and you are his subject, do you wish to bow down before a critic who is watching your performance? Do you wish to bow down before your teacher before you raise your hand and speak in class? Do you want to bow down before the tax collector? Ask yourself not only if you want to bow down, but whether a genuflection is *required*.

We may be concerned or anxious about how well we perform in front of these people because we realize that they may be able to provide us with things that we desire. Sometimes what we desire from them takes the form of love; other times it takes the form of opportunities for advancement. Still other times, it takes the form of avoidance—we desire to avoid the pain that they mete out when they are displeased. However, when you get yourself anxious in a performance setting, you are not usually talking about strongly preferring to get love or merely desiring respect or admiration. You are talking about something that sounds very much like dread, panic, or fear.

When you experience dread, panic, or fear, you can't perform, or you perform very, very badly. One component of your fear is a result of your being in the presence of your "sacred idol." When you create your own personal sacred idol, you magically turn humans into little tin gods. Then, when you are confronted with this god, you behave appropriately—you are struck dumb with wonder and awe.

This would be a perfectly appropriate response, if you were in the middle of Mt. Sinai and a bush was burning, and suddenly you hear a voice coming out of the bush which redundantly says to you, "put off thy shoes, from off thy feet" (Exodus 3:2). In that situation dropping your jaw, gasping with wonder, and being immobilized makes all kinds of good sense. The authors would probably do the same in that situation.

However, do you wish to turn auditioning before an unimportant, or even an important, director or agent into a burning bush? Does it help to be struck dumb with awe in front of a teacher? Does it help you to become struck dumb with awe when you are speaking to your colleagues? Certainly, it may pay to be appropriately concerned and try to be adequately prepared. But when you are struck dumb with awe, you are immobilized and may be too overcome to prepare.

Do you find it is helpful to be struck dumb with awe in front of any person? Even though it is a human response, is it one you wish to maintain for all the important people in your life. You might want to carefully choose the people to whom you give this kind of power.

When you go to a religious service you may find that as you watch, the majesty of the ceremony gets to you, and you may even be awestruck by it. If you go to see a show, you may hope to watch a performance that so enthralls you that you are inspired, at least for the moment. You may, while attending a museum exhibition, see a work of art that is so extraordinary that you feel yourself overcome by its power.

Spectators can afford to be struck dumb. However, when you are not a spectator, when you are the performer (i.e. speaker, a painter, or a teacher), does being struck dumb help? Did it help Sigmund? Reread the case history at the start of the chapter. See if you can identify the awe-struck thought, or the thoughts that produced that awe.

If you selected, "They have been in the business for years, and I am not worthy to be in their presence" or "Maybe I am not ready to audition before these big shots" or "If they don't like me, maybe I should just pack it in. Maybe I should just pack it in anyway," you correctly identified those thoughts that struck Sigmund dumb.

Are there any people in your life to whom you respond in this way?

Make a list. Write down your emotional responses to these people. What are you telling yourself about them?

Many of our clients have listed thoughts like these:

- "This is a person with life or death control over me."
- "Look, here comes a very important and powerful person. If I ever made a mistake in his or her presence, I would never be able to live it down."
- "Whenever I am in this person's presence, I shake, I quake, I quiver, I am uncomfortable."
- "Whenever I think about this person, I become a mass of nerves. I get so tight that I can't do anything right."

Any one of those thoughts is enough to immobilize us, and some people have them all simultaneously. What can we do to replace these kinds of self-defeating, immobilizing, awe-full thoughts?

Let's visualize a situation. You are in front of an audience, and you know that you are not very good at speaking in public. In fact, it's a new situation for you. There are many ways of de-stressing yourself. One of the classic ways, which almost every book on this topic includes (so why should ours be any different?), is not to see your audience as bigger or more important than you. One useful suggestion is to see them naked, or imagine them all wearing silly hats. You could try to see them as babies with rattles in their hands, rather than as gangsters with Uzis.

One client of ours used to say that whenever she walked into a meeting, she had this extraordinary, overwhelming perception of herself going into the Roman arena as a gladiator. She saw Nero looking at her with his thumb down and a hungry lion about to devour her. You can just imagine how well she would speak with that image in her head.

Try visualizing yourself in that same Roman arena. You are one of the Christians, and you discover that there is a hungry lion looking your way and licking his lips. What would you want to do in that situation? If you are like our client, we suspect that you are going to want to run out of the arena. You might want to cry. You might also want to pray for a safe deliverance.

While these might all be fine responses to either the lion or Nero, none of them are ultimately helpful approaches to performing in public. What would happen to your emotional response if rather than lions, you saw the arena filled with cuddly little pussycats or other cute and friendly creatures? Would you want to run? Would you want to hide? Would you panic? Would you shake? Or, would you want to pick up those kittens and cuddle them? You can try to do the same thing in front an audience—you can try to "cuddle" your audience. Many performers have learned this trick. Rather than showing the audience how afraid they are, they try to see the audience as nonthreatening, and therefore they respond to their audiences in an appropriate way.

If you are afraid of or struck dumb by your audience (because you perceive them as out to hurt you or kill you), you are understandably not going to do well. If you see the audience as threatening, you are going to crank up the volume of your anxiety. You will induce a stress reaction and may then perceive it as immeasurably more intense than you'd like it to be.

Your voice may quiver, which it is naturally going to do when you are anxious. But the more anxious you are, the more you are going to *experience* the quiver. You may go blank. You may forget your notes. You may even discover that your hand trembles so much that your notes fall on the floor; and all because you perceived the meeting room as the Roman arena, and the person or people you were making the presentation to as a bilious emperor Nero. In essence, what you did was turn your audience into vengeful, wrathful gods.

We are not saying that you should not see certain people as important to you. As we wrote in the previous chapter, "It is important because it is important." It is your right as a human to see some people as important, others as less important, and still others as very important. That is your prerogative. No one will ask you to dispute your belief that critics, agents, bosses, or teachers are important.

However, as we pointed out in the previous chapter, importance may be a matter of degree. It is possible for you to perceive someone as very important, maybe even 100 percent important to you, and still not be awe-struck. However, when you are struck dumb in someone's presence, you are saying that this person is more than 100 percent important. As your math teacher may have taught you, you can't have more than 100 percent of anything.

"Wait," we hear you say, "but this person *is* very important. The person for whom I am performing may make a determination that will influence whether or not I get a big contract. This person is going to make a determination that might lead me to get the job I've always wanted, or the part I've always wanted, or the gallery exhibition that I have been trying to get for years." While it may be indubitably true that these individuals have that power and authority, they are only human. They are *not* idols or little tin gods or bilious dictators.

For those of you who are devoutly religious, this awe-struck response may also provide you with another problem: namely, that you feel not only awe-struck but guilty at feeling awe-struck. When you make someone into an idol, you are also violating one of the Ten Commandments. The first commandment states, "I am your G–d, thou shalt have no other gods before me" (Exodus 20).

What must it be like to make your boss more powerful than the Lord himself? Is that what you really intended? If you do not appease your boss, do you expect him to respond as Jehovah did to the children of Israel who danced before the golden calf? You may have indelibly implanted in your memory the glorious, technicolor, Cecil B. DeMille production of that moment: Moses is in the desert and has gone up to the mountain. His followers are not quite sure what to do next. While they wait, they are persuaded to build a golden calf, bow down to it, and dance in front of it. When Moses returns, he is angry; he breaks the tablets, and the whole world seems to collapse as the earth opens up and swallows both the calf and the dancers.

When you feel immobilizing fear, are you turning your boss into a potentially vengeful god who might respond to your performance as the Lord did to the worshipers of the golden calf? When you give someone that kind of power, it only serves to distress you. You wind up distressing yourself if you believe "The critic is a god, I'd better try to appease her." "My teacher is a god, I'd better appease him." When you create these false gods, you make yourself scared, nervous, tense, and awe-struck. One way of combatting this form of performance anxiety is to change from idol worshiper to idol smasher.

Do You Enjoy This Image of Yourself?

Imagine yourself walking into a situation where you are about to perform. Vividly imagine the people you are about to perform in front of saying to you in a very imperious tone, "Bow down before me, kneel, prostrate yourself, and kiss my toe."

What emotions are you feeling? Do you like that feeling? Is that what you generally feel when you speak in public? When you speak or otherwise perform in public, are you acting as if you have been asked to kiss some particularly obnoxious anatomical part? If you do, then you are probably going to give a bad performance, and you may feel very tense, scared, angry, and possibly depressed.

Try Being an Idol Smasher

Try imagining yourself in the same situation as before. Close your eyes, take a calming/cleansing breath, and see yourself walking into the room where the performance situation is to take place. Recognize that you have created this monstrous idol. See yourself bowing down; see yourself kissing its toe. Then say to yourself, "*Stop*. I don't have to do this. This is not required of me; it is not *necessary*." See yourself stand up, square your shoulders, put out your leg, and kick the idol over. See yourself knocking it down and watching it crumble into dust. See a small human being, much like yourself, rise out of the dust. Now allow yourself to talk as equals to that other human being.

Practice this exercise for homework. It may help you to place critics, teachers, colleagues, and others into perspective. They're important, but they're not *awfully* important. They are merely important. Just as they are merely human. Many of you have probably been told any number of times, by any number of parents, friends, and self–help book authors, that *everybody* puts on their pants one leg at a time. Even though this person may be very important to you, it really is not in your long-term best interests to treat the person, in the words of one of our more loquacious acquaintances, as if his or her excrement was not malodorous. It is far better to develop a casual attitude toward your idols—an attitude that allows you to perform without anxiety. An awestruck attitude only encourages failure.

Down the Rabbit Hole and Behind the Wizard's Curtain

Children's literature provides us with two interesting role models for this approach: Alice and Dorothy. When Alice comes to Wonderland, she meets the all-powerful Red Queen, who has the unfortunate tendency to order people's heads to be chopped off. Alice at first thinks the Queen is rather powerful and tries to keep on her good side. During the "life or death" trial that ends the book, Alice finally realizes how fatuous it is to be afraid of the Red Queen. She says, "You're nothing but a pack of cards!" and becomes empowered. She doesn't take away the Queen's legitimate authority; rather, she changes her own awe-struck response to her. By changing her response, Alice takes charge of her life.

In *The Wizard of Oz*, Dorothy finally looks behind the screen and sees that the great and powerful Wizard of Oz is nothing but a tired old man. She's annoyed that she was awe-struck by him, but she too is then empowered to get on with her life.

We are not suggesting that you ignore or deny the legitimate power of certain people. Nor are we asking you to ridicule the legitimate power of the people around you. However, turning them into the Wizard, turning them into the Red Queen, turning them into Nero, or turning them into some substitute for Jehovah does nothing useful and only increases your anxiety and reduces your effectiveness. It is more effective to remember that the Wizard is just a tired old man, that the Red Queen is only made of pasteboard, and that the Emperor, by all accounts, is not wearing any clothes.

Render unto Caesar...

Marsha was a Ph.D. candidate in psychology who was becoming increasingly agitated and disturbed by "all the stupid requirements" she had to pass in order to get her degree. Whenever she contemplated getting her Ph.D. or saw others who had recently earned their degrees, she was awe-struck by the wonder of it all. She was also quite impressed by the power and authority that her professors had, and wished to eventually join their ranks. Marsha, however, was busily loading the gun with which she might shoot herself in the foot. "Why should I have to take language and statistics examinations, orally defend my research proposal, and then orally defend my dissertation? It's too much. Nobody should have to do it. Why can't they make the rules less onerous? I hate the whole process."

Marsha's sacred notions concerned the way people in authority should behave. She devoutly believed that all authority should be benevolent, that is, should treat her well and not cause her any discomfort. Since she did not like the requirements, she believed that they should not exist. Since she gave her professors her awe-struck attention, she also believed that she deserved to be counted among the faithful and given special privileges. Since her beliefs were not supported, she was contemplating "changing religions," that is, finding a new major and new professors to idolize—who she hoped would treat her the way she wished.

Marsha undeniably had the right to change majors, but she would have been better served by changing her logic and her philosophy. She devoutly believed that she should have to obey only pleasant requirements. She also religiously believed that any field of study that was truly enjoyable would not have any noxious requirements. By tenaciously maintaining these and other beliefs, she had created

---

The Gospel According to Marsha

1. Thou shalt not suffer any discomfort.
2. Thou shalt have to take only "relevant" courses.
3. Thou shalt have to obey only rules that appeal to you.
4. Thou shalt never have to take statistics or other maths.
5. Thou shalt have only professors who don't challenge your opinions.

Etc., Etc., Etc.

Do you have your own personal gospel?
What are some of your "religious" beliefs?

Unfortunately, Marsha didn't realize that every field of study has requirements—some noxious, some less so. She was denying reality when she told herself that only the requirements that she approved of should exist. In reality, the program's rules stated that all students were required to take certain courses. The rules may have been, and probably were, arbitrary and capricious. They may have reflected a different period of history and a different set of needs. Marsha's railing at them, however, did not change the rules and only served to increase her disturbance and ineffectiveness. Marsha had chosen a particular program and was well aware of the requirements before she enrolled.

A better approach would have been for Marsha to remind herself that all communities have rules, some useful, some not so useful, and some dumb. By choosing to join that particular community (her graduate program), she was tacitly agreeing to abide by the "rules of the land." Therefore she could have reminded herself to "render unto Caesar...," and thereby would have encouraged herself to abide by the rules. She could have said to herself:

"There is no evidence that Deans, or anyone else, for that matter, shouldn't make dumb rules. In fact, based on readily observable evidence, Deans should make dumb rules (because that is what they seem to do most frequently). Even though I most devoutly wish that the Deans wouldn't make dumb rules, neither I nor anyone else can take away their human right to do so. My demands that these rules not exist only help me to disturb myself and does *not* change the situation one little bit."

This acceptance of the requirements does not mean that she has to like them, or that she has to change her belief that they are dumb, arbitrary, or capricious. Her acceptance may allow her to see them as the dumb rules that temporarily guide her behavior while she is in this community.

Many people, when they first encounter this philosophy, think that we are recommending complacency and an endorsement of the status quo. This is *not* the case. We are merely pointing out to you that getting yourself angry, depressed, or immobilized in the face of dumb rules only serves to distress you and does nothing to change the powers that be. We are also pointing out that your distress comes from conflicting beliefs between you and the legitimate authority about what the rules "should be." When you get angry or depressed, you don't think straight, you don't think creatively, and you don't think strategically—all of which are needed if you are going to figure out how to change the rules, if possible, or to logically evaluate *if* they need changing.

Sometimes it is possible to work toward changing the rules; other times it is not. It is first necessary to determine whether working toward changing the rules is worth the time and effort involved. If it is, you may want to remind yourself to vigorously dispute your low frustration tolerance (LFT) concerning how difficult it is and why it *should move* more rapidly. If you decide that it is *not* worth your time or effort to work toward changing the rules, it would be wise to dispute your awfulizing about how terrible the rules are. It might also be useful to dispute any irrational beliefs that might lead you to feel angry or depressed about living in a world where such dumb rules are in effect.

Do you have any difficulty with the rules?

Can you dispute your belief that they shouldn't be there?

What would be a more effective response?

De-sacredize Your Symptoms

Many performers, both professionals and civilians, maintain another area of sacred ideals when it comes to their physical and emotional symptoms. They religiously maintain that they can perform only when they feel good. Therefore, when they experience physical symptoms such as dry mouth or jittery muscles, which often accompany any performance, they are struck dumb in the face of their symptoms and maintain a worshipful distance until their symptoms "choose to" fade. People who sacredize their symptoms maintain a worshipful response to their emotions as well.

Many civilians and theatrical performers devoutly believe that they cannot perform unless they are "up for the performance." If they feel emotionally down, they wait until they feel better, or they may self-medicate using alcohol or drugs, before they attempt to perform. Ironically, performers who suffer from performance anxiety rarely feel good when they contemplate performing. Therefore, they rarely, if ever, perform, or they PWI (perform while intoxicated). In either case, these performers experience the negative consequences of procrastination, missed opportunities, and loss of reputation, which may be worse than the consequences they were trying to avoid.

Do you have any sacred symptoms?
Do you stop yourself from performing because of your sacred symptoms?
Can you dispute your irrational beliefs about your symptoms?

De-sacredize Your Performance

Many performers have sacred ideals about the ritual aspects of their perform-ance. Writers, for example, may have sacred beliefs about the number of sharp-ened pencils they need before they can start to write. They may have sacred beliefs about the position of their chair in the room or the tilt of the computer dis-play. Musicians may "require" perfect silence or perfectly moistened reeds for their instruments. Writers, artists, sculptors, and composers may need to be "struck by the muse" before they can even begin performing. Many have so sacredized the entire process of performing that they are struck dumb by the wonder of their own activity, and may experience "artist's block" and an-guishedly await their muse's return. These sufferers religiously believe that be-ing an artist is a sacred duty and that their art is elusive. What they don't realize is that the more they make the process sacred, the more difficult they make it for themselves to function in it. Even civilian performers endorse a form of this be-lief when they see giving a speech as an impossible task that requires inspiration from on high.

The polar opposite of this sacred belief was espoused by the behavioral psy-chologist B. F. Skinner. Skinner was once asked to talk before PEN, the society of poets, essayists, and novelists. He entitled his talk, "On Having a Poem." In it he made a comparison between poets and chickens. He said, "Poets make poems, much like chickens lay eggs, and both feel better afterwards."

When you de-sacredize your performance ritual, you are merely reminding yourself that you can write, compose, or perform under less than optimal condi-tions. You are also helping yourself challenge any self-defeating or self-handicap-ping ideas that might ultimately do you in and stop you from performing. De-sacredizing the performance ritual allows you to perform without being awe-struck by your own performance (an activity better left to the audience). When we de-sacredize our performance ritual, we challenge our superstitious beliefs about what is necessary to our performance. We help ourselves let go of Dumbo's magic feather, or our lucky pencil, and perform naturally.

When we ask you to examine, challenge, and let go of your superstitious be-liefs, we do so fully aware that the world of the theatrical performer is filled with superstitions. We would not ask you to give up superstitious beliefs that connect you to your community and that are essentially harmless. We are not asking you to give up a reluctance to whistle backstage* or to stop referring to Shakespeare's "Scottish Tragedy,"[†] but rather to give up beliefs that *stop* you from performing.

---

*In the theater of the 1900s, sets and backdrops were raised and lowered by means of pulleys and ropes attached to sandbags. The stagehands would whistle to signal when a sandbag was to be dropped. The whistle was used to alert people backstage to get out of the way. An actor who inadvertently whistled backstage might unexpectedly come face to face with a sandbag.

[†]Many actors have a reluctance to casually say the name of Macbeth in a theater. The belief is that anyone doing so will jinx the performance and the performer. Actors who say Macbeth's name are required to remove the jinx by turning around three times and walking backwards out of the nearest door.

And Now, Class, Time for Homework!

De-Sacredize, Don't Idolize

Try to use the specific recommendations of this prescription whenever you find that your sacred ideals are having a negative impact on your performance or your willingness to perform. (You may also want to use the homework suggestions at the end of Chapter 5.)

1. Identify the sacred ideals that you are invoking.

   - Are they about important people in your life?
   - Are they about symptoms?
   - Are they about your performance rituals?

2. Take your emotional temperature after you invoke these ideals. (For example, how do you feel emotionally when you tell yourself, "My big boss is watching me. I had better be careful how I perform in his or her presence"?)

3. Try to dispute your irrational sacred beliefs. (For example, where is it written that you *can't* perform unless all of your pencils are perfectly sharpened? Where is it written that the dean *shouldn't* make dumb rules?)

4. Does this person, symptom, or ritual *really* require that you be struck dumb in its presence? If it does, is it in your long-term best interests to maintain that awe-struck response?

5. Try to de-sacredize.

   - Try to see the audience as non-threatening (page 115).
   - Try to be an idol smasher (page 117).
   - Try to remember the discoveries of Alice and Dorothy. (page 118).

6. What would be a more effective response, if you could do it? (Reread the coping strategy on page 121).

7. When you try to use more effective thinking, does it reduce your awed response to people, symptoms, and rituals?

8. Can you use cooler language?

Tolerate, Don't Musturbate

Have you ever had the experience of being in an "onion" situation (remember, an "onion" situation is one that is *un*fortunate, *un*wanted, and *in*convenient) and saying to yourself, "I shouldn't be doing this. I shouldn't have to be in this unfortunate, inconvenient situation. Why must I practice all the time? Why must I stand on line waiting to audition? Why do I have to send out a headshot right now, when I'd rather be doing something else?" If you recall from our earlier presentations, we talked about the concept of "I-can't-stand-it-itis." This concept occurs when you tell yourself that you *can't stand* any particular situation, behavior, or feeling. What happens when you tell yourself, "I must not be doing something I can't stand" or "I can't stand what I am doing"? You will probably feel anxious or angry, and you may even have a tendency to self-down because you are stuck in a situation that you shouldn't have been in at all. The reactions just listed are very common human reactions to unpleasant situations.

Musturbation Is Self-Abuse

Another very common, but equally self-defeating, reaction is to demand that the world and the people in it (including yourself) either *must be* or *should be* the way you want, or should *not* be the way they are. We call this response "musturbation." When you musturbate, you steadfastly choose to ignore the evidence you have received that the world, yourself, and others are behaving differently from the way you would prefer them to act. When you musturbate, you make yourself angry, anxious, and potentially depressed because things are not going **"as they must."** When you musturbate, you cast yourself in the starring role of Jehovah and then believe that you are entitled to act accordingly. This behavior can sometimes lead to people asking you, "Who died and made you G–d?" You can demand that "onion" situations not occur. You can demand that other people, or yourself, be different from what they are. You can demand anything, but **where is it written that you must get what you demand?**

We know that some unpleasant situations are necessary if you are going to get an acting job. Similar unpleasant situations are common if you are trying to get a job in another field or maintain a position in any field. You are going to have to audition, or you are going to have to stand in line. It would be best to try to tolerate these petty inconveniences rather than upset yourself about them.

The Case of Reginald: Reginald, an actor who attended one of our workshops, after hearing about musturbation, declared himself the "emperor of all musturbators." Reginald upset himself royally every time he had to put up with any unpleasant situation that went with his profession. He didn't believe that *he* should have to wait on line. He couldn't stand waiting around for hours until his turn came on open calls. He felt that he should not have to put up with petty details, and he couldn't stand the effort associated with dealing with casting agents. He believed that the audition process must be more logical and that only people who were going to be cast should be asked to audition. As a result, he couldn't stand the effort of learning lines for an audition where he only had a slim chance of getting the role. He couldn't stand the audition process at all. He stated that if he "got to run the business, he would do away with auditions, and cast from videotapes... never live."

Reginald spent a great deal of time telling himself, "The world should not be the way it is, especially in the theater. I should not have to put up with all of the nonsense I do just to get cast in a show or commercial. I can't stand it, and it must not be this way." Reginald's constant demands of how things in the theater *should be* kept him from working very much. He also lost a lot of friends and networking opportunities because others got tired of his constant angry demands.

If you are going to go for a job, you are most likely going to have to go through an interview process. If the job is an acting job, you are most likely going to have to tolerate the audition process, which Reginald did not want to do.

If you want to sell some product, you are probably going to have to routinely pick up a phone and make some calls. Your response of "I can't stand it" or "Why do I have to do this?" slows you down, gets in your way, and probably upsets you. It doesn't ever change the requirements of the external situation.

If you recall, we talked about disputing and arguing with yourself. We reminded you to stick to the objective facts of the situation you are in. Reginald's fact would be, "In order for me to have an opportunity to get the role, it is necessary for me to audition. If I don't audition, I have no chance of getting the role." If you are a salesperson selling a product, the facts of the situation are, "If I don't call on customers, I have no chance of selling the product." No one says that you are *forced* to do what the situation requires, but if you do not, you have no chance of meeting your goals. It's not written anywhere that you must be an actor or actress. It's not written anywhere that you must be a successful salesperson.

However, let us assume that you would prefer to be a successful actor, actress, or salesperson. Let us assume, as well, that you would like to get rid of your performance anxiety in these situations, or at least control it to some extent. When you are in a performance situation and find that you are telling yourself, "I shouldn't have to do this," does it enhance your performance?

Our experience and the experience of our clients has been that it detracts from performance. When our clients are in a performance situation and tell themselves, "I must not be doing what I'm doing right now" or "I must not have had this awful, intolerable thing presented to me," their anxiety increases, their physical discomfort increases, and their performance tends to deteriorate.

Try this experiment. Imagine that you are scheduled to do some public activity, and rather than saying to yourself, "Yeah, okay, sure, I can do that," tell yourself instead, "I *shouldn't have to* do that." How do you feel emotionally when you start thinking, "I shouldn't have to do this thing"? Do you feel good? Do you feel like you are ready to perform? Magnify the momentary discomfort or anger that you are experiencing by a factor of a thousand and you may get some sense of what it's like to respond in this fashion on a daily basis. If you do this regularly, you create a tremendous amount of suffering for yourself. Our prescription in this case is to *tolerate and not musturbate*.

As we said earlier, musturbation is saying to yourself, "I *must* not feel, do, think, or act the way I do right now. The world *must* not ask me to do the things I don't want to do. The world *must* not be the way it is." When you musturbate, you place yourself in a position of denying reality. The reality of the situation, at least for right now, is that someone is asking you to speak in public. The reality of the situation, at least for right now, is that if you wish to get a job as a performer, you need to audition. The reality of the situation, right now, if you are a student who must give an oral report, is that the teacher is basing your grade in part on your presentation. These are "onion" situations. They're inconvenient, they're unfortunate, perhaps they're even unnecessary in your judgment; but to demand that they shouldn't be there would be like saying that a car shouldn't have tires, or that a desk **should be** a chair.

When you *mus*turbate, you make demands about the world, yourself, and others, often characterized by use of the word *must. Musts* leave no room for argument. Can you prove, without a doubt, that the world must be as you want it to be? We call this a Jehovian demand, because when you make it, you are acting as if you were in charge of the universe.

Let's look at a really simple situation. You are driving along the highway and you pass a billboard advertising a home-style restaurant. You don't like billboards because it is your belief that they interfere with the scenery, and you tell yourself, "It must not be there." If you think about it, what are you saying when you say that something must not be where it is? Are you saying that you are Jehovah and that you have the right to demand that the highway authority of the state you are traversing respond to your demand and remove the billboard immediately? Can you prove that your demand, as a driver merely passing the billboard on that highway, should be more important than that of the people who paid for the advertisement?

Let's say that your demand is that you must not feel discomfort in new situations. If you make this demand, you will tend to increase your discomfort, and you will probably upset yourself. One of the common sentences that you will hear cognitive therapists who work with the concept of musturbation use is that musturbation is a form of self-abuse. When you tell yourself, "I must not feel what I'm feeling right now" or "The world must not provide me with the kinds of situations I am currently in," you do not change the world one iota. You do, however, make yourself feel lousy.

What's the alternative? The alternative is to at least temporarily *tolerate* those things that you don't like. If you wish to achieve a certain goal, such as auditioning or speaking in public, or placing yourself in the public eye to increase your chances for job promotion, you need to learn how to tolerate the things you don't like.

No one is asking you to like what you don't like or enjoy what you don't enjoy. There's a world of difference, however, between not liking something and telling yourself that what you don't like shouldn't be or that you can't tolerate whatever it is that you don't like.

When you say that you can't stand something, it suggests to your body that you are in the presence of something that will kill you, and your body cooperates. If you tell your body, "I'm about to die when I give my public talk," your body goes into defense mode. Your heartbeat increases, your stomach churns, you feel nauseous. All you are doing at that moment is creating further discomfort. No one is asking that you deny the reality that you are uncomfortable when you have to speak in public. That's true for you, and it may be because you currently are not terribly skillful at public speaking. If you see public speaking as dangerous to you and demand that you must not have to tolerate it, your body will react to it as a danger and will get aroused. What can you do to prevent this from happening? You can remind yourself that this activity may be highly uncomfortable for you because you're new at it, and therefore you will behave appropriately by being physically uncomfortable, but that you can stand it. In healthy bodies, those discomforts are merely signs that you are doing something new.

The rules of the game are that when you are in an uncomfortable situation that you'd rather not be in, but that you probably ought to be in to further your goals, teach yourself to tolerate.

Lessons in Tolerance

Use these situations to practice tolerance. First, write down a sentence that accurately reflects the situation. What could you say to yourself about these unfortunate situations that you may routinely find yourself in that would enhance your performance, rather than detract from it? Would it be a good idea to say, "I hate having to get up and talk extemporaneously; I must not ever be asked to do it"? Would it help to say, "I must not feel uncomfortable in new situations"? Would it help to say, "My bosses or my teacher must not ask me to do things I don't like to do"? What would be a better choice for a coping statement? Remember, a coping statement is a realistic thought that helps you to cope rationally. If you wrote, "I don't like it (whatever the situation might be), but I can stand it," you are right on target. Any variant on that sentence is accurate because you are not going to die from public speaking, even though you may feel highly uncomfortable. You can learn to be less uncomfortable and, in time, perhaps even enjoy the experience. We are saying that you can learn to accept the fact that the situation is uncomfortable for you, but that in the context of your job or your career goals, it is a necessary discomfort that it would be best for you to tolerate. If you want to have your dental cavities filled, you go to a dentist and put up with the necessary discomfort of holding your mouth open in a peculiar way and probably sitting in a chair that has been tilted backward in a peculiar way, because that allows the dentist to get the job done. You tolerate the momentary discomfort and inconvenience of the dentist's office to achieve the greater goal, healthy teeth. You tolerate the momentary discomfort of having a blood test taken to achieve the greater goal of finding out if you are in good physical condition. You learn to tolerate lots of inconveniences throughout your lifetime. When you tell yourself that you can't tolerate a situation, you're mistaking your discomfort for something that will kill you, and you only wind up making yourself miserable. We all have had this type of experience at some point in our lives.

Many of us learn musturbation from our parents. We are told from the time we are toddlers, "I can't stand it when you behave that way. You mustn't behave that way." How many times have you heard a mother say that to her child? What does she really mean? Does she mean the child's behavior is going to leave her lying dead in the playground? What she probably means is that she doesn't like the child's behavior and wants the child to behave differently. Watching a child throw a temper tantrum is certainly unpleasant, and is something that most parents dislike. However, watching a tantrum, while annoying, frustrating, and maybe even embarrassing to some, is still tolerable.

What does the child learn when a parent says, "I can't stand it"? The child learns to say, "I can't stand it. It shouldn't be there because I can't stand it." It's an interesting but very quaint idea, and it's inaccurate. No one likes to have to witness a tantrum. None of us likes watching someone misbehave, or having someone say something insulting to us. These are all sources of unpleasantness, but we as adults can learn to stand it.

Children have been known to believe that when anything unpleasant occurs, they can change it through intolerance (i.e., throwing a tantrum). Unfortunately, many children are reinforced in this infantile belief by their caretakers' caving in and either removing them from the "intolerable" situation or acceding to their demands.

Caretakers can also respond to infantile Jehovahs in other ways. They can use shame ("Shame on you, a big boy acting like such a baby"), or they may unfortunately use violence, that is, they beat their own demands into the child and force the child to comply.

Neither of these responses is preferable or effective.

If It Shouldn't Have Happened, It Wouldn't Have Happened!

When you musturbate, you say that something that did happen shouldn't have happened, and therefore it must not have happened. This denies the reality of what did happen. If some event mustn't have happened, it wouldn't have happened, because there would have been a law in the natural universe saying, for example, "Babies don't throw tantrums." There would have been a universal law that teachers never ask for oral reports or term papers or extra work to be done. There would be a law in the natural universe that says that directors have no right to listen to what they want to hear. If there were such a law in the natural universe, then no one would be doing these crazy things. No one would do the things we've just mentioned because they must not.

When you musturbate, you confuse your desire with natural law, the law of the universe. You may say, "I would much prefer not having to do things that make me uncomfortable." That's a perfectly natural and delightful desire. No one would like you to have a different desire. However, is it an immutable law of the universe that you or anyone else should never experience discomfort? The law, probably more accurately stated, is that as a human, you will feel uncomfortable. As a matter of fact, when you perceive danger, you're supposed to have a rapid heartbeat. That is the law of the body. When you say to yourself, "I can't stand this very natural thing," you upset yourself more, and your body responds with even greater discomfort. That seems to also be a natural law. Therefore, it is in your best interest to remind yourself to tolerate the situation that caused you discomfort.

Don't Confuse Forgiveness with Forgetfulness

The Case of Barbara: Barbara was in a loveless marriage. She had been married to her husband for ten years and "got nothing out of it except grief." Every two or three weeks her husband would become violently angry and would strike her. She would beg him to seek help, but she also believed that a good woman stands by her man. Every fight would end with Barbara and her husband tearfully making up and her tolerating his behavior and forgiving him. As the battles wore on, Barbara become more confused:

"He hits me. I tolerate it and forgive him, as I must. Then he hits me again. I thought if I forgave him, he would learn that I love him and would stop hitting me."

Barbara confused forgiveness with forgetfulness. She assumed that her husband, who enjoyed violence like a vinophile loves fine wine, would give up his violence just because she forgave him and she wanted him to give up his violence. He didn't stop his outbursts because they were effective (babies' tantrums are also often effective). Barbara needed to be convinced that he wouldn't change just because she wanted him to, and that his behavior was illegal in her state. I used the following analogy of the bear to help Barbara see that her tolerance of her husband's bad behavior was not an effective means to encourage him to change, nor was it an effective strategy for her own safety.

What Do Bears Do in the Woods?

A story is told of a naturalist who enjoyed going out into the woods to hike and camp. He relished the clean pine air and the babbling brooks, and when evening fell, he would seek out a large oak tree and sleep beneath its boughs. As luck would have it, the naturalist picked a tree that was the "dumping ground" for a large grizzly bear.

The bear headed for the tree and, oblivious to the sleeping naturalist, did what bears do in the woods. The naturalist woke up and was about to get angry and argue with the bear, when he realized that the bear probably did not speak English and so forgave the bear for its transgressions and went on his way.

The next night the naturalist returned to the same tree to sleep. He reasoned, "I like the countryside that it is in, and besides, the bear won't do that again—especially since I was so forgiving." That same night the bear returned to the tree and...

When you confuse forgiveness with forgetfulness, you too forget what bears do in the woods.

Barbara was helped to see that her husband was the bear in the woods, doing what bears do best. I helped her see that she had a number of choices:

- She could tolerate the ordure, which I would not recommend in cases of spouse abuse.
- She could get out of the woods.
- She could sleep under another tree.

Barbara began to work on her irrational belief that her husband must change just because she forgave him, and then offered him the choice of getting professional help on his own or by court order. She quietly stated that she loved him, but she was unwilling to tolerate his behavior any longer. She also told him that she was prepared to go to a women's shelter if necessary. She saw that his Jehovian demands and her saintlike tolerance were ineffective tools for building the kind of relationship she wanted. As a result, she began to work toward changing both herself and the marriage.

We would encourage you to also work toward changing those things you can change. It may very well be true that eventually you can tell your teacher, your boss, and even certain directors, "I would much prefer that you handle the project in a different way." Some of them may listen to you, and indeed you might be able to organize enough support to effect social change.

One particular woman, who is well known in the community, was very unhappy, and rightly so, about drunk drivers. Rather than merely saying that people shouldn't be allowed to drive around drunk and that others mustn't find it amusing, she organized her strategy and her community and developed the organization Mothers Against Drunk Driving (MADD). This organization eventually did bring about change. We no longer find visual images of a drunk driving down the road weaving back and forth a good inspiration for laughter. We no longer assume that it's perfectly okay for anyone to leave a party intoxicated, and in fact, designated drivers are becoming the norm even among college students and adolescents.

The woman who originated MADD didn't like the behavior she saw, but rather than musturbate about it, she organized and achieved some change. Musturbation alone, or saying, "We shouldn't do this; this is stupid, this is foolish, this is degrading," will not accomplish anything. She didn't just say, "It must not be." She said, "I don't like it, and here's what I can do to alter it." In order to alter it, our guess is that she had to tolerate a huge amount of discomfort, possible inconvenience, and a lot of negative feedback. She probably was called a party pooper at some point, and some people who enjoy their alcohol and do not think consequentially probably told her, "Ah, come on, everyone gets a little high. Ah, come on, you're only young once. Ah, come on,..." She, however, stood her ground rather than merely saying, "It must not be" and helped change our perceptions as to whether getting drunk and driving is cool. The popular belief now is that we must not drive when we're drunk, rather than that anyone can drive and in any condition. By tolerating the discomfort of social opposition and working toward change, she eventually was able to use evidence to change social perceptions. We owe her a debt of gratitude because the world is a safer place because of her work.

Many other such people have existed in the world, and what we are saying to you is not that you should passively sit by and allow things that you dislike to continue on indefinitely. If you truly believe that some behaviors need to be changed or some parts of the social world need to be changed, by all means go out there and work toward change. But in the meantime, tolerate what is until you can make a difference.

There are situations in the world in which you cannot make a difference. You are not going to be able to eliminate a job interview if you want the job. You are not going to be able to eliminate an audition for a role in most cases. Therefore, you need to recognize that there are situations in which, even though you feel uncomfortable and you tell yourself "It must not be this way," it will continue to be so. If you want to succeed in these situations, you need to tell yourself something that will help you tolerate them, get through them, and succeed.

*What are the situations in which you use the word **must** or say, "It must not be"?*

*In what situations in your job, in getting a job, or in trying for a promotion do you use the word **must** or the words must not be?*

Write them down.

After you have listed two or three musts, write down what you can tell yourself instead of "It must not be this way." An effective coping statement for "It must not be this way" could start out with, "I don't like this very much, but I can't change it and therefore I can tolerate it because _____ or I can tolerate it and _____." Fill in the blanks in a manner that is appropriate to the situation you are in.

Notice that we are constantly saying that you don't have to like something in order to tolerate it. We are asking you to use the thought, "I don't like it, but I can tolerate it and _____." What is your specific "and"? Some of our clients have used the following "ands":

1. and I can learn to function effectively within it.
2. and learn how to cope better.
3. and work to see if there's any way I can change it, if it's in the changeable category.

You probably are not going to get a director to change the audition rules, unless you are a superstar. Even superstars have occasionally been requested to audition for specific roles. You are not going to be able to get all teachers to see that they can make an exception in your case. Everyone else has to give a speech in order to get the grade, but you don't have to. Is this fight worth fighting? You may want to pick the areas where you think you can be effective.

Musturbation demands that the world change. And while in many situations that might be desirable politically, socially, and economically, how will hinging your success on the world's changing help you become successful today? The odds are very, very strong that even if the world does change, it is going to take a long time for that to happen. You may be one of those rare selfless souls who says, "I don't care how long it takes, but I am willing to devote my entire life to getting the world to change, and I am willing to give up my own personal happiness, health, and chances at having a successful, productive life in order to do so. I'm going to let those all go by the board until the world changes."

If you're that kind of individual, then you probably don't have performance anxiety because you are already out there on the barricades. But if you are that individual and you do have performance anxiety, the first step is to tolerate and work with yourself to cope with your own anxiety and then change the world. You can almost picture a mother telling her young and upcoming revolutionist child, "Listen, dear, before you change the world, finish eating your spinach. Then go clean your room. A good revolutionist is a healthy, clean, and neat revolutionist. It's not right to storm the barricades before you wash your face."

This may sound rather silly, shallow, or even demeaning, but there is a grain of truth in it. The grain of truth deals with the concept that it's easier and more expedient to work on changing your behavior, than it is to change the political infrastructure. That doesn't mean that if you think the political infrastructure needs to be changed, you don't work toward changing it.

> *The Case of Frederick:* Frederick, a Protestant minister, had always dreamed of becoming an agent of social change. He pictured himself bringing industry to underdeveloped areas and teaching the impoverished to grow their own crops, and all would become good and thankful churchgoers because of his good works.
>
> Frederick, with all his dreams, hated his day-to-day existence. He didn't like the politics involved in conducting a congregation. He didn't like the petty arguments involved in the perfunctory board meetings that he had to constantly attend. He told himself, "I can't stand all this pettiness when the world is so full of important problems." He also told himself that if he were really strong and useful, he would be out in the world solving the problems of the poor and the hungry. When he had to do pastoral counseling and listen to his parishioners' problems, he told himself, "I can't stand to listen to all these petty little things. These people should not be taking up my valuable time with their mundane little situations."
>
> Frederick became more and more unhappy as time went on. It was not until his bishop visited him because of complaints from his congregation and pointed out all of the social ills that existed around him that Frederick was able to see that change could begin at home and could count. Frederick was then able to change his behaviors in order to tolerate what he saw as petty and mundane. In doing so, he realized that for the present he could work most effectively on changing the poverty and unhappiness in his own parish.
>
> What was Frederick's real problem? Frederick saw himself as an agent of social change, but only in the bigger world picture. He never seemed to realize that problems exist all around and that his not being able to stand petty problems would keep him from doing his job. Frederick learned the lesson that the revolutionist child's mother taught, "Start with the more immediate and doable changes, before moving on to the grandiose."

Is it always in your best interest to work on changing the things that you don't like or that you think need changing? Are there situations in life that cannot be changed? Let's say that you are a medical student. You decide that you should not have to take the Medical Boards that are required for licensing and specialization designation. You rally a group of your fellow students who also hate the idea of taking examinations, and you send your petition to the Medical Board. Are you going to effect change? You probably are not going to have an impact because the rules have been established to set a minimum requirement for competence in the field. Therefore, when you decide that you personally do not like something, before you try to change that thing, it would be best to determine if it really needs to be changed, and why it has been established the way it has.

   The Case of Simone: Simone, an art student, always believed that the world should be different from the way it was. However, she was not interested in social change and injustice or poverty. She was interested in having a color–coordinated world. She believed that cows, rather than being the color they were, should be green so that they would blend nicely with the meadow. She believed that roosters should be bright, bright red so that they would look good on weather vanes. She could never figure out why nature had made such mistakes and why cows were not green.

   Simone had heard a little bit about genetic engineering while in school and decided that one of her missions in life would be to color-coordinate animals. She believed that a green cow would fit more perfectly into nature.

How realistic are Simone's goals? Should she bother trying to see them through? Would she be wasting her time, trying to change something that is immutable? How do you determine what you can realistically change? You first need to determine whether what you want to change realistically needs to be changed. Do cows need to be green? Is there a strong biological reason to effect this change? Is this goal an achievable goal? Can a cow be made this color, and is the cost worth the investment?

These are only some of the questions that you need to ask yourself when you try to decide whether you want to work on changing a situation. If the situation cannot be changed or does not merit the effort and cost that would be required to change it, it would be best if you could acknowledge that fact and learn to tolerate the situation.

When deciding whether to try to change a situation or to acknowledge that the situation is the way it is and learn to tolerate it and deal with it, you also need to look at the possible consequences of your actions. Let us say that Reginald, our emperor of musturbation, organizes all of the actors in New York, and they all decide that live auditioning is out and that submitting videotapes is the only way that they will audition. The directors and the producers all insist on live auditions. What will be the probable consequences for Reginald and his fellow actors if they insist on having it their way? What will probably happen is that the producers and directors will recruit other actors from other locations who will meet their requirements. Therefore, it is in your best interest to ask yourself, "What are the consequences of my not tolerating things as they are, and what are the possible consequences of insisting on change in the situation I am in?"

What coping statements could you use to help you avoid the mistakes that both Reginald and Frederick initially made and the error that Simone continued to make? Try using the following:

1. "I can change myself, but I can't insist that anyone else change."

2. "The world should be the way it is, because that is how it is. This means that a fact is a fact is a fact. Blue is blue and yellow is yellow. Cats are not dogs, nor should they be."

3. "I can stand something even if I don't like it. I can learn to tolerate it, and I don't need to like it."

4. "I can learn to tell myself that situations I don't like aren't intolerable, just unpleasant."

And Now, Class, Time for Homework!

Tolerate, Don't Musturbate

Try to use the specific recommendations of this prescription whenever you find that you are musturbating about the world, yourself, and others. (You may also want to use the homework suggestions at the end of Chapter 5.)

1. Search for your musts and shoulds and list them. Dispute your irrational belief that the world, yourself, and others *must be* the way you want them to be.

2. Develop a list of coping statements that you can use to short-circuit your musts. Read them to yourself as you begin to experience the rage that comes from people's ignoring your demands.

3. When confronted with a *bear*, or an *onion*, do a reality check. Remember what onions and bears are supposed to do.

4. Practice tolerance, when it is in your long-term best interest to do so.

Prescription 8

Use "Why Not?" Not "Why Me?"

The Case of Thomas: Thomas, a mild-mannered purchasing agent who was employed by a well-known chain of merchandising marts, always presented himself well and hoped that no one would notice how unsure he was of his skills. Since Thomas was a pleasant and accommodating employee, his boss often volunteered Thomas's services to train a new employee or take a client to lunch. Thomas would become very anxious, but the only person he would let in on his little secret was his wife. He would often sit in front of the television after a day's work, wringing his hands and muttering, "Why me?"

One day, Thomas's boss called him in and asked him to conduct an orientation seminar. Thomas could handle one-on-one contact without his anxiety being too visible; however, he was terrified of groups. He began to shake and said to his boss, "Why ask me to do this? Why not ask someone else?" Thomas's boss, who had never seen him behave this way before, stood and watched, totally mystified, as Thomas fled from the office in panic.

Are you terrified of challenges, like Thomas?

When someone asks you to try something new or different, how do you respond?

Do you run and hide, or do you welcome the invitation as an opportunity for adventure?

The Difference between "Why Not?" and "Why Me?"

Let's say that you were put in a situation similar to the one in which Thomas found himself, but instead of an orientation, you were invited to try a new type of role if you are a performer, or teach a new way if you are an instructor, or sell a new product. What would your first thought be? Write it down. How would you feel if you received such an invitation? Write that down as well.

Many people, presented with these opportunities, would feel a little tense or nervous, but would tell themselves, "Wow, I can hardly wait. This is probably going to be exciting, interesting, etc." They would therefore experience the eustress associated with this type of challenge. We will call this type of response the "Why not?" response. Many others would instead experience you-stress. They would probably tell themselves, "This is horrible and difficult. I don't want to have to do this. Why don't they give this to someone else?" These individuals would feel a great deal of discomfort and possibly some anger, or at least annoyance, and might end up self-downing if they look back at the opportunity they dismissed. These are the "Why?" or "Why me?" responders.

Let's look at a slightly different scenario. You are a salesperson for a major soft drink company. Your salary is excellent, and your commissions are even better. The company decides to introduce a totally new and different soft drink product aimed at a different population of consumers. Since you are one of the top salespeople, you are asked to take on the burden of selling this product. There are many risks involved. No one knows if the product will really sell. No one knows what it will do to your commissions if it doesn't; however, the company is willing to raise the commission percentage because of this risk. If it does sell, you could double your commission earnings. What would you do?

Would you ask your boss, "Why did you pick me?" Or would you say, "Why not? I've always wanted to sell a new product or at least try to do it."

When you ask why, you are essentially asking, "Why me?" Why am I being singled out to do this horrible, horrendous, horrific task? Why do I get all the hard work?" When you think that, what are your emotions? Do you feel good emotionally and physically on top of things? Do you flip the switch and start the anxiety cycle rolling? When you say, "Why did he or she ask me to speak in public?" what's your next thought? What do you believe is going to happen if you get to do this? When you ask, "Why did they ask me to do this?" does your paranoia kick in? Do you begin to think, "Are they trying to make me feel bad? Are they trying to get me in trouble?" What would happen if rather than asking "Why," you responded, "Sure, why not"? Which response would get the better reception from the boss? Does the person who says, "Why me?" feel good about himself and feel good about the possibilities within the situation? Who conveys an attitude that is more upbeat? Remember, in many cases, you are playing the role of the worker or of the person looking for promotion or more money. Saying "Why not?" suggests that while you may not be great at this new activity, you're at least willing to give it a try.

One client, Claude, who is an actor, was asked to do some improvisation at an audition. He was instructed to "Just take a moment and go with it and see where it leads you." He had never improvised before. He was terrified of the possibility of making errors. He kept thinking, "Why am I being asked to do this? I don't know how to do this. Why are they asking something so stupid of me? After all, don't they know I don't know how to improvise?" If Claude had said to himself, "I am not really quite sure why I am being asked to do this, but why not? Director have the right to ask for any kind of silly thing they choose to. What's the worst that can happen?" he still might not have been great in the improvisation, but he would not have come out a basket case, which he did. He left the audition feeling very blue and having done a bad job at the improvisation, because he kept on ruminating about all his whys, instead of concentrating on his improvising.

Next time someone asks you to do something that is not life threatening, immoral, or illegal, you might try the "why not?" response. You certainly would not want to try the "why not?" response if someone asks if you would care to mug someone, or rob a bank. But is speaking in public equivalent to killing someone or robbing a bank? If someone says to you, "I need to have a few more cold calls made. I know that you've never done this before, but I'm sure you'll be able to handle this assignment," what would you say? Would you respond, "Why not? Sure, I'll try it," or would you say, "Not me, I don't do those well"?

We call the "I don't do those well" response *rehearsing a symptom*. The more you refuse to do what you don't do well, the less skillful and more upset you become. By saying, "Why not?" you increase the odds that you might include some new skills in your repertoire. This is not a guarantee, but nothing is guaranteed in this world. If you use the "Why not?" approach, you are opening up the door of possibility. This door leads to the possibility of improvement, the possibility of perhaps even having some fun, and the possibility of increasing or broadening your horizons. Can you think of other possibilities that opening the door of "Why not?" might lead to?

"Why not?" allows you to perhaps experience a playfulness that you didn't experience previously. Since you are not yet an expert at this new activity, you don't yet carry the burden of having to be good at it. You are just allowing yourself to try on the experience for size and comfort. Why not take the risk of doing something new? If you have gotten this far in the book, you know that something new doesn't place your work in jeopardy, nor does it place your ego in jeopardy.

Since there is some stress associated with all new activities or events, even if it is eustress, you may feel physically uncomfortable for a while. Nothing dangerous will happen. "Why not?" implies that you are aware of all of these things. So why not take the risk and see where it leads?

The "Why not?" response allows for a playful attitude, since you're acknowledging the thought, "Why not? I'll try, and I'll see what happens," rather than demanding the certainty of the known. The words "I'll try" imply the idea that "I cannot predict the outcome, but let's see what happens. I might turn out to be very good at this, or I might need some help."

What could you do in a playful way if you truly believe, as we are hoping you do by now, that nothing permanent is at risk, or at least not in a dangerous, life-threatening way? How might you playfully respond to a request for a public speech? How might you playfully respond, even if it's only inside your head, to an opportunity to audition? Why not give it a try? Why not ask that person whom you have been admiring for a date? Why not? The "Why not?" response includes the concept of "What's the worst thing that could happen?" Look at all of the ways we can use what we have already learned by responding with "Why not?" You don't have a chance to awfulize, because you are asking yourself, "What's the worst thing that could happen? The worst thing that could happen would probably be that you might find out that you're not very skilled or talented at the new activity, or that you don't really enjoy the new activity. How terrible would finding that out be for you? You are not saying that the situation should not be the way it is. What you are saying is, "Yeah, why not? You want it done that way…fine, why not? I can try it that way." If that way doesn't work for you, it's not the end of the world, and you have cooperated by making the attempt at the new activity.

One Interesting Exercise

In order to see how well you've accepted the idea of using "Why not?" instead of "Why?" try this next exercise. Imagine that you work as a volunteer for a local charity. At the end of each year, right before the summer break, the volunteers are given a thank-you dinner, at which each volunteer group entertains. It is done in fun, and no one thinks anything of it. Your group decides that it is going to stage a chorus line type of dance number in which the men dress as women and the women dress as men. Both sexes dance in the line and do kicks. You have always regarded yourself as clumsy. When you are approached to participate in this activity, how do you respond? What do you say to yourself? How do you feel as you anticipate the skit and its chorus line?

If you responded, "Sure I'll participate; why not?" you've gotten the idea of the chapter. If you feel a little nervous about the anticipated appearance in front of the other volunteers, that is totally normal. After all, since we are assuming that you are clumsy, you are not a professional dancer. Most people do not have to stop themselves from the fun of participation just because they feel a little nervous. Remember that eustress may include some nervousness. You may even have been able to tell yourself, "This may be fun, and if it is embarrassing, who cares? I'll be up there embarrassing myself with a crowd."

If you responded by saying, "Why me? I don't want to do that," try rereading this chapter as well as Prescription 10, "Be a Participator, not a Self-Spectator." Then try responding again. Ask yourself, "What is the worst thing that could happen if I get up and dance in this crazy chorus line?" You could say that the rest of the audience might laugh. Would they be laughing at you or at everyone? Aren't you going to be laughing at them when it's their turn? Ask yourself what you lose by not participating. If you don't participate, you probably miss out on the shared group experience and cohesion. You may also miss out on a lot of fun and the opportunity to try something that you probably have not experienced before. Try vividly imagining yourself as part of that chorus line. How do you feel imagining it? Is it awful? Is it humiliating? Is it the material of which shame attacks are made? If it is, go for it, and tell yourself, "I can tolerate this and survive to tell about it another day."

And Now, Class, Time for Homework!

Use "Why Not," not "Why Me"

Try to use the specific recommendations of this prescription whenever you are in a performance situation and find that you are stopping yourself from acting playfully. (You may also want to use the homework suggestions at the end of Chapter 5.)

The next time you have an opportunity to perform, try using "why not?". Dispute your irrational beliefs that you should not be asked to do something new. Reframe the situation as a shame attack if necessary.

Prescription 9
Act "As If"

The Case of Sean: Sean, although an honors student all through school and through his MBA, was very nervous about his executive skills. He believed that an executive should always be strong, decisive, and able to act on a moment's notice. To Sean, a true executive was a person who always had complete command of what was happening around him, and like a superhero, would rush in and save the day immediately.

Sean viewed himself as just the opposite. He thought that his good grades were just the result of chance. He saw himself as weak and wimpy, and never as strong and decisive. He could not imagine himself in an executive position, and he therefore always applied for jobs that were well below his qualifications. Of course, he found these jobs boring, but he was afraid to go any higher because he feared that he wouldn't be able to meet the demands and responsibilities. When he was finally promoted to an executive position in the company he had been with for a number of years, he found that he was unable to sleep and developed many of the symptoms related to anxiety. He calmed down only as he considered writing his letter of resignation.

Many people who experience performance anxiety state that one of their beliefs concerning this problem is that they will *always* act the way they've habitually acted. Some of the beliefs that we've heard are

1. "I've been shaking; I will continue to shake. There's nothing you can do about that."

2. "I always get nervous; I will never not be nervous. There's nothing you can do about that."

3. "Other people aren't as nervous as I or other people seem to get their act together and perform well or speak well, but I will never do that."

It is certainly possible that some people may not improve, or at least not improve sufficiently to meet their demands. However, it has been our experience that when you tell yourself that you will never get better or that that's the way you are, you will probably create a self-fulfilling prophecy. The prophecy you create means you will not get better or you will not improve your skills. As you may recall, a self-fulfilling prophecy is a prediction of doom and gloom that stops you from working on the very problems you need to work on in order not to fail. Since you are not doing the necessary work, the failure you predicted will probably occur.

Walk This Way...If I Could Walk That Way, I'd Be a Different Person

One way out of this dilemma is to try to approach it as an actor's exercise. Even if you are not an actor, pretend that you are for a moment. Visualize yourself as an actor who knows how to act. I hear you saying, "Wait, but I am not *acting*, I am actually shaking." We know you are, but have you ever seen anyone similar to yourself who can get up in public and not shake, or who can get up in public and speak clearly and who appears, at least to the naked eye, to be very much at ease? For just one moment, could you pretend to be that person? Could you say to yourself, "I will act as if I were the person I would like to be"?

Psychological research has shown that many people, especially young people, imitate those whom they respect and admire. One way of learning to master a new skill is to act *as if* you were the person you respect and admire, performing the new skill you wish to master. This may be the way you learned to tie your shoes as a young child. This is one of the ways you could show your parents, for example, that they had influence over you. You may have stood in front of a mirror and made the faces that go along with shaving. You may have watched someone garden and then imitated the digging and raking that went along with gardening.

What are some of the behaviors that go along with performing without anxiety? Well, there seem to be people standing up, speaking in a firm voice, and seemingly being relaxed when they speak. Could you pretend that you are one of those people?

If you are a professional actor, you take on roles all the time. Civilian performers who suffer equally from performance anxiety take on roles too, but may not be as aware of it. Why not attempt the role of the "fearless performer"? You can make believe that you are braver than you would ever expect to be. You can make believe in many respects. How would you act, if you could act as if you were calm? Who would you pretend to be, inside your head?

Can you think of a person, be it a media name, a personal friend, or a colleague, who has the very qualities that you aspire to have—in this case, bravery? Can you act like that person for the moment? What do you imagine that that brave person who is unafraid of speaking in public would think? List some thoughts that you think would enable you to pretend (for the next five minutes) that you were unafraid of speaking in public. You could tell yourself, "Well, I could act like X [the brave person you've chosen] and see if I could fool my audience, because they possibly don't really know that I am a coward about this. I could clear my throat when I feel the quiver coming on, and speak slowly." Many people who speak in public do not rattle off like a runaway railway train when they are speaking. Many speak in a slow and deliberate voice. You could do that too.

Could you pretend for a moment that you were a more experienced speaker? Take your book and walk to a mirror. Look at yourself in the mirror. How would a person who is comfortable appearing in public stand? Would he or she stand exactly as you are standing now? If your answer is yes, read the next four sentences of this book aloud, pretending you are very calm. Did you notice what you had to do to make the pretense happen? What did you have to say inside your head? Did you tell yourself, "Well, this is just make believe, it's not really me"? Did you say to yourself, "I could do this in my living room or in my bedroom, but I know it is really going to be different in the outside world"? Did you say, "How does this help me? I'll do this because this is what the authors are suggesting, but how does this help?"

If you remember the little kid you once were, you might realize how this helps. When we make believe, we take on the qualities that the person who is more experienced and capable than we are seems to possess. Make-believe worked for us when we were children. We did not have anyone else to compare ourselves to, so we would imitate daddy or mommy, or the big football hero or the magician we saw at a birthday party. We then developed some of their skills through imitation and observation. We can do that same thing now, because it doesn't change. The only thing that changes is your age, and all your years of telling yourself, "I can't perform without discomfort. I can't perform as capably as the more experienced people do." You too can learn to perform without discomfort. You can learn to perform in a more professional manner if you first imitate.

When they first go to art school, many artists are taught to imitate the work of artists who are more accomplished than they. The students copy those who are more experienced and more influential than they. In doing so, they learn different styles and techniques, which they can later modify to create their own unique art. Imitation in this case not only serves as a way of learning, but also helps you try on different disguises until you find the one that is yours.

I remember teaching my first college-level course. I was in the same school I had attended as an undergraduate. I had taken classes with a couple of teachers I really respected and admired. Not having any teaching style of my own when I began, I imitated my most respected teacher, a man I loved and admired. Unfortunately, I imitated him in front of a group of students who had had him the previous semester. They came back to me at the end of the day and said, "That was a good lecture you gave, but it was a bad imitation of Dr. Bauer." While I was chagrined at being so easily uncovered, I also felt somewhat happy that people recognized who my source was. They saw that I was trying to imitate a person I considered one of the best psychology professors I knew. Within a year, I was no longer "doing" John Bauer. I was beginning to "do" Mitchell Robin, but it took me a year of learning, experimenting, and developing my own style.

Turning the Copy Machine Off

Could you give yourself that same year? Imitate the people who do the job you'd like to do. Copy their posture if you need to; copy their style of humor if that's what you think is missing in your delivery. Copy their histrionic quality, if that's what you think would make most sense for you. And then, as you become more expert and experienced, try to stop imitating them and instead try to institute you. How would the person you'd like to be as a speaker behave? Do you want to be very relaxed, or do you want to be a little stiffer? The style that you choose is a judgment call or an actor's choice. Do you want to tell a joke immediately (which is what they recommend in many books), or do you want to let the jokes sneak in at another point in your presentation? Do you wear a suit and tie at every presentation, or do you occasionally wear a turtleneck? These are all actor's choices or judgment calls that only you can make for yourself. You can learn to be you at any meeting.

If you are an actor, you can develop your own unique style. Many people start out doing bad imitations of Laurence Olivier. They discover that they are not Laurence Olivier, but they are very good actors nonetheless. You could try doing Denzel Washington, if that's the style of acting you like, but you will probably discover that over the years you develop your own style.

Whistle a Happy Tune

Imitation works. Remember the lyric in the song that opens Rogers & Hammerstein's immortal *The King and I*. Anna and her young son Louis are traveling to Siam, a foreign, mysterious, and frightening land to them, to meet the ruler of that country. They are standing on the ship, and they see people, dressed in a way that they are not used to, approaching them in boats. Louis becomes fearful, and his mother, in an effort to calm him down and cheer him up, tells him that being afraid is okay, but it is also okay to pretend you're not afraid. In fact, she tells him that by **pretending** to be unafraid he will not only convince others but himself as well.

What do you need to say to yourself in order to get through the next ten minutes of a scary speech? What do you need to say to yourself in order to get through the next half hour of talking to someone on a date? Some males in the 1940s and 1950s used to imitate Cary Grant, a romantic, but very human movie hero. Many an adolescent or even an adult may imitate those heroes and heroines they saw in the movies, who looked very romantic and very self-assured. This type of imitation often works, at least temporarily, until eventually through practice you discover your own style.

What can you do to act "as if"? List the settings or situations that for you would require acting as if. Is it going to an audition and acting as if you have done it many times before in your life, when this is the first time? Is it going to a job interview and acting as if the job really isn't that important? After all, if it's very, very, *very* important or too important, you may act nervous rather than acting in a confident manner.

You may have noticed the choice of words here: acting nervous, acting confident. Is your nervousness as much of a response to your suppositions as your confidence? You convince yourself that you are nervous. Remember all the examples that we gave you in preceding chapters. You convince yourself that you're terrified because of the real or imagined dangers involved, and therefore you act *really* terrified. In fact, you might act so terrified and give such a convincing performance that you might qualify for an Academy Award. Unfortunately, if you act nervous when you are trying to get a job, you are probably not going to get that job as readily. You could try acting confident; and eventually, you may not only convince your audience that you are confident, you may also convince yourself.

At this point, some of you may be saying, "But how can that be?" As you read through this, do you believe that this technique can work for you? We suspect that not everyone believes that this will work. After all, how can it be that if you convince others, you can convince yourself? Let's talk a bit about a very simple experiment that was done a few years ago and written up in the psychology journals. It's called *facial feedback,* and the research concerned emotional response.

The researchers discovered that people who are forced to smile eventually assume that they are happy, and that people who are forced to frown eventually assume that they are sad. They then attribute meaning and find a reason to be happy or a reason to be sad. This research was conducted on undergraduates who were looking at neutral photographs and were told that they were being studied for distractibility. They were shown non-emotionally laden photographs while one of the researchers stood behind each student and physically manipulated his or her facial muscles, either down into a frown or up into a smile. The student was then asked to rate the pictures that he or she had been looking at. The students tended to rate the pictures that they'd been forced to frown over as sad, and the pictures that they'd been forced to smile over as happy or pleasant.

Why did the researchers get these results? They concluded that the muscles are sending the brain a signal that the face is smiling. The person responds to that signal by *feeling* happy. "I must *be* happy because the only reason I smile is when I *am* happy." If the muscles are being manipulated downward into a frown, the person reasons, "I must be sad since I am frowning."

If you act "as if", you convince yourself, even when someone forces you into it. Try this as an experiment to see what happens. Look in the mirror again and frown. Frown at yourself, and stare at yourself as you do. Try to say something good about your day while you *force* yourself to stay in a frowning mode. Can you say a pleasant sentence with your face in a frown, and does it sound convincing to your ears? My suspicion is that the harder you try, the sadder you sound. Now try looking into the mirror again and grinning and try to say a sad sentence in a convincing way. Grin, not a big toothy grin, just a nice, basic, "I'm glad to meet you" grin. Grin at yourself, and say out loud if you need to, "The weather is miserable, and I feel terrible." When you say that as you are grinning, do you believe it? Is it difficult to sound convincingly miserable and unhappy when you bring your face up into a smile? Do you discover that when you act as if you are happy, it's hard to be as convincingly sad as you were? If you act as if you are sad, it's hard to experience happiness. Try it again, but on a bigger scale.

Try this exercise on the next four people you meet. If necessary, tell yourself that it is a shame attack. Greet these people as though they were your best friends. See what happens. They could be strangers, or they could be enemies. Greet them pleasantly, as you would someone you are happy to see. What occurs in the interaction between you and these strangers? Greet the next four people after that, whoever they may be, with frowns. Act as if you are not happy to see them. Do you get a different reaction?

Let's try another experiment. Do you ever order food from a restaurant? If you ever call a restaurant to deliver food to you, whether you are ordering a pizza or something elaborate, speak to the person on the other end of the phone as though you were a captain of industry. What would it be like to speak in front of an audience of 10 or 15 or even 200 pretending you were that captain of industry? In each case, when you act as if, you give yourself a chance to try on the skills that you need to learn in order to do the job that you want to do.

Lies that Sound like Truths and Vice Versa

When we work with our clients, they will sometimes respond to our suggestions to act as if with the following reply: "You want me to pretend that I am something or someone that I am not. You want me to pretend that I am not anxious or that I am not afraid. I know I am anxious and afraid. I won't live a lie!" What does it mean to say that you *are* afraid or that you *are* anxious? Are you afraid in every cell of your body? Are fearfulness and anxiety in performance settings written on one of the branches of the DNA/RNA double helix? If you *are* anxious, does it means that anxiety is an immutable quality that you possess, like your gender, eye color, or height? To say you *are* anxious is the same as saying that you *are* a 5'10", brown-eyed male or female. It tells others, as well as yourself, that this is your unchanging, biologically fixed reality, and that there is nothing that you, or anyone else, can do about it.

Do you really mean to convince yourself that there is no hope of changing your performance anxiety? How do you feel emotionally when you tell yourself that there is no hope of something? When you convince yourself that a personal characteristic is beyond repair, you sabotage your own efforts to change and make yourself miserable and immobilized.

What would *you* call a person who tries to convince others of something that has no evidence to support it? *We* would call such a person a charlatan or a liar. When you convince yourself that you can't change the quality of your behavior, at least to some degree, and you act accordingly, you too are a convincing liar. It may be that the choice boils down to which "lie" you want to believe about yourself: the self-sabotaging one that emanates from your crystal ball and concludes that the future is bleak and hopeless because you are incapable of change, or the more hopeful one that concludes that the future *could* be better, since some change is possible. The choice is yours. Ladies and gentlemen, choose your lies.

> *The Case of Joanne:* Joanne, a cellist, loved to play with a small symphony orchestra. She loved the music and the musicians she worked and traveled with. She began to panic when the orchestra decided to do outreach in the local schools. Each musician had to speak before a group of sixth graders and explain what he or she did, his or her training, and how he or she came to be there. Each then had to demonstrate how the instrument sounded. Joanne was terrified of speaking to any group, even sixth graders. Jerry, another of the string players, adored addressing assemblies. He told Joanne to imitate his style and presentation. Even though she was terrified, Joanne found that by imitating Jerry, she was able to get through and fulfill her contract.

Could you act like Joanne and imitate someone you are close to, whether you are placing an order on the phone, conducting a class, or merely learning to greet people you know? Acting as if could work for you as it did for Anna and Louis in *The King and I* and for others in all walks of life.

And Now, Class, Time for Homework!

Act As If

Try to use the specific recommendations of this prescription whenever you want to try on a new set of behaviors and see if they are more effective. (You may also want to use the homework suggestions at the end of Chapter 5.)

1. Dispute your belief that you *are* a particular way. Remind yourself that you *generally act* in accordance with your beliefs. If you *believe* something is frightening, you *act* afraid; if you believe something is good for you, you *act* happy.

2. In your next performance situation, try to act *as if* you are confident. Imitate someone who acts more confidently than you and dispute your belief that this is wrong or that you are lying to yourself.

3. How would you like to act in performance situations? Identify some role models and study their techniques. At your next performance opportunity, try to use some of these techniques. Shamelessly copy their methods *until you can find your own style,* and then turn the copy machine off.

Prescription 10

Be a Participator, Not a Self-Spectator

The case of Juan Q.: Juan was an artist who had developed "painter's block." Every time he approached the empty canvas, he would begin to wonder if his strokes would be bold and courageous enough. As he put paint to canvas, he would not only stand back from the canvas to observe his work, but also attempt to observe himself as he was painting. "Was that last stroke too timid and not expressive enough? Did I get enough paint on the brush?" He would also observe himself observing himself and would think, "Why am I doing this? Am I being too judgmental, or not judgmental enough? I wonder what the art critics will think when they see my painting. A good artist would be able to just paint without agonizing over every stroke. I need to relax and just paint, but if I just paint, it won't come out the way I want it to. Why did I ever think I was an artist?"

The more Juan paid attention to himself, the less he paid attention to his painting. The more he acted as a spectator, the less he acted as an artist. Juan was experiencing you-stress rather than eustress from his painting. You-stress occurs when people are deeply involved with (1) disturbing themselves about the significance of their physical symptoms or (2) disturbing themselves about their ego and their esteem. Juan's you-stress resulted from his plumbing the depths of his navel rather than the depths of his art. The deeper he delved, the more disturbed he became until he eventually stopped painting altogether.

If You Want to Watch the Show, Buy a Ticket

Many performers are like Juan Q. They try to monitor their performance while they are performing. They assume that if they watch themselves while they work, they will be able to make immediate adjustments that will positively affect the outcome. Many vocal coaches, in an effort to stop their students from self-spectating, remind them that "You can't sing and listen at the same time." These coaches will tell you, "By the time you hear yourself sing off key, it is too late to do anything about it. The time to worry about technique is when you are practicing specific skills." Many therapists have had clients who have attempted to listen to themselves while they are talking about their problem. These clients are usually very concerned about how their therapist views them. They believe that if they can monitor their words, the therapist will not come to an unflattering perception of their mental health. Unfortunately, since they are self-monitoring or self-spectating, they don't say what is really on their minds, but rather attempt to control the therapist's perception of them. I once had the occasion to tell such a client, "If you want to sit in my chair, you can, but we might make more progress if you do your job and let me do mine." When you are in a therapist's office, your job is that of client. When you leave the office and are back on the street, you can assume any job you wish, including that of a person who is practicing what you have learned in therapy. When you paint a picture, your job is that of a painter. You can take on another role, such as critic, at a later time.

You Can't Dance with One Body at Two Weddings

The rule we suggest you use is similar to an old middle European expression, "You can't dance with one body at two weddings." You can use this expression to remind yourself either that you can't be in two places at the same time or that you can't be a painter and an art critic at the same exact moment. No one is suggesting that you not attempt to avoid mistakes, or that you stop working to improve your skills. The intent is, rather, to remind you that when you single-mindedly self-monitor, you inhibit the flow of your own performance, which is the antithesis of the creative act you are hoping to produce.

...And Now I Am Picking Up the Can of Soup...

We would like you to try an experiment. Try doing some ordinary household task while you give a running narration, a precise description of everything you do, think, or feel. Try to be observant of every passing moment, and tell yourself about it in a richly detailed stream of consciousness. For example, open up a can of soup, and from the moment you begin to walk in the direction of the cabinet in which you store the cans, describe it! You might discover that your monologue sounds something like this:

> I am standing in the hall wondering whether or not to do this exercise. I feel pretty dumb talking aloud to myself, but there must be some reason those idiots want me to do this, so here goes. I am walking into the kitchen. As I pass the hallway, I notice that the floor needs mopping. I wonder if it's my turn to do it, or if I should remind someone else to do it. This is really annoying. I wonder if I should tell myself that I am getting annoyed. Now I am in the kitchen, and I am walking over to the cabinet. I wonder if I described that in enough detail. How much detail am I supposed to use? I wish I had more information. OK, I opened the cabinet and picked up a can of soup in my right hand. It is a can of vegetable soup. Do I really even like vegetable soup? I am now looking for the can opener. Now I am beginning to feel somewhat self-conscious. I am also aware that I am beginning to become frustrated because I cannot find the can opener. Is this vegetable soup worth the effort of looking for the can opener? Now I wonder where the pot is.

How easy is the "simple" task of opening up the can of soup, pouring it into the pot, heating it up, and then eating it, if all the while you are keeping up a running commentary? More importantly, how much did you enjoy the experience of cooking or the experience of eating the soup? When you watch yourself, or act as a spectator of your own life, you may discover that you stop yourself from enjoying the direct experience of living. Spectators experience the world vicariously. They, like Chance the gardener in *Being There*, like to watch rather than do.

When you are a self-spectator, you take yourself out of the action and place yourself on the sidelines. While sitting on the sidelines may be a useful location for a member of the audience, it is a useless location for a member of the team. If you have ever seen a game where an active member of the team has been side-lined, you may recall seeing that team member impatiently waiting for a chance to get back in the game and nagging the coach for that opportunity. If you engage in self-spectating you may have also watched yourself wondering when you will get your chance to be in the game. When you sideline yourself, you reduce your chances of success. You also get the bittersweet opportunity to watch yourself do poorly and feel miserable.

I *Could* Have Lived My Life, *but* I Didn't Want to Get Involved

Many of you may remember from a number of years ago the story of a woman named Kitty Genovese, who was brutally assaulted and murdered on a street in New York while numerous witnesses calmly stood by and watched from the relative safety of their apartment windows. When those witnesses were ques-tioned, they replied, "I didn't want to get involved." When you act like a specta-tor in your own life, you too watch without involvement, and the results could be equally unpleasant.

What stops you from performing and keeps you on the sidelines?
Write down some of your thoughts.

If you are like some of our clients, you may have written down some of the following:

- Whenever I begin to perform, I am aware that I might fail, and so I stop myself before I begin.
- I really dislike it when my boss tells me I have to perform, and so to as-sert my independence I try not to.
- I am very aware of my physical distress when I perform, and I would rather stop performing than have to face it.
- The more I am aware of myself on stage, the more self-conscious and inhibited I become.
- It's like I have these two little observers sitting on my shoulders—you know, like in the cartoons—who tell me whether or not I should do something. Unfortunately, I am usually told not to.

Do you, like that last person, also have "observers" sitting on your shoulder who increase your self-consciousness, telling you not to do something, or who are telling you to be inappropriately cautious?

The Case of Herman A.: Herman A. was an in-service sales trainer for a large telecommunications corporation. Although he liked his work, Herman tended to try to be a member of his audience as he was doing the instruction. He found that he couldn't make this work. He spent a great deal of time trying to guess how stu-dents were receiving him. He would say to himself, "What did they think of that scenario or this pun? I wonder how it came across. They don't seem all that atten-tive, and they are not laughing very much. I wonder if they understood. I wonder how they will evaluate me at the end of the course."

Herman did not realize that by playing the spectator at his own presentation, he was causing himself problems. He was not aware that each time he ran this script in his head, he would halt his lecture and seem lost in thought. His students would then become restless and begin to doubt that he knew what he was talking about. Therefore, rather than keeping his students engaged, he was doing just the opposite. He could never understand it when the feedback he received indicated that he seemed lost and not to have a command of his material.

Herman is a fitting example of what can happen when one becomes a spectator at one's own performance. Herman thought that doing this would help him, but it only impeded his performance. His observer, "little Herman" who sat on his shoulder, did not give him very good advice. As a matter of fact, listening to little Herman's advice almost cost Herman his job.

Herman came to a workshop and was able to see that his only choice was to get rid of the spectator/critic on his shoulder, and instead immerse himself in his work. He was able to realize that he could tolerate the discomfort of not knowing how he was doing from moment to moment. Not knowing was allowing him to speak in a more assertive and knowledgeable fashion. Maybe you, like Herman, need to brush the spectator off your shoulder.

Many of us recall watching cartoons in which the hero is about to do something when two little spirits appear on his or her shoulders. These spirits are typically represented as a little angel and a little devil. The angel encourages the hero to keep to the straight and narrow, while the devil encourages the hero to do something pleasant, but usually forbidden. If you suffer from performance anxiety, it is likely that your "angel" is encouraging caution and your devil is encouraging you to take the forbidden, and possibly "shameful," risk of performing at your current level of competence (or lack thereof). If you recall these cartoons, you may also remember that when the hero makes a decision to listen to either voice, it usually results in the distracting observer being lifted from his or her shoulder and forcefully placed in a convenient sack or trash can. You can do the same thing with your distracting observers' voices. While we would encourage you to listen to your angel when it encourages caution about assault, theft, or equally antisocial behaviors, we would also encourage you to forcibly remove that selfsame angel when it cautions you against performing in your long-term best interests.

Tell Your Back-Seat Driver to Shut Up or Go Home

Who are your observers? Are they the little angels or devils of cartoon fame, or are they people you know? When you are self-monitoring, do you have an image of someone either sitting on your shoulder or looking over your shoulder at everything you do? It may feel like you have a perpetual back-seat driver. What image do you have? Is your image one of a critic, or is it the "good" self/"bad" self, an old teacher, or your boss sitting there with a little pad checking off your accomplishments and failures? Do you enjoy the image of this person constantly monitoring you? Does the observer's monitoring improve or impede your performance while you are performing? If your answer is that your performance is impeded, why not try picturing yourself asking that observer to sit in the audience where he or she belongs, and then get on with the job of living? If you see your observer as a little genie in a bottle, picture yourself putting the genie back into the bottle until it is needed. You could also encourage the little genie to sit in the audience and tell you *a day later* how well you did.

Once you've gotten that spectator to agree to talk to you after the show, you are ready to return to the job of living. However, you may experience some concern about what happens next, or about what you will do without that little voice. The more telling question is, What have you been able to do *with* that little voice? When you stop the monitoring, you are not stopping your fine-tuning of your performance, nor are you stopping your desire to improve your results. When you stop acting like a spectator, you are merely completing your performance as a performer, then examining it afterwards when it is finished.

You will probably need to dispute your irrational belief that if you don't watch yourself every minute, you will undoubtedly fail. You will probably also have to dispute your belief that you *can* watch and do at the same time. Remember, even directors who act in their own movies have to see the results on film afterward to truly know how well they did and if they have to refine their own performance.

And Now, Class, Time for Homework!

Be a Participator, Not a Self-Spectator

Try to use the specific recommendations of this prescription whenever you find your-self beginning to act as a spectator in your own life. (You may also want to use the home-work suggestions at the end of Chapter 5.)

1. Remind yourself about the results of the "and now I am opening a can of soup" exercise. Ask yourself if you really need to act as a spectator to your own life.

2. Dispute your belief that you can prevent poor performance while you are performing. Remind yourself that the way to improve is to practice be-forehand. If you are aware that you made a mistake while performing, tell yourself to continue and try not to down yourself. You might also want to read the next two prescriptions.

3. As you get up to perform, ask your little genie or back-seat driver to sit in the audience and talk to you after the show. If it is persistent and demands attention, take a calming/cleansing breath and tell it to "shut up or go home!"

Be Process-Oriented, Not Product-Oriented

The Case of Peggy S.: Peggy S. was a dance student who was about to perform at her senior recital. She knew that the school invited the directors of some of the city's major dance troupes to attend this recital. Many of the school's former students had been successfully placed in these troupes. Peggy had prepared many years for this moment, and now it had finally arrived. Peggy was at the practice barre when she began to visualize herself dancing perfectly. She saw herself going through each of the combinations perfectly. She imagined the thunderous applause that would greet her curtain call. She then began to experience doubt. "I will never be able to dance so perfectly that I receive an ovation," she thought. "I am fooling myself if I think that I have a chance of getting into any troupe, let alone a major dance company." The more she dis-stressed herself by imagining the "awful" consequences of not getting into any troupe, the more she become physically tense. As her physical tension grew, she saw it as a sign that her belief was correct and that she would never be accepted in a dance troupe. "After all," she thought, "my body wouldn't lie to me. I wouldn't be feeling this way if it were true that I could make it as a dancer."

There Is the Dance, the Dancer, and the Dancing

Peggy's you-stress got in the way of her performance, as you can well imagine. She became so involved with watching herself dance, hoping that she could do a "perfect" recital, that she wound up not dancing well at all. Peggy lost sight of the fact that her job at the moment was to be a dancer, not a critic or a company director. She was so focused on the potential outcome of her performance that she had trouble performing. Peggy confused three different issues: the dance, the dancing, and the dancer.

All performances consist of the following components:

- *The product* (the dance). The product occurs as a result of a performer's using a process. Products are generally complete and can be compared and evaluated. In Peggy's case, the product she was trying to complete was a senior dance recital.

- *The process* (the dancing). The process refers to the actual activity of making a performance happen. Processes are transitional and ever-changing. Processes can be evaluated in terms of how useful they are in creating specific results (remember our tool kit dispute). In Peggy's case, it was the dance steps, the technique, and the style of dancing that she was taught.

- *The performer* (the dancer): The performer is the person who uses the process to produce or create the product. The performer brings his or her own training, ability, élan, talent, and desire to both the process and the product. Performers can be compared and evaluated on their ability and their willingness to successfully use specific processes to arrive at a desired result. When you ask directors about certain problematic actors, you may hear, "He or she is wonderful, but can't be trusted to arrive on the set on time, or take reasonable direction, so I don't think we can use her or him." In Peggy's case, the performer was Peggy herself, a senior in a dance school, with her own unique mix of personal assets and liabilities.

Peggy was so caught up in her desire to deliver a finished and perfect product that she lost sight of the process that helps make a performance memorable. By focusing on the product, she stopped enjoying the process and became self-conscious about her failings.

Have you ever had Peggy's experience? Did you ever get so caught up in the finished product that you ignored the process that takes you there? Many people who suffer from performance anxiety are so anxious about the speech or the performance or the ball game that they ignore the little details that carry the day. They may also assume that since they are incapable of delivering the finished product perfectly, they should quit attempting to deliver it at all. You may remember that in Prescription 1, we called this type of belief magical thinking. The aforementioned perfectionists may have looked into their crystal ball and seen failure. They are partially correct—since they are human, they *are* incapable of perfection. Despite that "failing," they are still highly capable of performing well, or at least learning how to perform well.

Don't write the review until after the performance is over

When you, like Peggy, focus on the outcome, you get ahead of yourself and are already reading a review that hasn't been written yet for a play that has not yet been performed. Staying oriented in the process allows you to focus on the two other components of the performance situation: the dancing and the dancer. When you switch your focus to the process, you allow yourself to become aware of variables that might have an impact on your performance: your aptitudes, skills, and training, and your unique assets and liabilities that will influence how well you use those skills. As one of our colleagues who runs in the marathon put it, "Don't concentrate on winning, concentrate on running."

Let us assume that your goal is to be able to speak up at a PTA meeting.

- *Speaking up* is your product.
- Now let's focus on the process. What skills do you already have that allow you to produce that product? Are there any skills that you are lacking that you might be well advised to learn in order to create that product?

- Now let's consider the performer. What are your unique personal assets and liabilities? What qualities or attributes do you have that you could put to good use if you were to speak up at a PTA meeting? Is the topic one that you feel passionately about? Is the issue one that you feel might have an adverse effect on your children? Have you prepared your argument beforehand? Do you have other qualities or attributes that might get in the way of your speaking up? Are you afraid of appearing foolish? Do you think that people might act in a disapproving manner if you were to speak up? Are you horrified by the thought of their potential disapproval?

By focusing on the other two components, you can take stock and begin to make adjustments in the things that you can control that will influence your performance:

- You can improve your skills, if you wish to.
- You can dispute your horror of not being perfectly prepared or of possibly being disapproved of.
- You can calm yourself down before you perform and thereby improve your chances of having the appropriate level of stress for the situation.
- You can practice recovering from your known liabilities.

You notice we said that you can control the process and the performer, but you cannot really control the product as fully as you might like. You may want to manufacture a car. You can control the steps to manufacture it. You can take other steps to ensure that the final product you come up with is a car and not a bicycle. However, you cannot guarantee while you're working on a car that you will not wind up with a lemon. You may have observed that almost every automobile manufacturer has, at least occasionally, invested untold millions in unavoidably producing citrus fruits. They didn't intend to set up a juice business, but the public has some input into whether or not a car will sell. You can have a goal of manufacturing a car. That is a realistic goal. Having a desire to produce a popular car is an understandable desire. Demanding that you must produce the perfect popular car is irrational. You may be fully in touch with the pulse of the public, but publics have been known to develop arrhythmia.

The Case of Professor H.: Professor Alvin H. was a well-known presenter at conferences on the politics of health care reform. He was very knowledgeable and able to convey his points well; however, this had not always been the case. When Alvin had been a just beginning lecturer in the field, he had developed the bad habit of writing his reviews before presenting his paper. He would second-guess his colleagues in an effort to appear erudite when responding to the inevitable questions that would be posed. However, he found that as he prepared for these questions, he was seeing more holes in his presentations. This led him to be a dry, overinclusive speaker. He was unaware of this until one of his mentors asked if his presentation at a certain meeting was going to start with the beginnings of modern health care, that is, Galen and ancient Greece.

When Alvin realized that he could not write his own reviews of the finished product without damaging his talk, he relaxed and began to tell himself, "If I leave something out, it will be just too bad...and I am sure that one of my colleagues will catch it. I am here to present my paper, not to evaluate it." Alvin H. was a professor who thought rationally and did not need help to reach this conclusion. He found that he, and his audience, had more fun with his talks when he was able not to worry about the product and merely enjoy the process.

Do you think that you, like Professor H., can find some reward in just enjoying what you are doing without evaluating the outcome? Try it, and see if your result, like Alvin's, is more positive than your past results.

But Can't I *Decide* to Write a Best Seller?

You can decide to write a book, but best sellers are a judgment of the marketplace. You may intimidate yourself if you try to write a "great" book, or a best-selling novel. A more realistic goal is to write a book and then see what the reviews say and how the marketplace responds. If you tell yourself ahead of time that your book must be "a best seller or else," it will only take your mind off the process of writing. If you tell yourself that it is presumptuous of you to try to write unless you have something major to say, this only takes you out of the writing arena. A better response would be to try to write and then see what occurs. You may discover that you have something to say while you are in the process of saying it. You may discover that what you have to say intrigues the public. You may even discover that you need to learn how to spell and punctuate, or that you need someone to assist you with those chores.

You notice that we haven't said you shouldn't *prefer* to do well or to get good reviews. Those preferences are highly appropriate, but it is unlikely that you will always get what you prefer, and therefore the better strategy is to keep your eyes on the process.

Many people who come to our workshops are surprised when we say that they can't *control* the outcome. They have read somewhere that if you visualize yourself doing the job perfectly, you will *automatically* do it perfectly. While we do use visualizations, we do so rationally. Visualizing success may help you see the necessary steps to take to make success more likely. Visualizing these steps and then actually taking them or learning how to take them increases the likelihood of your being successful. But it has been our experience that many people substitute the visualization for the physical practice of actually doing what needs to be done.

Another, and perhaps better, form of visualization for success is to visualize yourself successfully overcoming problems in your performance or overcoming failure. Success is an outcome that may be elusive. Recovery from error is an ongoing process that may bring eventual success with it. Many novice performers experience failure, or at least partial failure, while they develop their skills. When you practice recovery skills and rational or effective coping statements, you can inoculate yourself against the emotional upset that often accompanies a disappointing performance. We are not saying that you will stop being disappointed or that you will enjoy failure, but you may be able to place it in perspective so that it is not awful and is only disappointing. One way of inoculating yourself against failure is to develop Plan B.

Developing Plan B

Most people who have a strong desire to perform well assume that discipline, talent, and persistence are all the personal skills that are needed. In addition to this list, you may also want to add having a Plan B. Plan B is the plan that is activated when Plan A goes awry. Plan B could be a totally different goal: Plan A is I become an actor; Plan B is that I teach speech. Plan B could also be having two different but compatible goals. Having an alternative plan enables you to place a less then sterling performance into proper perspective so that you can then activate the "at least" response:

- I am planning to audition for a major role. If I don't get the part I want, I will call my friend and try to cheer up. That way, if I don't get the part, I can *at least* have someone to commiserate with. Even if I don't get the part, *at least* I will have learned to audition for the director.
- I am planning to give an impressive speech. I have prepared well, but I am also trying to use my preparation to teach me something about the topic that is new to me. That way, even if the speech is a dud for some reason, *at least* I learned something new.
- I am hoping to paint a great picture, but I am also attempting to gain a greater understanding of dry brush technique. This way, if I don't produce great art, *at least* I have learned a new technique.
- I normally stutter when I speak. Plan A is to speak without stuttering, Plan B is to speak at all—either way I win!

Placing Failure into Your Vocabulary

To repeat: We are *not* advocating that you wish to fail or that you enjoy failure, but rather that you plan for failure so that it doesn't throw you for a loop. You have heard the sentence, "Failure is not a word in my vocabulary." When we advocate that you place *failure* into your vocabulary, it is to help you see that it is not horrible but just another onion. You can fail at an activity, recover from the failure, and go on to achieve success in another arena, or in the same arena at another time. Even very successful people fail, and are still considered highly successful.

Let us look at professional baseball players as a prime example. If the objective of playing baseball is to hit the ball so that you can get on base, then most professional ballplayers are failures more frequently than they are successful. If we understand the concept of a batting average, it reveals the number of times out of 1,000 tries that a particular batter actually connects with a ball and gets on base. A professional ballplayer is doing well if he hits .300 and is overjoyed to be batting .400. This means that they *don't* get on base six to seven times out of ten, and yet they are considered highly proficient. The product is to play the game; the process allows for home runs, hits, *and errors.*

And Now, Class, Time for Homework!

Be Process-Oriented, not Product-Oriented

Try to use the specific recommendations of this prescription whenever you find yourself focusing on the product of your performance rather than the process. (You may also want to use the homework suggestions at the end of Chapter 5.)

1. Examine your own performance situation in terms of the dance, the dancing, and the dancer example. What skills do you need to do your dance? How many of them are currently in your repertoire? How many do you need to develop? What personal qualities do you have that will help you in your performance? What personal qualities may get in your way? What strategies can you develop to overcome or minimize your liabilities? Dispute your belief that you will do better if you focus primarily on the dance.

2. Remind yourself not to write the review before the performance is over. Allow yourself to perform without the distraction of worrying about the outcome.

3. Before your next opportunity to perform, try a recovery visualization. Vividly see yourself in the performance setting. Picture yourself performing, making a mistake, and recovering from it. You may need to practice taking calming/cleansing breaths before, during, and after this exercise.

4. Develop your Plan B. For every performance situation that you may be in, try to have an alternative objective. Try using the "at least" response if you can realize only your secondary objective. Dispute your irrational belief that you must always reach your objective.

5. Remind yourself that Babe Ruth struck out 1,330 times!

Prescription 12

Stay in the Moment

Imagine, if you will, a person getting up to make a speech. As she begins, she starts out strongly. She's aware of her notes; she's aware of the point she's going to make. Over the course of her speech, she begins to think, "How is the audience receiving me? I wonder how I sound." At that point, she pulls away from her task for just a moment to listen to herself talk. As she does so, she gets distracted because she hears her voice getting tighter. She is aware of her heartbeat, and she suddenly loses her concentration. She begins to worry that the audience will notice her distraction, and she now starts stammering with greater frequency. Finally she discovers that she can't continue without pausing "shamefully."

This is not an uncommon experience. Many performers in everyday life find that there are times during their performance when they become distracted and lose their concentration and focus. Professional actors and actresses have also been known to experience loss of focus. When this occurs during a rehearsal, the director will probably say to them, "You've lost contact with the moment. Stay in the moment!" What does that mean, "You've lost contact with the moment. Stay in the moment"?

Again, imagine that you are an actor in a play set in the south of France in the middle of the seventeenth century. During the course of the rehearsal, you suddenly start to think about your accent. You become worried about whether or not you sound like a Frenchman of the seventeenth century. At that moment you are no longer either acting in or rehearsing the play. You are now acting as a critic or as a dialect coach or as something else.

Imagine yourself as a singer who, while singing, begins to become distracted and concerned about vocal quality. At this point, you are no longer singing your song but wondering if you might have sung that last phrase off key. When you do that, you are no longer in the moment of the song. You are somewhere else, thinking about the mechanics of vocal production.

If you are a public speaker and you are aware of a distraction or wondering how the audience is perceiving you, you too are not in the moment of producing your speech, but are somewhere else (possibly sitting in your audience). Staying in the moment means staying focused on the task at hand, whether it be speaking in public or doing some mundane chore.

The Case of Martin Z.: Martin was a middle manager for an insurance firm. Although he was quite competent at his job, he hated the mundane "housekeeping" that went with the job and would put it off as long as possible. As a consequence, Martin's office and desk became a cluttered mess. He knew that he would be able to function more efficiently if he cleaned up the clutter, but he could rarely bring himself to do it. Every so often Martin would start the chore of cleaning off his desk, but he would soon become distracted. He would stare out the window or reorganize the paper clips. He would frequently come upon a magazine or other publication that he hadn't read, and would riffle through it. Martin soon discovered that unlike some other people, he couldn't riffle while he worked. When he did, he rarely completed these minor chores to even his own highly flexible standards.

Don't Riffle While You Work

Actors, actresses, and other professional performers are typically expected to ignore all other distractions and, if they possibly can, stay within the "imaginary moment" of the script. An actor or actress is expected to, and typically receives training on how to, stay focused on the interaction between his or her character and the other characters on stage. They generally are expected to be aware of themselves not as John and Marsha, but as the nobleman and serving wench in the south of seventeenth-century France that they are playing. Staying in the moment means temporarily losing self-awareness so that you are acting appropriately within the setting of the play. Paying attention to distractions that pull your focus away from the appropriate behavioral and emotional responses of a seventeenth-century French nobleman are counterproductive, but unfortunately are all too common.

What can you do? You can remind yourself that you can always go back to practicing and rehearsing the skills you need to speak with a better accent or sing on key or use punchier language in a presentation at another time. The time to rehearse is in rehearsal; the time to write your script or your outline is weeks before your presentation, or days or hours before your presentation if that's all the time you have. However, today is the presentation day. Right this minute or for the next twenty minutes or for the next three hours, depending on what you are doing, the moment requires performance. Performance is not rewriting scripts; performance is not changing or worrying about vocal technique. Those are all preperformance tasks. Performance is certainly not anxiously scanning the audience to see if they're all smiling in rapt appreciation.

You may recall doing some of those things and feeling uncomfortable because you had lost your concentration. Staying in the moment means trying to stay focused on the task at hand and not losing your concentration, or at least trying not to. If you discover that you have lost both concentration and focus on the task, then staying in the moment means taking a cleansing/calming breath, clearing your head or challenging your beliefs, and getting back into the moment rather than awfulizing and self-downing about it. Calling yourself stupid or saying to yourself, "Isn't it dumb of me to have lost my focus" is counterproductive and immobilizing. Instead, try telling yourself, "So all right, I'm human; I got distracted. Back to the storyline (or back to my presentation)."

Any number of parents can remember seeing their children losing concentration in a school play or assembly program. Their child is performing the central role of the Buttercup in the award-winning assembly program "Welcome, Springtime," when suddenly the child looks out at the audience and waves. The child is probably thinking, "Where is mommy, where is daddy? Is everyone looking at me, and roundly applauding me as they must?" If you were to do that as an executive at a business meeting, it might be amusing. It wouldn't be terrible and awful, but it's certainly *not* staying in the moment, nor is it the kind of image you are trying to convey.

Do you recall the Shakespeare quote we cited in the beginning of the book about how we are all players performing on stage? If you are that executive who is giving a speech, you might want to try reframing it as "I am playing the part of an executive who is giving a speech." Try casting yourself in this new role. You are playing the part of an executive in an office meeting attempting to sound professional, grown up, and reasonably self-assured. In Prescription 9, we talked about acting "as if." Right now, if you stayed in the moment, you could act as if you really had all the confidence that you think you need to have. Staying in the moment in this case means keeping to the script for an executive presentation. Staying in the moment means talking about the product (if that's what the presentation is about), talking about its benefits or its drawbacks, talking about the expenses that might be incurred in producing it. Looking around at the audience and figuratively waving to your friends and family or wondering if everyone is appreciating you will only upset you and cause anxiety. This latter point is especially true if you have already discovered that you are the type of individual who says, "I must be loved and appreciated by everyone or else it is awful."

Do Not Accept This Invitation to Feel Awful

Let's examine another opportunity to feel awful. You're giving your speech. You've lost your concentration because you were worrying about how well it was going to be received, and you discovered some member of the audience yawning, another member of the audience scratching his ear, and a third audience member rustling through notes, all providing you with a challenge to straight thinking. If you were in the moment, you would probably pay little or no attention to them because you would be too busy doing your job. What is your job? Acting like an executive. If you are a performer, what is your job? Singing or dancing or painting on the canvas. When you anxiously ask yourself, "Will the audience love me?" or "Will the art critic love every stroke and realize how much I sweated to produce it?" you are not staying in the moment. Instead, you are critiquing yourself before the moment is over.

The moment that we are referring to may be a real one, or it may be an imaginary one portrayed on stage in a play; in either case, staying within the confines of the moment will enable you to do a better job. The moment, if you are an actor, may be in the seventeenth-century king's bedchamber. The moment, if you are an executive, may be today in the meeting room. If you are "acting" in either role, you will do better if you stay focused. Anything that you pay attention to that is inappropriate to the role of the king of France or to the presenter's role distracts you and inhibits your performance. Staying in the moment means staying in character, paying attention to how the king of France would behave, and trying to act in a consistent fashion throughout. *In the moment* you are not John pretending to be the king of France, but *the king himself* responding to an interesting opportunity. *In the moment* you are not the distractible Marsha making a presentation, but rather *the presenter herself* responding to an interesting opportunity.

Stay in Character

The Case of Genevieve: Genevieve, a young musical comedy specialist, was really skillful at presenting her songs when she was with her vocal coach. However, she found that when she was performing with her partner, she would lose her concentration and focus. Genevieve loved to sing show tunes, especially duets. She adored the show music of Gershwin, Porter, and Berlin, a great deal of which is better done with a partner. Unfortunately, because of her lack of concentration and focus during a performance, more than one male partner had given up on her.

Why were Genevieve's partners abandoning her? Genevieve asked her vocal coach to come to a performance that she was giving with Ron, her current partner, to see "what I am singing incorrectly."

You can probably guess by now that Genevieve's problem had nothing to do with her vocal technique or ability. After witnessing a performance, Genevieve's coach came backstage and asked her, "What goes through your mind while you and Ron are singing?" Genevieve replied, "First I wonder what Ron thinks of my singing. I don't want him to be overwhelmed or angry with me. I want him to like me. I then wonder if I used enough mouthwash, because I don't want to offend him and have him leave me because of it. After that, I look around the audience to see if they are bored, of if they are looking at their programs instead of us. If there are other singers waiting to go on, I look to see how they are reacting to our music."

If you were Genevieve's coach, what would you say to her? What Genevieve's coach did say is, "Did you ever think about the *meaning* of what you are singing and who you are singing it to? There you stand with Ron, who is your beau for the moment, singing a charming love song. If you are not singing it *to* him, will the audience believe the song? Stay in character. Be Ron's lover (for the moment). How can you be in the moment with your lover if you are not singing like a lover, and are instead taking the audience's emotional temperature concerning your performance?"

What advice would *you* give Genevieve? Her coach told her to look at Ron, or whoever her partner might be, and think about the meaning of the song. She was then instructed to communicate this meaning to her on-stage beau. Genevieve's coach reminded her to stay in character, to stay in the moment of the song and of what she was singing in the song—otherwise she might have to resign herself to singing another chorus of "The Man that Got Away."

How would a competent executive respond if he or she had an opportunity to present before major people in the corporation who he or she wished to impress? If you are trying to be impressive, suddenly worrying about whether you are impressive takes you out of the moment. Right now, at that moment, you are cast in the central role of an impressive speaker. You have a number of effective alternatives:

- You can act *as if*.

- You can participate and not self-spectate.
- You can stay process-oriented.
- You can stay in the moment.

No matter how well, or poorly, you are doing, worrying about your product (that is, worrying about whether you are really delivering an impressive speech) takes you out of the moment. We all have products we are trying to deliver. You may be trying to deliver an impressive speech, or to make your point at a PTA meeting, or to complete your assignment for a class. If you are a skater, you may be trying to deliver a triple axel. Worrying and saying to yourself over and over again, "Will I do it? How am I doing? Can I do it? Will the audience accept it?" is not helpful. These may be interesting and even useful questions to have answers to, but they are not the questions of someone who is in the moment. They are the questions of someone who is paying attention to the product before the product has been produced. You can't examine a product before it is completed. The performer is making the product at that moment. Staying in the moment allows you to enjoy the sensations you are experiencing and the process of manufacturing the product. Later you can play another role, that of observer, critic, or judge, if you so choose.

If you stay in the moment, you also allow yourself to enjoy the process. Staying in the moment ultimately means acting as if, not self-spectating, and staying process-oriented.

And Now, Class, Time for Homework!

Stay in the Moment

Try to use the specific recommendations of this prescription whenever you find yourself becoming distracted or making yourself anxious about things external to the moment you are in. (You may also want to use the homework suggestions at the end of Chapter 5.)

1. When you find yourself slipping out of the moment in your daily activities, remember that you can't riffle while you work. Take a calming/cleansing breath and ask yourself. "What is the moment I am in?" Enumerate the demands of the role and then try to fulfill them, within the limits of your current level of ability.

2. Dispute your irrational belief that you must not ever slip out of the moment and that you are stupid if you do so. Remind yourself that humans are distractible and that you are a human, then get back into the moment.

3. Try visualizing yourself losing the moment, then visualize yourself recovering and staying in character.

Prescription 13

Rate Your Behavior, Not Your Soul

During one of her acting classes, Miss Stella Adler, a world-renowned acting coach, asked her class to rise for a silent moment of tribute. She said, "A man of the theatre died last night. It will take a hundred years before the harm that man has done to the art of acting can be corrected." The man she was talking about was the famous Lee Strasberg, the founder of The Actor's Studio.
Hay (1989) *Broadway Anecdotes*, Oxford University Press p. 359

Would you have expected something so damning to be said about such a respected man in the world of theater? What does this tell you about how we think? It says that people's evaluations of themselves and others are often idiosyncratic. How do you rate Lee Strasberg if you are in the theater? What does this suggest to you about how you might respond to your own foibles?

The "Tissue Box Dispute"

Before we discuss this problem, try the following exercise. Get a tissue box or a large notebook that you are willing to destroy. Do you have your tissue box full of tissues or your notebook in your hand? We are now going to ask you to list your qualities in three different ways. Qualities are attributes that you think you possess.

- List those attributes that you think are good, worthy, or desirable.
- List those that you think could use some improvement, but are not so bad.
- List those that are pretty lousy, awful, and rotten as far as you are concerned.

Now, if you are alone or, if you are in public and you don't mind what those around you think, take one tissue out of the box or one sheet of paper out of the notebook and identify it as one of your qualities. You might, for example, say, "I'm a good friend" as you pull one tissue out of the tissue box and let it drop to the floor. "I don't get things done as quickly as I'd like to" and drop another tissue or piece of notebook paper on the floor. Don't remove all of the tissues or all of the pages of the notebook. Leave some available, because no one can truly know all of his or her qualities, whether good, bad, or improvable.

Try to list at least a dozen of your attributes, or more if you can. They don't have to be perfectly balanced: three good, three bad, and three mediocre. Once you've done that, look at the clutter around you. (By the way, you may want to dispute your low frustration tolerance about having to pick up the mess you've just created.) You now have this little bit of clutter, representing all your qualities and attributes, strewn on the floor around you.

Are You the Tissues or the Box?

Now ask yourself, "Which one of these tissues (or pieces of paper) *is* the tissue box (or the notebook)? Which one of these pieces of paper represents the container?" Write down your answer.

Now ask yourself a more personal question: "Which one of these attributes *is* me?" A functional response to both questions is "none of them." None of the tissues *is* **the tissue box**. None of the pieces of paper *is* **the notebook**. They're part and parcel of an entire package, but **they're not equivalent**. They're the contents, not the container. No person is one attribute.

Do Not Confuse the Contents with the Container

You are not your skills, your charm, your appearance, or your dysfunctional behavior. People who get themselves upset and who stop themselves from performing or become anxious about their performance, routinely confuse the performer with the performance. You may have many good qualities or indifferent qualities, but they are not you as a human being. They represent the things you do. Confusing the two is a very common error, but it can be a very dangerous one for your personal well-being. It would be better to separate your behaviors from your total being. It is best to see your behaviors as things that you do and are concerned about and wish to show improvement in, but not to see them as necessarily being you.

The Impossible Task of *Self*-Improvement

We want you to improve your behaviors whenever you can, but how do you improve *you*? We know that you probably got this book out of a section of the bookstore or library entitled "Self-improvement." We would have preferred that this book be placed under a category called "Behavioral Improvement," *because that is really what we are trying to help you do. Many people, as they approach the task of "self-improvement," begin to believe that it is an impossible task. What does it mean to improve your self? What does it mean when you say, "I am a bad person"? What does it mean when you say, "I am a good person"?* These are phrases that are very common in our culture and in our vocabulary.

Little Jack Horner and You

Let's start with the last one first, "I am a good person." Like Little Jack Horner of Mother Goose fame, we tend to believe that if we do something good, we *are* good. Many of us heard sentences like that as children: "Oh, what a good boy; you ate all of your vegetables," or "Oh, what a good girl; you helped mommy." That's nice, and it's probably even pleasant to hear, but it's misleading. It assumes that because you *did* something nice or *behaved* appropriately or pleasantly, your value as a human being suddenly escalated. Every part of you turned good because you ate your spinach. If eating spinach has that power, Popeye must be the best person in the world.

If you helped mom with a chore and you are a good person, what does that mean when you refuse to help mom with a chore? Does it mean that your personhood suddenly takes a nosedive and you no longer have the ability to be good? If you refuse to eat your spinach, does that mean that you are no longer a decent human being and deserve to be incarcerated? Remember, people tend to think illogically. The type of statement that equates your worth as a human with a single act such as helping your mother or eating properly is a prime example of the illogical equations we wrote about in an earlier chapter. While this type of thinking is common, it is certainly not helpful.

Let's look at another example of this type of faulty reasoning. Many of us had to take competitive exams to get into college or graduate school or for job placement. Many of us have been trained to confuse our grades on these examinations with our identity or our worth. If you are doing relatively well in school, you may go around boasting and bragging, "I *am* an A" or "I *am* an honors student." If you've done poorly, you may conclude, "I am a loser, totally and completely, because I can't pass calculus." This kind of confusion, while common, as we said before, is self-defeating.

As you are reading this, we can hear some of you saying (because many of our clients have said this to us as well), "Do you mean we shouldn't want to do well, or shouldn't be concerned about how well we do?" Certainly we want you to be concerned about how well you do. We are not telling you to give up your concern. We *are* saying that it would be best not to confuse how well you do with how good you are. Don't confuse how poorly you do with how stupid, rotten, or worthless you are. These are qualities you possess. Look back at the tissues on the floor. Look at all those qualities you've strewn about and remember that some of the tissues represent good qualities, some represent bad qualities, and some represent qualities that need improvement. You can attempt to improve those that need improvement because you may get better results, which may be one of your goals.

But if I tell you that your goal is to improve your self or your soul, that's an insuperable task, and you would rightfully shun doing it because it cannot be accomplished. You can improve the quality of your performance:

- If you are singing off key, you can learn to sing on key.
- If you are typing forty words a minute, you can learn to type eighty words a minute.

If there are no physical limitations, you can probably show dramatic improvement in whatever you are doing. Even if you have physiological limits, **you can usually show** *some* **improvement**, depending on the skill or area you choose to work on. If you are a male, no matter how hard you try, you can (probably) never give birth. If you are very short and very thin, you probably will never be a champion muscle man or weight lifter. If you are five feet tall, you will probably not be asked to join a chorus line of six-foot-tall chorines.

The Rating Game—The Game that Everyone Loses
Why bother playing the rating game at all? As members of the society we live in, we've been taught to use markers for accomplishments. How many pages can I

write? How many baskets can I sink? How many problems can I solve on this exam? How many lines do I have to memorize? How many canvases must I complete before I can show my paintings in my own show? Those markers of achievement are very helpful because they can give you some point of comparison that you can use as feedback concerning whether or not you're showing *improvement*. But that's all they show you.

Reaching any or all of the markers doesn't *prove* that you are a worthy human being. You would be hard pressed to show me how reaching your goal suddenly makes you a worthy person, or, if you haven't reached your goal, that you've suddenly lost your worth.

"But wait," I can hear you say, as many of my clients have said to me, "Isn't it true that if I do poorly over time, I won't keep my job? Won't I be worthless in that regard?" Yes, I would agree that if you continue to do poorly, you may not keep, or get, a job, and in that regard some employers might describe you as "worth less" to them than a more reliable employee.

Sergeant Friday's Precincts of Worth

Since it seems to be both self-defeating and irrational to globally rate yourself on the basis of one, or even a few, criteria, what would we recommend? You may recall the *Dragnet* dispute (Sergeant Friday to the rescue). When you use this form of dispute, you look at the facts, without editorial comment. The facts are that there are many areas in which you could rate your behaviors if you so chose. We therefore need to look at "precincts" of worth. You could certainly talk about your economic worth, or your worth as an employee to a particular employer. We could talk about your worth to a particular person as a sex partner or as a spouse. You may not be terribly worthy as a spouse for person A, but that does not mean that you would not be worthy as a spouse for person B.

> *The Case of Selma:* This reminds me of a client named Selma, who, after a very messy divorce, came in for some supportive therapy. During our first session, Selma told me, "I am a failure as a woman because I am divorced." That's a pretty weighty statement and a very sad one. The client who says, "I am a failure as a woman because my marriage broke up" is engaging in what we would call *global self-rating.* She was rating her entire womanhood on the basis of one very unfortunate and unpleasant incident, the dissolution of her marriage. This was certainly an unpleasant, unhappy, and unfortunate event for her. Let's look at the logic and the rationality of her rating system. If she had rated her behavior as (1) her usefulness or (2) her aptness as a spouse for her previous husband, *maybe*, it would have been okay to say that she was a failure as a partner for him (whom we nicknamed Mr. Wonderful). She might have been an inappropriate spouse for Mr. Wonderful, but on reflection we also realized that probably no one would have been the greatest spouse for Mr. Wonderful. We might say that (3) Selma failed as a partner in a relationship, but that would not be totally accurate, either. We might have said that she didn't have certain specific wifely skills that she thought it was appropriate to have, and maybe it would have been a good idea if she had had those particular wifely skills. One could equally argue that even if she had possessed all of the wifely skills she demanded, this is no guarantee that she would have remained married to Mr. Wonderful.

There have been innumerable Mr. Wonderfuls in various women's lives who agreed that even though their women "did all the right things," they still didn't want to stay with them. What can we conclude? The only thing that it is factual to say is that Selma's marriage broke up (remember, editorial comments usually result in irrational beliefs). To conclude that she lost her X chromosomes because her marriage broke up would be bizarre. She is a woman. She may have failed at her goal of staying married to Mr. Wonderful forever, and that alone may be pretty sad and unfortunate for her.

As we were working on a peripheral problem, Selma divulged that her goal in life was to find "*the* man" and stay married to him until she died. Even though we could debate the appropriateness of that goal, or how realistic it was, it still was her goal, and she had failed at it. That is certainly sad and unfortunate as it stands. How much more sad and how much more unfortunate could her failure be? How much more immobilizing and self-defeating did she make it? By going to the next step, the step where she editorialized and said, "Because I didn't achieve my purpose in life, I am a failure as a human being whose sex happens to be female," she managed to globally rate herself in a negative way.

How does one fail as a woman? I can see how you fail in your attempt to be a good student, but I can't see how you fail as a woman. You are given an exam, and you don't pass your exam. You have then failed as a student in that class on that specific examination, but not in any other way. If you stay specific and very, very focused, you will still feel sad. No one is trying to rid you of negative emotions when they are appropriate and functional. We are not that saying that you must feel good all the time. It would be inappropriate to feel good when you are not achieving your goals in life or when you are suffering a misfortune. The secret is to feel appropriately, but not dysfunctionally, sad and to continue to live. The secret is to live through and cope with these foul-smelling, unpleasant onions without assuming that your total worth has been irremediably and negatively affected.

It is much harder to cope if you globally rate yourself or others. No one likes to be treated badly, and many of us don't like to be around those who treat us badly. If you conclude that because an individual treats you badly, that person is globally worthless, you only increase your anger or hostility, and that doesn't help the matter. Increased hostility doesn't help you perform in front of someone who you think is a total and complete moron or a total bigot. Every one of us has some redeeming social value. It may be hard to locate in certain people, but it is there.

Introducing the All-Purpose It

The way to respond to your bad or problematic behavior, whether it be procrastination or a shaky voice or an inability to memorize lines, is to recognize that those things are not desirable behaviors and say, "I don't like those behaviors." With some of our clients, we refer to it as the *all-purpose "it."* The client is taught to say, "I don't like 'it'" or "I don't like myself with 'it,'" rather than "I don't like myself because of 'it.'"

Which of your behaviors don't you like?

> *What are some of your "its"?*
> *Write them down on a piece of paper.*

Now, complete the following sentence: "I don't like 'it' [fill in the behavior that you don't like here], but until I can change 'it,' I will accept myself with [this behavior] (again, fill in the behavior).

> *The Case of Xavier L.:* Xavier L. was a perfectionist about his work skills. He was head of the computer programming department of a major mailing house. He was very proud of the meticulous way in which he ran his department. He told himself that all departments should be run the way his was, and that there was *no excuse* for the slovenly way in which the nonperfectionists in the company dealt with their work.
>
> When he had to attend marketing meetings and other staff meetings, he acted in an arrogant manner and made demeaning comments to the others around him because he told himself, "If these people need help or make errors, it proves that they are rotten people. If they are rotten people, why should I have to treat them nicely?"

Since Xavier did not treat the other staff members as humans, he was excluded from many meetings and company excursions. He received only perfunctory raises and was never offered a promotion. Xavier could never understand why this was happening and blamed it on the others' being jealous of his perfectionism and efficiency.

Xavier L., like many other global self-raters, was globally rating not only himself, but others as well. He evaluated each of his coworkers based on what he saw as their work efficiency. Xavier believed that if someone was efficient, he or she was a good person. But if the person was found to be even slightly lacking in efficiency, Xavier thought that person was a total loser. No one likes to be seen as a loser, and because Xavier was forthcoming concerning his feelings, everyone on the staff knew where he stood. He could not see that it was his global ratings and not jealousy, that was keeping him from being promoted.

I Hear that Attila the Hun Was Good to His Dogs

Have you ever looked at another person, whom you have globally rated in a negative manner, and asked yourself, "What are some of this person's good qualities?" Why not try that? Take a piece of paper and write down the given name of someone whom you might globally rate as undesirable. Write down the attributes you see that make that person appear globally bad to you. Now try writing down his or her good qualities. You still may not like the individual, and you may decide that the particular person you are imagining has no place in your life, but is that person totally without redeeming characteristics? Think of a coworker that you are having difficulty interacting with at work. If you imagine this individual's good points, you may find it easier to get along with him or her.

Xavier L. luckily attended one of our workshops and was able to see that some of the people he was globally rating on his idiosyncratic "personal efficiency rating" were nice people who actually did a pretty good job. He later reported to us that as he continued to picture each of them as a unique human with varying strengths and weaknesses, he found himself being friendlier and having an easier time getting the information he needed. He also found that these people were nice to interact with, and that it was more pleasant being with them than being isolated as he had been at work.

We have pointed out that humans often globally rate themselves and one another based on behavioral characteristics. Humans also tend to globally rate themselves based on one feature of their appearance.

The Case of Serge: Serge, a fund raiser for a non-profit organization, was very fussy about his appearance. He had a wart on the back of his neck that kept reappearing despite repeated excisions. He also had freckles on his arms. Serge could not tolerate freckles. He often wore an artistic-looking scarf to work, and he wore long-sleeved clothing, no matter how warm the weather was. He told himself that if anyone were to see the wart on his neck or the freckles on his arms, they would laugh at him and tease him unmercifully. He avoided any intimate contact because he "knew" that no other human could ever accept him because of these horrible anomalies. Serge therefore remained alone. He did not date anyone for fear that she would find out his horrible secrets, and he never accepted social appointments during the summer so that people would not question his ways of hiding his "terrible flaws."

As you can see, Serge made himself very unhappy by globally rating his essence on the basis of one wart and his freckled arms, which he found totally unacceptable. He made the fallacious assumption that others would see these flaws in the same exaggerated manner that he did. His attitude toward himself and his global self-rating forced him into isolation and loneliness.

Do you rate yourself on one physical characteristic?

If you rate yourself in this way, which characteristic do you use to ascertain your worth? Is it your nose, your eyes, your height, or your weight? Try this exercise. Stand in front of a full-length mirror and look at yourself. Which of your many physical characteristics don't you like? As you rate each characteristic, what do you tell yourself about that characteristic and about you as a person with that characteristic? Do you tell yourself that the characteristic causes you to be worthless? Do you tell yourself that the characteristic is worthless? Look at your hands in the mirror. Are they worthwhile, or are they totally worthless? If you said, "Worthless," what is worthless about them? Are your fingers totally worthless? Are your knuckles or your palms totally worthless? Do you have totally worthless shoulder blades? Remember Katasha in *The Mikado*, whose shoulder blade drew crowds even though she was not considered attractive.

Now that you've rated each characteristic, which one of these represents the total you? If you mentioned any characteristic that defines you, we would like you to prove it. Let us say that you said that your eyes are too small and that your eyes are you. Prove it, right now—prove that your eyes are you! What about the other 99 percent of your body—has it no importance? If your eyes are really you, how do you rate your non-visible characteristics, such as your charm or your style?

Even though you are bombarded (daily through the media) by the belief that you *are* your appearance, is this provable? It is obvious that our culture emphasizes and worships what it considers to be physical attractiveness. Does this mean that you must rate yourself solely on the basis of your physical attributes? If you do, what happens as the cultural definitions of beauty change? What happens as you age? Do you become unacceptable? Remember that one major reason why appearance is pushed by the media is to make money. Television relies on the advertising dollar to make a profit, and advertisers must convince you that you need to change by buying one of their products. But do *you* profit? How does buying or owning the advertiser's product affect your self-worth?

I am a Falllibble Human Bean

Since you are totally human, you are imperfect by definition. You are also fallible. We have not yet met a perfect or an infallible person. You therefore almost certainly have some undesirable attributes. Were you ever taught that a rotten apple spoils the barrel? Remind yourself that you can always rid yourself of the rotten behavior. Also remind yourself that a rotten behavior does not make you a rotten person, just as a rotten apple doesn't ruin the entire barrel. If you consider yourself to be of reasonable value, what we would encourage you to do is to remind yourself that behaviors are changeable. If you do not consider yourself to have value, try reminding yourself that you have worth just because you are on the planet and alive. You don't need to do anything or to have anything in order to create your value and your worth.

What are the prerequisites of worth? Carl Rogers, a fellow psychologist, talked about conditions of worth. He stated that if you set your conditions of worth at too high a level, it becomes almost impossible to be worthy. Xavier L.'s standards for his colleagues were much too high for any of them to attain. Rogers also wrote about "unconditional positive regard." We would like you to adopt a slightly different concept than Rogers'. We would like you to think in terms of unconditional, positive self-acceptance. This is discussed in depth in Prescription 14, "Accept Yourself, Warts and All." If you decide that you are totally worthless, just remind yourself, as a start, that the chemicals in your body have some worth.

In the first part of this book, we discussed the fact that everyone has a philosophy of life. We also discussed the philosophical dispute (what would the old philosopher say?). When we talk about self-worth, we are discussing a philosophical issue. We are pointing out that every being has worth just because that being exists.

When we talk about rating behaviors, we are not talking about your having worth because you exist. Instead, we are talking about the worth of some of your characteristics and behaviors to yourself and others. You may have to have specific skills to have worth to an employer. One of these important skills might be punctuality. You may have to have a certain attractiveness or enjoy certain things to have worth to a particular sex partner or friend. You may need to be sensitive to that person's emotional needs. Those behaviors may require some effort initially or maybe even continuously in order to maintain your level of skill. However, let us remind you once again that no one attribute or behavior defines the total *you*.

The Leopard's Spots

Your goal is to pay attention to and work on those behaviors that you can change. You can't change your personhood. Many of you have learned to say that "the leopard can't change its spots." We would agree with that concept; however, the leopard *can* learn to do other things. It can learn to run figure eights and it can learn to lick behind its ears if it needs to, in order to get food. The leopard is capable of changing many of its behaviors. Its spots are not its behaviors. If you were going to say that a leopard can't learn to breathe under water, we would again agree. Leopards probably cannot learn this particular skill, but neither can humans without assistance.

Try Using "It's Only"

If you're motivated to change and you don't engage in self-defeating behaviors, you frequently will change. If you say, "Why bother? After all, I did this one bad thing and I can never recover," then you probably will not be motivated to try to recover. You may even get entangled in a self-fulfilling prophecy. You may create a self-fulfilling prophesy that leads you to not be motivated, and therefore you get the expected result and you do not recover. If you then say, "Wow, my prediction was correct. A worthless person like myself doesn't succeed," the only one you will be fooling is yourself. A person who says, "I am separate and distinct from my behaviors" has a much easier time of it. Change becomes easier, because you can use the "it's only" argument. Change then becomes, "*It's only* learning to type a little faster, *it's only* learning to sing the song better, or *it's only* learning to hold my tongue rather than saying the first thing that comes to mind in social settings. That's hard enough for me to do, but I can do that." However, if you set out to change everything about yourself instantaneously, you are asking the impossible. We are not asking the leopard to change its spots or the tiger to change its stripes. We are asking a human being who is reasonably intelligent to learn to separate behaviors from being, and to work on changing attributes and not being.

Remember that all humans are unique and that there is no one exactly like you in all ways in this world. Your uniqueness in itself bestows worth.

> *The Case of Matilda P.:* Matilda P., an actress, was doing her first one-woman show on the life of Emily Dickinson. She was totally unfamiliar with the special efforts needed for this type of presentation. She was very nervous the first night and tripped on many of her words. When the reviews came out the next morning, her stuttering and tripping rather than the strengths of her performance were highlighted. Matilda was devastated, but she still had a choice. She could accept the reviews as more than what they said and rate herself as a lousy actress and an awful person for giving such a lousy first-night performance, or she could take the reviews under advisement and work on her lines and delivery. Happily, Matilda did the latter and improved her presentation for the remaining performances.

Matilda rightly decided to rate her behaviors and not her soul. It would be in your best interest to follow Matilda's example and do the same.

To help you act like Matilda, you might want to try to use some of the following coping statements.

1. Just because I acted poorly, that does not make me a bad person.
2. Just because I acted wimpishly, that does not mean that I am a wimp.
3. Just because I acted wormily, that does not mean that I am a worm.
4. Just because I acted unselfishly, that does not make me a saint.

Another exercise that will help you to separate your behaviors from your worth as a human would be to pick part of your life—your job, for example—and list all the things you do as part of the job. Try writing all the different aspects of your work on a piece of paper. Next to each aspect, write down a performance number indicating how well you do each task on your list. A score of 1 indicates poor performance, and a score of 10 indicates superior skills. Then look back, take one of the skills you listed, and say, "Because my performance on this skill (e.g., computer programming), was a three, does that make me a bad person? It may suggest that I need to work on my skills as a programmer, but it means nothing about my worth as a person."

Rochelle and I Work as Psychologists

Another exercise that we would like you to try is to list all the activities you engage in this week. Take each activity, such as your job, your relationships, and your hobbies, and rephrase the way you say it. Let us say that you teach. Instead of saying, "I am a teacher," we would like you to say, "I work as a teacher." The reason for this is that your whole life is not made up of the hours that you stand in front of a class or grade papers. Rochelle and I work as psychologists, we are not psychologists. This means that every cell in our bodies is not psychological. Most people lead lives that include a myriad of roles. You may work as a parent, as a spouse, at your job, as a driver, as a shopper, as a Little League coach, etc. These are the things you do. If you say, "I work as a psychologist," or "I work as an actor," or "I work as an executive in an ad agency," or "I work as a parent or a homemaker," it helps you to gain perspective. People are going to stop you and say, "But what are you?" You can then say, "I am a human." At first, this declaration may seem silly or shallow; however, on reflection, it tells you what you are and then helps you to separate your behaviors from your essence by allowing you to state the many things you do and roles you play. If you learn to think in this way, if you lose one of your many roles—for example, if you retire from your job or are no longer acting in a direct parenting role because your children are grown and have left home—you will not see the loss as the end of the world because you will not have lost your identity. You will just have stopped performing a certain task or a certain role. You may then be ready to either take on new roles or increase the time spent on other activities in your life. You will not have lost your essence by giving up one role, even if it is the major role with which you identify, because you will see yourself as being more than any one role can define.

And Now, Class, Time for Homework!

Rate Your Behavior, Not Your Soul

Try to use the specific recommendations of this prescription whenever you find that you are confusing your self with your behavior. (You may also want to use the homework suggestions at the end of Chapter 5.)

1. When you feel the urge to globally rate your self, use the tissue box dispute and remind yourself that the contents are not the container.

2. Try responding to questions about what you *are* with what you *do*. (e.g., "I am doing the job of fathering today" or "Today, I am working as a computer programmer").

3. When you experience failure in any performance situation, try a narrow rating rather than a global one (e.g., "I failed in my attempt to learn today's tap dance lesson" rather than "I *am* a lousy hoofer").

4. When you are attempting some behavioral change, try to use "it's only" (e.g., "I am only trying to learn to talk for five minutes without stuttering" rather than "I have to learn to talk better" or "I am only changing my posture" rather than "I am trying to be more manly").

5. Try to look for the good in others as well as yourself.

Prescription 14
Accept Yourself, Warts and All

The Case of Amy L.: Amy L., a fashionable young marketing executive, had been approached by a headhunter to interview for an executive position with a major corporation. When notified of the date of the interview, Amy became very anxious. She broke out in an itchy rash that covered her arms and torso. She found that whenever she thought about how she would dress for the interview and how she would present herself, she began to hyperventilate. As the date of the interview neared, Amy spent more and more time looking at herself in her full-length mirror and critically examining every feature of her appearance. She tried on numerous "appropriate" interview suits and rejected each one in turn, because she believed that each magnified a fault that she did not want noticed.

Amy increasingly told herself, "No one could ever hire me for an executive position because my hair is too fuzzy and my figure is pear-shaped. No major corporation would want an executive representing them who has fuzzy hair or who is not tall and slender as a reed. I know that I'm good at what I do, but my good qualities won't count for anything because of my appearance. All of my shortcomings will prevent me from getting this position or any other similar position. Why should I even go to the interview if I can't get the job because of my appearance?"

One of the most difficult lessons that we must learn as humans is how to rate our behaviors and features without globally rating ourselves. In the previous chapter, we showed you the results of globally rating yourself. Using a pragmatic dispute, we tried to get you to reconsider the usefulness of confusing your behavior with your self. We tried to show you that evaluating how well you do a task makes far more sense than globally identifying yourself as deficient or defective. The corollary to that behavioral self–acceptance is to also work on accepting yourself within your physical limits, and, if possible, to work at changing those limits that are changeable.

The formula that we recommend our clients use is the all-purpose "it." An example of such a formula would be to start with, "I don't like myself *with* 'it.'" For "it," you may substitute performance anxiety, the physical symptoms of stress, your physical appearance, or other physical, behavioral, or emotional characteristics.

What were Amy's "its"?

Remember, Amy was anxious because of her fuzzy hair and her pear-shaped physique. While she *could* go through the expense, bother, and discomfort of cosmetic surgery, the more "elegant" approach would be to work toward accepting her unchangeable physical characteristics. She could then concentrate on working on the problems that get in her way behaviorally. Once again, the formula is, "I don't like 'it,' but I can accept myself with 'it' while I am working to change."

In the previous chapter, we encouraged you to remind yourself, "My behavior may not be helpful, but it doesn't help me to put myself down or condemn myself because I have that bad behavior. While I work on changing my problematic behavior, I can work on accepting myself with it. I am not a globally worthless person because I have problematic behavior."

This new prescription encourages you to say, "I am not a globally ugly person because I do not like the way I look. I am not globally ugly or unattractive even if others may not like my appearance. I can accept myself, even if others do not. I can also, if I choose to, change my physical appearance through diet, exercise, or cosmetic surgery, if I think it will improve my chances of performing better."

What are your physical "its"?

Are your "its," like Amy's, characteristics that cannot be changed? Let's say that your "it" is your short neck. You can begin to help yourself by telling yourself, "I can accept myself with my short neck. I cannot change the length of my neck, but it does not help me to become anxious or upset because my neck is short. I can work to change my anxiety and upset, but for now I can accept myself with both my short neck and my anxiety."

Now that you have focused on the quality or qualities that you don't like about yourself, what are some of the physical characteristics you possess that you do like? List them. You may have a short neck, but you may also have a winning smile and a charming manner that attracts people. Is your entire personhood contained in your neck?

The Woman Who Mistook Her Bosom for Her Self

I once worked with a client who believed that her whole being was contained within her breasts. She had had innumerable breast augmentations and reductions. She devoutly believed that in order to be accepted by her lover of the moment, she had to look as he seemed to prefer. While she acknowledged that no lover had ever explicitly demanded that she undergo corrective surgery, she could never believe that any lover would continue to accept her unless she looked like his fantasy woman. She could not imagine that even if it were objectively demonstrated that her breasts were somehow inadequate, she had other redeeming physical, emotional, and behavioral qualities that were attractive and that would help her attract and maintain a lover's interest. By seeing herself as one-dimensional, she felt not only unattractive but depressed and anxious whenever she was in a public setting.

Over time, I was able to get her to challenge her belief that she was only a bosom. As she began to change her global rating and practice "warts and all" self-acceptance, not only did her emotional outlook improve, but she functioned more effectively in social settings and (as an added benefit) incurred less expense.

"...With a Caricature of a Face"

Even if you are objectively physically unattractive, where do your smile and your way with others fit in? Gilbert and Sullivan in *The Mikado* remind us of the multidimensionality of humans in a most humorous way. Katisha, the comic villainess, is considered rather unattractive. The character is often played using outlandish costuming and extreme makeup. When sarcastically reminded of how others see her, Katisha responds, "You hold that I am not beautiful because my face is plain.... Learn that it is not in the face alone that beauty is to be sought. My face is unattractive...but I have a left shoulder blade that is a miracle of loveliness. People come miles to see it. My right elbow has a fascination that few can resist." Remembering Katisha is a good way of reminding yourself that your self does not consist of only one characteristic.

The notion of self-acceptance requires work in two areas: accepting yourself behaviorally and accepting yourself physically. We have already discussed and will continue to discuss techniques to assist you in changing those behaviors that you would like to change.

People like Amy use their body image as an excuse so that they do not have to perform. They may categorically tell themselves, "I won't perform because I don't like the way I look." "I won't go out on a date because of my appearance." "I won't speak to a new person." "I won't ask for a raise because of my appearance." "I won't go for an audition because I don't look the way I am 'supposed to look.'" We discussed the tyranny of the "shoulds" in an earlier chapter. If you *should* have had a slender build, *should* have been six inches taller, and *should* have had a different face, you **would have had those features**. It's unfortunate that you do not look the way you'd like to look, and you could probably make *some* adjustments to look more the way you want to look. It is up to you to decide if it's worth the time, the effort, the money, the aggravation, and the potential pain required, in order to change your looks. A much less expensive and far more effective solution is to change both your attitude toward and your evaluation of your appearance.

We have all been exposed to the thoughtlessness or jesting comments of others regarding our appearance throughout our lives. When we were children, a parent, or possibly a teacher, a neighbor, or an older sibling or grandparent, may have made offhand disparaging remarks regarding one of our features, or the way we dressed, or our weight. The comments may have zeroed in on our freckles, or the size of our ears, or the shape of our nose. Depending upon how sensitive we were to seeking the approval of those around us, especially those who were important in our life, we may have taken their comments to heart and even as children told ourselves that we would never measure up.

Beauty Is in the Eye of a (Hopefully Blind) Beholder

You have often heard the adage that "beauty is in the eye of the beholder." You have also probably heard, and possibly said, "Love is blind." You may rationally desire that these two beliefs be maintained by the people who look at you. We have no control over how others see us. Many people, even lovers, may see your flaws but choose not to see them as fatal defects. Some, unfortunately, may have the ill grace to point them out to you. You only wind up disturbing yourself if you irrationally believe, "If he or she *really* loved me, he or she would be blind to my defects and shortcomings." It is in your best interest to remember that you can learn to control *your* thoughts, but not the feelings, thoughts, or perceptions of others.

"Mirror, Mirror on the Wall..."

You can, however, teach yourself to look into your own mirror and say, "I may not be perfect, but I am beautiful to me. "If you are able to do this, you reaffirm the fact, you like yourself and you like your looks, despite the biases that might exist within your family, community or culture.

Two Possible Drawbacks to This Approach

A word of caution is in order before you do this exercise. There are two negative results that can occur. If you say, "I am beautiful to me," you may ignore changes that it may be necessary for you to make in order to maintain your health. The second problem that could arise is that if you use this statement without caution, you may not be ready to see or change those things that it would be best for you to change or to hear objective criticisms from others that might well benefit you in the long term. A better statement for you to begin with might be, "I like the person I am, but if a change will benefit me, I am open to considering it."

> *The Case of Joe W.:* Joe was a massive ex-football player who had gained an enormous amount of weight after he had retired from playing. He now weighed over 300 pounds. His weight was putting a strain on his heart, resulting in cardiac problems. If Joe were to say, "I am beautiful to me," he might use this statement to avoid doing what was necessary to reduce his present weight and maintain a healthier one. I encouraged Joe to see that self-acceptance includes the acceptance of helpful health practices.

Changing the Culture One Person at a Time

Weight and physical appearance are major sources of concern and unhappiness in our culture. The result is that we act like weight and appearance bigots. What that really means is that we treat people who don't fit our stereotype of beauty badly. Many of us can remember a classmate being laughed at in the schoolyard, and possibly being taunted, because that poor child did not fit the current definition of an acceptable-looking child. We can remember how the members of the group encouraged one another to indulge in that bigotry. We also hear people make disparaging remarks about others who may be too fat, too thin, or too unmuscular. This bigotry, in any of its forms, is one of the most unpleasant features of our cultural climate.

While we may not have an immediate and direct control over the community value system, as much as we might desire to and as much as we might attempt to change it, we can have an immediate and direct control over our thoughts, feelings, and actions. With time and with effort, community values do change, as evidenced by our response to drunk drivers and unwanted sexual overtures in the workplace. However, we can typically effect a personal change without waiting for years to pass and for laws to be enacted.

When you attempt to change the culture, you are trying to influence the attitudes, opinions, and behaviors of millions. When you attempt personal change, there is only one person who has to be convinced, and that is yourself. Perhaps an appropriate thing to tell yourself would be, "Other people may be bigoted, but it does not help me to be bigoted about myself."

A Minority of One

I once had an occasion to work with a client, Martin Q., who was tremendously self-bigoted. He disliked everything about himself and put himself down for a variety of reasons, every opportunity he had. As a way of intervening, I finally wound up saying to him, "It occurs to me that you are your own KKK. And you treat yourself as the only minority group in town. You act as both the bigot and the minority group. Would you care to change that perception?" Martin was a little taken aback and then admitted that that was exactly what he was doing. He was behaving in a very unpleasant, very self-condemnatory way, and as a result in a very destructive way, towards himself. He began to slowly work on accepting the idea that although he might not look terribly handsome in the eyes of others, that did not mean that he deserved to be lynched. It did not mean that he deserved the hounding he was giving himself.

Quitting the S.B.B. (Self–Bigotry Brigade)

Once he began to accept that fact and endorse his new self-perception, overtime, and with help, a number of interesting changes began to occur. He started walking differently. His posture improved. His vocal quality changed, because as he began to think of himself as at least worthy to exist. He began to talk in a more assertive manner. About three months after that change, he came back all smiles to report that somebody had told him that he was attractive.

Now, what changed for him? His weight hadn't changed; his height hadn't changed. He hadn't gotten better clothing. He hadn't added any extra muscle tone. What had changed was the message he sent to the world, as well as the message he sent to himself. The message he now sent out was, "I am acceptable. I am worthy. I am, if not perfect (no human is perfect), at least capable of attracting people to me." He learned to act like a social magnet, and thereby attracted people to him.

As part of our work together, we discussed well-known actors who became famous even though they never even closely approximated the culturally ideal body type. Among those we both were able to identify were Jackie Gleason, who was much heavier than was acceptable for males; Wally Cox and Don Knotts, who were both much smaller and skinnier and lacked the physique of popular male heroes; and Anthony Perkins, an accomplished actor who was tall, reedy and angular—not what one would consider a physical idol. Martin was able to point out that their physiques never seemed to get in the way of their goals. They became famous because of their ability, despite their not fitting the popular mode.

I Am All Ears

Another example of how warts-and-all self-acceptance is beneficial occurred during the 1992 presidential debates. You may all recall one particularly memorable moment when Ross Perot was speaking to someone and caught himself in an interesting and revealing sentence. He looked at the camera, then at the questioner, and said, "Go ahead, I'm all ears." He looked abashed for a moment, then started to laugh, and said, "Yep, that's right; I *am* all ears," and continued with his remarks. Mr. Perot did what we have encouraged our clients to do for years: Accept what is real about you, rather than bemoan it. We don't know what his past was like, we don't know what his childhood was like, but at that moment he exhibited the kind of self-acceptance that we are trying to teach. One could probably say in a kindly way that Mr. Perot's ears are larger than most people's ears. That may be accurate, but that editorial piece that we constantly warn you against would be, "I can't stand it. I could never succeed or accomplish anything because of my oversized ears." There have been editorial cartoonists who treated Ross Perot badly because of that look. But Ross Perot has not allowed that poor treatment to stop him from making a fortune or functioning effectively, even though he might not (and we have no way of knowing this) have been thrilled about the way his face looked as a result of that prominent feature.

If you don't take yourself out of the performance setting as a result of your appearance, you have a better chance of getting what you want. Any number of actors will tell you stories of directors who have refused to cast them because they did not fit the director's image of what the part called for. Many directors will tell you equal numbers of stories of actors who, when hearing of their requirements, said, "Oh, you need someone who is gray; I can dye my hair gray" or "If you need someone six inches taller, I can play taller."

If a director has a particular type in mind, you may be rejected not because of your acting ability, not because of your talent, and not because of your personhood. Rejection in this setting may simply be a result of something beyond your control, that is, the director wants somebody who looks like his or her stereotype of the character. In this situation, it is in your best interest to work toward accepting the fact that while you may be very capable and even very good looking, in the director's eyes at least, you are not "right" for the part.

Even if you are aware of the directors biases, it is still in your best interest to attend the audition, not avoid it. You may fit the director's stereotype of another character, either in his or her present production or in a future one. If you do not audition, the director will not be aware that you exist.

When you ask someone for a date and you are refused, as sometimes happens, you may be told no because you may not fit the other person's stereotype of what his or her date "should" look like. If you foolishly conclude that since you were rejected for one date, you will be rejected for all dates, you will probably stop trying to get dates and wind up even more unhappy than you currently are.

Just because you don't fit the observer's stereotype of a date or a character, it doesn't mean that you are not capable and talented, or that you necessarily must respond as a victim. When you are treated badly, is it necessary or helpful for you to become dysfunctional? We once worked with a participant at one of our workshops who used to jokingly say, "If someone goes out of their way to be mean to me, the least I can do is be hurt."

Staying in the Arena

You know that we live in an imperfect world where bias still exists. Do you want to act in a biased way toward yourself, take yourself out of the arena of life, and thereby limit your own opportunities? What could you do, think, or say to yourself that would be more helpful?

- You could try to evaluate yourself in a rational and honest way.
- You could also try to separate those physical features and behaviors that you can change from those that you cannot.
- Try a personal cost-benefit analysis. You can do this by saying, "Is it worth my time, effort, and energy, given the possible potential gain, to work on transforming my body?"
- Even if the answer is yes, it would be in your best interest *not* to take yourself off the stage or out of the arena while you work on that change. It may take you five or ten years to achieve the body you want, but it will probably take you far less time to challenge and rearrange your thinking so as to tell yourself, "Okay, I may not like the way I look, and that's pretty unfortunate. Other people may not like the way I look, and that would be pretty unfortunate as well. But I can accept myself, my failings, and my body while I change them."

I *Would* Do It, But...

There are attributes other than body image and appearance that people may have difficulty accepting. We often hear our clients say, "I would get up and speak, but I cannot because I...." Many people's "because" is a behavior, such as "because I lisp," "Because I stutter," or "because I shake." Some people tell us that they cannot perform their jobs because others will see that they are anxious, and that too is unacceptable to them. Other characteristics besides appearance are used to stop performance in any and all situations. Some of the things that individuals allow to stand in the way are visible and some are invisible, such as upset stomachs, dry mouths, or nervousness.

Do you have some "becauses"? Write them down.

Do you have some nonphysical attributes that you allow to get in your way? We can classify these other attributes as either behavioral, emotional, or cognitive. You may decide that your stuttering, your anxiety, or your way of thinking is unacceptable for others to see and, therefore avoid performance situations. We referred to this in our chapter on sacred ideals.

It is difficult for you to perform if you are struck dumb by these negative feelings and undesirable attributes. You may say, "No one can perform when he or she feels as depressed as I do." That type of statement severely limits your options. You can also severely limit the quality of your performance if you think, "People who catastrophize the way I do can never get up and read a paper in class. It would be foolish of me to try. Everyone would see the way I think, and I would end up being embarrassed and humiliated."

Even though it seems that we have listed many ways of rating yourself that can interfere with performance, there is one more type of important rating that people give themselves that stops them cold. They rate their likelihood of giving a good performance in a given situation. Since they believe that the probability of their performing well is low, they get angry and depressed about "having to perform." They then attempt to avoid opportunities to perform, and as a result they never learn to perform well. They may say, "I cannot give speeches in public; people should know that. I cannot accept the idea that this job has that requirement. I cannot accept the idea that this class requires me to read my essay. I cannot accept the idea that I must expose myself to criticism."

How can you rephrase "I cannot accept" so that it becomes an invitation, rather than a barrier, to improvement? You might try saying:

- "I don't like what I have to do, or I don't like this attribute, but I am able to perform even if I don't like it. Where is it written that I should avoid things I dislike?"
- "I am going to see what happens. My undesirable attributes don't have to stop me from performing."
- "I can accept that performing is a requirement. If I am to get a good grade, I have to perform."

This last statement looks like it includes the kind of Jehovian demand that we warned you about. However, if you recall the first prescription, you remember that not all shoulds, musts, or have to's are self-defeating. This last statement includes an acceptable "conditional should." A conditional should indicates that in order to reach a goal, you need to fulfill certain requirements. If you are a student taking a college course in public speaking, the chances are slim that you will be able to pass or do well in the course if you do not get up and give one or more talks. Unfortunately, the course you are taking or the job you are employed in has certain requirements, and arbitrary or capricious though these requirements may be, they are there not only for you, but for every other person in that position. You have a choice. You can continue to rail against what is and say that it shouldn't be that way, or you can accept that this is the way the situation is and work on tolerating it. When we say accept yourself, we even mean accepting yourself in these personally unpleasant, unwanted, and inconvenient onion situations.

Saying "It's really terrible that I have to be in a situation where I am required to perform" immobilizes you and increases your misery. If you have any tendency to self-down, to feel depressed, or to become emotionally distraught, this is an invitation for you to indulge in that kind of self-defeating behavior.

How can you avoid accepting that invitation? What would be a better way to respond? Remember what we taught you in the beginning of the book. Dispute; call in Sergeant Friday to the rescue. What are the facts without further embellishment or editorializing—just the facts?

- If you are a student in a speech course: The fact is that the course has a requirement that students in the class will have to get up and speak. If you don't get up and speak, you will not meet the requirements for passing the course.

- If you are a graduate student trying to qualify for your doctorate: The fact is that if you go for a doctorate, you will be required to learn a language or two and be tested on that language. You will probably also be required to complete a dissertation and to present that dissertation in a public arena and defend it.
- If you are an executive in many corporations: The fact is that you will be required to do public presentations.

Those are the facts. Where is it written that it shouldn't be that way? How would you respond to a person who says to you, "they shouldn't have a requirement that makes people speak in public"? How would you respond if someone said, "My teacher shouldn't require that people read their research papers aloud"? What would be the rational response? Write it down. If you wrote, "Where is it written or what is your evidence that a person shouldn't be doing what he or she is doing?" you would be right on target.

Now, what would be a more effective response? Try this problem: You are confronted with the interesting dilemma of wanting to meet a new person and having that person's phone number. You realize that if you don't call that number, you are not going to meet this new person. Now, you could say, "I shouldn't have to do that." Indeed, if you do not want to meet that new person, you do not have to do it. However, if your goal is to meet a new person and you have that phone number, it would probably be a better idea for you to do it. You don't want to say, "Why should I have to?" because that phrase may tend to immobilize you. Remember, you are not being forced or coerced into doing something, and therefore you don't need to rebel to assert your independence. But if you think it would be a good idea for you to do it, what would be a more helpful response? You could say, "If I ever want to meet this new person, it would be in my best interest to make the phone call."

Picture yourself sitting in a dark well, and outside there is a beautiful sunny day. You really want to go out in the sun, but you don't want to make the effort of climbing up the ladder on the side of the well in order to get out of the well into the sunlight. How are you going to get to the sunlight that way? If you don't make the effort, you don't get to the sun.

Right now, you may not like the situation that exists, but if you recall the child you once were, there were probably many foods you didn't like. You parents may have told you that zucchini and cauliflower were good for you. You may have also been told that these vegetables were an acquired taste. You may possibly even have acquired a taste for some of the foods you initially turned up your nose at. You may be treating public speaking the way you once treated zucchini. You may turn your nose up at it now, but you might discover that you like it.

And Now, Class, Time for Homework!

Accept Yourself, Warts and All

Try to use the specific recommendations of this prescription whenever you find yourself beginning to make yourself upset about your physical appearance. (You may also want to use the homework suggestions at the end of Chapter 5.)

1. List your physical, emotional, and cognitive attributes that you believe stop you from performing.
2. Where is your evidence that it would be completely impossible to perform with these attributes?
3. Where is your evidence that having these attributes is terrible, rather than inconvenient?
4. Are you behaving like the woman who mistook her bosom for herself?
5. How does confusing your attributes with your self help you to perform or help you to improve your performance?
6. Every morning when you wake up, look into the mirror and say, "Hi, gorgeous" or "Hi, handsome." If you have trouble doing that, what are you telling yourself that makes it hard for you to see yourself as good looking?
7. Try acting like Katisha. What are some of your physical qualities that may be *unusually* attractive? Write down three or four sentences that demonstrate your acceptance of your appearance and use them in daily conversation (e.g., "I have always thought my eyebrows were my best feature" or "I have always thought that narrow chins were signs of a pointed wit").
8. Try quitting the S.B.B. (Self–Bigotry Brigade).

If You Must Compare,
Compare Downward

The Case of Rob: Rob, an aspiring young comedian, had problems getting up to perform at clubs. He had written his material and rehearsed it well. He knew his routine, and he had prepared for hecklers and other problems that he could encounter. However, he would not take advantage of the opportunities to perform that came his way. He kept telling himself that until he could perform in as polished a way as Bill Cosby or Robin Williams, he could not get up on stage.

Rob's friends encouraged him to perform and often accompanied him to comedy clubs. Rob strongly refused to get up and perform, even with their support and backing. He told himself, and them, that anything short of a "Robin Williams performance" would be an embarrassment to all and that he would not and could not tolerate that. Rob's own personal rating game was doing him in.

Comparisons Can Be Made in All Directions:
Upward, Downward, and Sideways

It is probably inevitable that while you are working on these prescriptions, you will continue to rate yourself and others. You will probably give in to the temptation of comparing yourself to others. You might discover that the neighbor next door has a better income or a higher standard of living than you do, and coming out on the negative end of the comparison might lead you to self-down about your income. If you are in the theater, you might decide to compare your talents to those of famous performers and say, "I wish that I had the stage presence of Lynn Redgrave or the film presence of Tom Cruise." If you are a classical singer, you might say, "I wish I had the voice of a Jessye Norman or a Luciano Pavarotti."

This type of wishful comparison is understandable and very human. No one is going to ask you not to make comparisons. It can however, become self-defeating when you compare upward and use the "evidence" you find to keep you out of the performance arena. Rob's comparisons kept him from reaching his goals. It was probably true that **at this point in his career** he was not as polished a comic as Bill Cosby or Robin Williams. By saying that he would risk performing only if he could be assured of their comedic sense and delivery, he kept himself from attaining the stage presence he would need to become a good comedian.

Comparisons Are Odious, Upward Comparisons Are Noxious

Every parent will tell you that comparisons are odious. You are different from the people around you. Children and siblings in the same household are often different from one another yet there is often a tendency for others to make comparisons between them because they are members of the same family. Making comparisons is a human tendency. It is generally not a helpful tendency, but it is very human. We are not going to ask you to stop making comparisons, but we *are* going to help you to make them in a different way.

Imagine, if you will, that you are a beginning piano student. You've just completed six months of lessons, and you've gotten beyond Happy Fingers—Book One. You are beginning to put together your left hand and your right hand, and the sounds you make occasionally even resemble music. Your teacher may have inquired as to your musical preferences when you began your studies so that music you like could be included. If you like classical music, you may have been given a simplified classical melody. If you indicated jazz, a simplified jazz number may have been included. These pieces are similar to the ones you would like to play. You then began to quietly explore Beethoven's "Ode to Joy," or you begin to tinkle out Scott Joplin's "The Entertainer." At this time, you are probably going to be tempted to listen to some highly proficient pianists. If you are interested in classical music, you may listen to Horowitz. If you are interested in ragtime, you may listen to Max Morath. You may even decide to attend a concert and watch how a specific pianist approaches his or her work, or you may choose to listen to a recording of a professional performance. What an opportunity to gain inspiration, but what an opportunity to also think about it irrationally. If you suffer from performance anxiety and you listen to a more proficient expert you might be foolishly tempted to say, "I will never be as good as that pianist on the recording. I will never be as good as that concert pianist. I will never play as well as the jazz performer in this club. I may as well stop now, since I will never be able to play as well as they do." Ironically, if you allow yourself to stop learning and practicing, you definitely will never play as well as they do. By stopping the activity, you stop growing.

Downward and Onward!

You make downward comparisons when you look at people who are less proficient or who have less in life than you do. If you recall what we wrote in Chapter 5, Thomas Wills found that people who compare downward typically are happier, possibly because they realize that they have more out of life than some of the people around them. They may, as a result, agree with Georg Simmel, who wrote, "There is something that doesn't displease us in the misfortune of our friends."

On a less misanthropic note, this may also be the time to remember Pollyanna and play a "glad game." If she was sick in bed, she would say something like, "Even though I have to stay in bed, at least I can look out the window." When we, like Pollyanna, use "at least," we are making downward comparisons. It may put you in mind of the old adage, "I cried because I had no shoes, until I saw a person with no feet."

What can you say "at least" about? You may say, "I may not be able to do
_____, but at least I can do _____." Fill in the blanks for yourself. "I may
not have this, but at least I've got that."

If you are a beginner who is just starting to play the piano, it is our experience
that when you compare your playing to that of people who are less proficient
than you, but are similar to you in background, training, and experience, you
probably are in a position to make far more useful comparisons:

- If you have done even a little practicing, you are probably far better
  than those who never practice.

- If you have been practicing even slightly, you are probably far better
  than beginners who are starting off today.

- You probably do not play piano anywhere near as well as George
  Gershwin, because you have only been practicing for six weeks, or after practicing the trumpet for three months, you are definitely not going to be able to play as well as Wynton Marsalis; however, both of
  these performers are people whom you can emulate. You could say, "I
  would like to sound like them at some point in my life." That would
  probably be a good goal for you to have as a performer. These are good
  eventual goals, but they are not good *immediate* goals.

Goals for Now and Later

Many people make themselves disturbed about goal attainment because they
confuse immediate with eventual goals. They believe that they should be able to
attain their long-range goals immediately, and they develop low frustration tolerance (LFT) and start to self-down when it takes them longer than immediately
to attain them. There is no reason you must experience success quickly, or at all,
for that matter. You are more likely to achieve success if you set realistically attainable goals and accept yourself, and the rate of progress you make, as you
slowly work towards attaining them. Confusing currently unattainable eventual
goals with possibly attainable immediate goals leads to loss of motivation, emotional upset, and some spurious "proof" about the impossibility of eventual success. Monitoring the progress you make toward your long-range, eventual goals
is typically a good way to maintain motivation while you are learning.

Our goal is to encourage you to keep learning and to keep growing. We also
would like to teach you to tolerate the discomfort that many people feel as the
days, weeks, and months wear on and seemingly no improvement occurs. When
you compare, don't compare with where you want to be. Compare with where
you've been, not where you're going.

Imagine that you have been practicing your new performance skills (whether
it be playing the piano or speaking in public) for eight weeks. Ask yourself:

- Is my performance any better than it was when I first started practicing?

- Is my performance any better than it was last week or the week before?
  - If your answer is no, what are your choices?
  - Are you practicing enough?
  - Have you reached a plateau?

- Are you attempting a task that is too difficult for you at your current level of proficiency? These may all be reasons why you are not improving.

- Are you possibly stopping yourself from improving because you are scaring yourself? Are you telling yourself, "I don't sound the way I am supposed to. It is not coming as quickly and easily as it should"?

- What would be a better response for someone who has those thoughts? You could say, "If it should have been quick and easy, it would have been quick and easy. However, it doesn't seem to be that way, and that is just too bad."

Right now some of you are probably saying (as some of our clients have said), "But that means I am always going to be confronting very, very hard things, and never getting any better."

Can you prove that prediction?

Where is your evidence for that belief? What are the facts? Is it appropriate to say that you are never going to get better at playing? You don't really know that, nor do you have a way of knowing that now. Is it appropriate to say that it is always going to be hard? You don't know that either. Remember what we wrote in the first prescription: When you attempt to predict the future, you may be engaging in magical thinking. We cannot predict the future, and neither can you. The odds are that with practice, it will probably get somewhat easier. The odds are that with practice, your playing and performing skills will improve, and performing in general will become somewhat easier.

We have far greater evidence for this prediction than for one that predicts future failure. Think back to the first time you tried to ride a bicycle. You may have had a bicycle with training wheels. The first time the training wheels were taken off, you probably wobbled. The second time you attempted to ride, you probably wobbled a little less. With practice, you were able to ride evenly and steer the bicycle.

Other things in life are similar. They take practice. If you expect to do new, unusual, and stressful things perfectly the first time, you are going to be very disappointed, and you will probably end up pretty bumped and bruised. Therefore, when you attempt something new or are working to improve a skill, remind yourself of the bike-riding analogy. It's going to take some time. It probably would not be sensible to compare yourself to ninety-day racers. Therefore, it might be in your best interest to do a sideways comparison.

Sideways Comparisons

When you compare sideways, you compare yourself to yourself. You look at your past behavior and past performance, and compare it to your present performance. You may find yourself saying, "Oh, wow; when I first started out, I couldn't do this as well." Rather than self-downing when you compare yourself to a more experienced performer, an alternative response would be to speculate as to what you could sound like after three, six, eight, or ten more months or years of practice. You might then say, "Wow! I can hardly wait."

You could also say, "How do I sound in comparison to where I was when I first started playing?"

Many of you who are reading this book may have attempted to speak in public for years, but, despite your attempts, you still suffer from performance anxiety. Public speaking has become your bête noire, your worst nightmare. In fact, you may have discovered, like some of our clients, that it gets more difficult every single time you try to do it. One possible explanation is that every single time you attempt to speak in public, you get yourself terrified. You may have scared yourself about the significance of your physical symptoms. You may have scared yourself about the significance of doing poorly. You may have gotten yourself so anxious about what is at risk that by the time you get around to trying to practice, you are a basket case. Since you have seemingly not experienced much success, you may believe that sideways comparisons may not be useful for you. But you would be wrong!

It would not be appropriate for you to compare yourself to highly confident speakers, or to people who speak well all the time. You may falsely believe that you can't compare your present level of performance to your previous level of performance, but indeed, you may discover upon calmer reflection that only some of your symptoms have gotten worse. You may also discover that some of your performance skills have actually improved. You may have learned to prepare in a more timely fashion. You may have learned to look at your notes more frequently. You may have made some skills improvements each and every time, but your performance is not yet perfect.

Downward comparison will also work in your case. "How well am I doing as compared to others who are immobilized with terror? Not everyone speaks effortlessly. I certainly don't," might be a sentence we would encourage you to say. "How well am I doing as compared to others who speak with effort?" It is unlikely that you are the only person frightened or terrified by the opportunity to speak in public. How well are you doing as compared to them? Did you get up at all? Did you at least get one sentence out? Did you at least say yes to the invitation to speak? Did you at least say something, even if it wasn't perfect? If you completed any of these public speaking-related tasks, you may be able to rate your public speaking behaviors more favorably than previously. Many people who are terrorized by the opportunity or idea of public speaking do not get up at all. Try using the "at least" phrase. "Well, at least I got up to speak." "Well, at least I had something to say." "Well, at least I didn't faint, as some people have." Therefore, the downward comparison will also work for you. It is helpful to remind you that you are not the sine qua non of either perfection or lack of perfection. There is always someone around to whom you can compare yourself profitably. And while it may sound cold–blooded to compare yourself to people who are doing worse than you, it has a valuable effect. If you suffer from performance anxiety and you compare yourself to people who do better than you, you may get discouraged, and you may not want to try again. If your eventual goal is to ultimately do as well as you can, upward comparison is self-defeating. If you use downward or sideways comparison, then you are more likely to see that you are showing some improvement and may yet get to be someone else's role model. So then that person can say, "I hope, someday, I can do as well as you do." For the present, maybe your goal is to say, "I may not being doing as well as I could be, but I am doing a lot better than those who are not trying at all." And, if you are one of those who is not doing at all, maybe your goal is to say, "Well, at least I am now working at making a change." Some folks who suffer from performance anxiety are not even working to make a change. They have decided to accept the fact that they will never perform. And while there may be some value and benefit in that particular kind of self-acceptance, it certainly doesn't put you in the running for a Tony Award or any other achievement award.

One homework assignment you might want to try this week, even if you are pretty good at not comparing yourself to others, would be to create a list of those people whose skills in a specific area are not as good as yours. This may sound hard to do, especially if you think you are the worst there is or the lowest of the low. If you cannot think in terms of a skills area, analyze a skill into its component parts and compare yourself to others on each piece. Remind yourself that you don't have to do perfectly well to be successful. Use the "at least" comparison that we wrote about earlier: "At least I have some skills." "At least I can do certain parts of the job." While it may seem a cold comfort, you could also remind yourself, "At least I don't have to learn it all from the beginning and, if I want to make the effort, **at least I can learn!**

An Unpleasant Discovery

A moment ago we told you to look around for people whose skills are less than yours. One of our clients, while doing that exercise, made an unpleasant discovery. In fact, the discovery was a real onion. While he was looking around at his coworkers he saw, as we pointed out, some with more experience who were better performers, and some at his level who did not do as well as he...when along came Mary.

> **The Case of James J.:** James, a middle manager, wanted a promotion. He decided to check out the competition and discovered that Mary, at his same level in the company, was far more proficient at speaking in public than he and was far more adept at computer expertise than he. She was also more skilled at making cold calls than he. James had better organizational skills than Mary. He wanted to be competitive, and he wanted to improve.

> *What could he say to himself, and believe diligently, that would keep him motivated and not immobilized? Write down your response.*

Could he say, "Well, they are bigoted against males; therefore there is no sense in my trying. Affirmative action won't let me succeed"? Would that have been an effective response? Could he say to himself, "I may not do as well as she does in those areas, but I can perform as well as she does in others, or if I want to I can work towards improvement"? Which do you think would be the better response? Which would help him stay motivated? James could also do a skill-by-skill comparison. He could gently remind himself that even though he excelled in some areas, it would be in his best interest to work on improving his skills in the other areas as well. He could compare his computer skills now with what they were a year ago and see whether they had improved. If not, he could investigate the steps necessary to help him make the grade without globally rating himself because of his deficiencies.

Remember the global rating game: people who rate their totality on the basis of one characteristic. James could have said, "Just because I don't do well with computers, that means I am a total and complete failure." He also could have said, "Just because Mary can work with computers, that means she is totally and completely perfect." Those beliefs get us in trouble on both sides. James may not be as good as Mary in some of these areas; therefore, what's his solution?

Mary *is* better than James in computer, cold calling, and public speaking skills. Who could James compare himself to? If he compares himself to Mary, he's inevitably going to feel rotten. If he thinks that it is terrible that he is not as good as she, he may be awe-struck or feel depressed or angry. What might he do that would be more effective? He could again say, "Well, it's true she's better than I am in X, Y, and Z, but with effort I can improve."

Some of you may be thinking, "At least James had some good qualities, but everybody is more experienced than I." If that's really the case, you are probably a new employee, and maybe you need to compare yourself downward, or laterally. How well are you doing in comparison to the other employees just hired? How well are you doing in comparison to those who are scaring themselves about the significance of not doing well? Even if your peers are that much better than you, you might want to look at that fact and tell yourself that this is an ideal invitation to work harder, rather than an ideal invitation to self-down. If you can successfully dispute your LFT which invitation would be a better one for you to accept? If you accept the invitation that says, "Because other people are doing better than I, therefore I am doomed to failure," you are not going to have any success or fun. If you accept the invitation that says, "Well, so there are people who are doing better; what an interesting challenge," you might have both some success and some fun.

And Now, Class, Time for Homework!

If You Must Compare, Compare Downward

Try to use the specific recommendations of this prescription whenever you find that you are stopping either preparation, practice, or performing as a result of comparing yourself to others. (You may also want to use the homework suggestions at the end of Chapter 5.)

1. Try some upward comparisons. Compare your performance to that of the best experts in your field. Remind yourself that they are very superior to you. Take your emotional temperature. Does making an upward comparison help you feel better or help you get or stay motivated? If you would like to be as good as they, what behavioral, emotional, and cognitive roadblocks will you have to overcome? Can you dispute the irrational beliefs that might impede your performance?

2. Try some downward and sideways comparisons. Take your emotional temperature. Compare your response with that in the previous exercise. Which response is more helpful?

3. If you have been trying to perform for a while and have a tendency to feel bad about your relative lack of progress, make a list of *all* the skills needed in your particular performance area. Check off the ones you are capable of. Remind yourself that you have made some progress, even though there is still more progress to be made. Then use the "at least" technique. "I may not know how to do _____ yet, but at least I can do _____."

Prescription 16
Give Yourself Permission to Be

Our last prescription, give yourself permission to be, could also have been our first prescription. While you are working on any new behavioral skill, you need to give yourself permission to *be the way you are right now*, while you work on changing. You may need to tell yourself, as we have taught you to say in other prescriptions:

> "While I may not like my behavior, I can accept myself, warts and all, while I change. I don't like the fact that I am jittery, anxious, or nervous. I don't like the fact that I seemingly have to put myself into onion situations (at least if I want to get, or keep, the jobs I desire). However, I can give myself permission to feel uncomfortable. I can give myself permission to feel jittery. I can also give myself permission to do things less than perfectly."

All of the different prescriptions are summed up in this final one. We are asking you to acknowledge that while you would strongly prefer to change, if for some highly unlikely reason change was impossible, you would still be OK, although you probably would not feel as happy, or possibly be as successful, as you would prefer to be. REBT philosophy reminds us that there is *no universal law of nature* that says that you *have to be* successful, that you *have to be* a performer, or that you *have to* ever speak in public in an unjittery way. If you are reading this book, however, it is highly likely that you have a strong desire to accomplish some, if not all, of these objectives. By giving yourself permission to be, you reduce your chances of developing performance anxiety about your reducing your performance anxiety.

This could have been our first prescription, and we then could have gone on to the prescription "De-stress Yourself, Don't Dis-stress Yourself." We had many discussions as to where this prescription belonged, but ultimately we felt that it was a good summary prescription. It ties all of the other prescriptions together and presents them in one sentence. It is essentially what you will need to say to yourself in a variety of different circumstances.

Giving yourself permission to be means not only giving yourself permission to be jittery and perform, but also giving yourself permission to rid yourself of your irrational beliefs. You are giving yourself permission to get rid of your nutty thinking in small increments. You don't have to get rid of all of your anxieties at once. You don't have to go from imperfect to perfect or from one extreme to another.

Use this book. Read and reread it from time to time. Allow yourself to improve in steps. If you need to, use this book again and again to work on any prescription that applies to you, as long as you need to work on it. You don't have to do it perfectly the first, second, third, or even the three hundredth time you attempt to work on your performance anxiety. You may discover that there are things that require your constant attention because they are connected to core irrational thoughts that you have practiced for many years. These things may not disappear easily or all at once, but you may discover that if you work on them routinely, you can keep them under control.

I Have Permission to Change Slowly

You may be reading this book with the hope that your performance anxiety will magically disappear by the final page. We certainly would be thrilled if that happened, but the likelihood is that your work will begin once you have finished this book. Giving yourself permission to be also means giving yourself permission to go slowly, or even to occasionally take steps backwards, which is also part of the process of change.

I Have Permission to Be on a Plateau

Human change seldom occurs linearly. We rarely go from 0 percent to 100 percent smoothly. There are always regressions and plateaus. You may experience a plateau, or some situation where things are going well, but you don't seem to be making much progress. You may not be doing as poorly as you used to, but you are still not doing as well as you hoped. Giving yourself permission to be also means giving yourself permission to be on a plateau and saying, "All right, I don't seem to be making much progress, but at least I am holding my own."

I Have Permission to Relapse and Recover

When you give yourself permission to be, please remember to also give yourself permission to have relapses. When you have a relapse, you seem to slip backward. You can remind yourself that humans have relapses. You can work on accepting yourself, warts and all, or relapses and all. Try to accept yourself with the relapse as you work toward getting back to where you started.

When people are on diets, for example, and have a relapse, they sometimes beat themselves up. We would recommend that rather than beating yourself up, you remind yourself that you can always get back on track (return to dieting) despite your relapse. Accepting the relapse doesn't mean abandoning your goal. It just means accepting the reality of the situation. Let us suppose that you "humanly" ate a piece of forbidden chocolate. Rather than beating yourself up, say to yourself, "That was a good-tasting chocolate, and while I would like another piece, it would be better for me to continue my diet. It was very pleasant to have this momentary relapse, but now I am back on target." Then start right back in on your diet.

The same strategy can be used in working on improving your performance skills and decreasing your performance anxiety. You may discover that with a little practice, you can easily and readily incorporate some of the things we have suggested to you. You may discover, however, that while you're doing so and beginning to feel some success, one of the things you thought you had under control resurrects itself. You can remind yourself that "old habits die hard," and that change may take you a little longer than you thought.

By giving yourself permission to have a relapse, you are not encouraging the relapse, but you *are* tolerating the relapse. You can remind yourself of Prescription 7, "Tolerate, Don't Musterbate":

"I really wish I hadn't had my relapse, but I did; that's unfortunate, but it's okay. I have permission to be human."

You may have spent a good deal of time in the past hiding your performance anxiety from those around you. At times you may have been successful at hiding it, but at other times you may not have been as successful. Have you ever discussed your performance anxiety with your family and friends? Has anyone where you work or in your professional network ever told *you* about his or her own performance anxiety? Remember, fear of public speaking is among our top ten fears, rated as more frightening then the fear of death.

Try This Exercise

If *you* suffer from performance anxiety, how many other people around you probably suffer from it as well? Why not look around you and see if you can spot your fellow sufferers: those people who also are trying to avoid performing or who seem to have trouble in a public arena. Take an informal poll of the people around you and see how many of them share this problem with you. You can do this verbally, in daily conversation, or you can make up your own written survey. Once you have completed your poll, you may want to take the risk of telling a few of your close friends, family, or fellow "members" of A.P.A. (Anxious Performers of America) that you too are dealing with this challenge.

You may ask, "Why should I do that? I would be ashamed of telling anyone about my performance anxiety." There are good reasons to share your performance anxiety with fellow sufferers:

- If you work on changing your behavior with the support of those around you, it is sometimes easier than working on it in isolation.

- By "coming out of the closet" on this issue, you can challenge your shame—and overcome it.

- Knowing that you are not alone sometimes benefits you as well, because it gives you a network of people who can not only help you work on your skills, but also help you challenge your beliefs.

- You can help others as well, by pointing out what you have learned.

Remember, this last prescription, "**Give Yourself Permission to Be**," also means giving yourself permission to be you *with* your performance anxiety. This includes giving yourself permission to share your problem and work on solutions with supportive others. In the beginning you probably will not want to share your challenge with strangers who may not suffer from performance anxiety, for fear that they may ridicule you or be nonsupportive. You might want to remind yourself of a common reaction to reading about well-known people who either experience or suffer from performance anxiety: "I didn't know *they* suffer from it too—My gosh, they are as human as I am." When we read about such people, our respect for them tends to increase because we realize that they either successfully overcame a debilitating problem or are still working to overcome it. We expect that you may have the same reaction to your own fallible humanity.

I Have Permission to be Human

When you give yourself permission to be, you give yourself permission to be human; that means fallible and capable of making mistakes. It would probably be a good idea for you to accept your own fallibility and not give yourself any grief about it. You may want to remind yourself that if you shouldn't make mistakes, have relapses, or take a long time to learn, then you wouldn't be capable of making mistakes, having relapses, or taking a long time to learn. If *all* humans shouldn't be fallible, then you as a representative human would be physiologically incapable of making mistakes.

When you use this prescription, you are essentially saying to yourself, "I am OK, even if my behavior needs work." You may not like your behavior, but you can give yourself permission to be fully alive, fully human, and fully imperfect (although perfectible)! You can give yourself permission to be less than capable while you work on improving your capability, if you choose to. In fact, you can give yourself permission to be less capable than you'd like to be, and still experience some happiness, some success, and some contentment. You can say to yourself, "I have permission to feel jittery, anxious, and nervous while I am working on being less jittery, less anxious, and less nervous. I don't enjoy my jitters, my anxiety, or my nerves, but they're okay, and I am okay with them. They're okay, at least for right now."

If you are suffering from rather than merely experiencing the symptoms of performance anxiety, it is probable that not only are you jittery and anxious, but you are also not performing, speaking, auditioning, or rehearsing. While that's not okay given your long-range goals if you wish to perform or get a better job, it is still appropriate to say to yourself that you are okay with those symptoms, even though those symptoms are not wonderful. When you give yourself permission to be, you are telling yourself, loudly and clearly,

> "I am not necessarily thrilled with some of the symptoms I'm experiencing. I'm not necessarily thrilled with some of the behaviors I am engaging in that may be self-defeating. I'm not necessarily thrilled with the situations I find myself in as I work on improving, but it's okay to be there. I can work on improving anything that's not great. I can work on changing anything that I *can* change, if I choose to change. But for right now, it is okay to be the way I am, or at least the way I act, because I have permission to act that way."

We are assuming that the way you are acting is neither illegal, immoral, nor self-destructive. We wouldn't want you to give yourself permission to be a more effective mass murderer. We wouldn't recommend that somebody who was an ax murderer, or was working hard and diligently to become one, say to himself or herself, "It's all right; I have permission to kill people." But in this particular context, what are you asking of yourself? You are asking yourself:

- To work on improving your general skills

- To get over your discomfort about appearing on stage, or in public
- To cope with feelings of physical and social discomfort and perhaps to reduce their power or rid yourself of them
- To enhance both your performance skills and your coping methods

All of these goals are well within the guidelines for a happy, healthy, well-adjusted life. Therefore, while you work on showing improvements in those areas, you are probably well advised to give yourself permission to be, or at least to act the way you are acting. This prescription is not meant to encourage a smug, narcissistic, self-satisfaction that is oblivious to making useful changes; rather, it is meant to help you place things into a perspective that will allow change to occur. It has been our experience that when you demand perfect and instantaneous improvement of yourself, you wind up achieving only depressed immobilization or unreasoning anger.

Will demanding that you must change force you to do so?
Will being intolerant of the time that the change requires make you
change any faster?

You are giving yourself permission to be *you*, not Laurence Olivier or the chair of General Motors (even though that may be your ultimate goal). Since you are working toward a goal, you can remind yourself to be process-oriented. You are in the process of change. It may be very difficult for you to see change because it is a process that goes on throughout your life. If you think of it that way, you realize that it is truly okay to be where you are, because you are not yet finished.

Try saying to yourself as you start your work on overcoming your performance fears and anxiety, "I give myself permission to be human." That's a good place to start as well as a good place to end.

And Now, Class, Time for Homework!

Give Yourself Permission to Be

Try to use the specific recommendation of this prescription whenever you are practicing the other prescriptions. (You may also want to use the homework suggestions at the end of Chapter 5.)

Class Dismissed.

Appendix A
Commonly Asked Questions About Rational-Emotive Behavior Therapy

Question 1 This approach seems so simple—why do I sometimes experience difficulty in making it work for me?

Answer You may be confusing "simple" and "easy." The methods outlined are fairly simple and straightforward, but they are not easy to implement. In order for this program to work, you will have to overcome many ingrained habits and beliefs. You may not find this all that easy to do, and you will probably experience some disappointment and frustration along the way.

The question that you may want to ask yourself is, "Is it worth it? Is the possibility of my future success worth the certainty of my current discomfort?" We have both worked with clients who answered that question, "No, it is not worth experiencing all these hassles in order to change. I am content in my misery. Change is too hard."

There is no reason anyone with performance anxiety must overcome their problem. Many people live happy and productive lives and never push themselves to perform in public. They change their life goals and experience success and fulfillment in other endeavors. If these clients had also been willing to conclude that their lack of accomplishment, while disappointing, was not devastating, they would have ended up emotionally intact. However, many such clients also conclude that they are total failures, and their misery increases.

Question 2 Isn't this approach too shallow? Other approaches appear to be much deeper. This approach seems to stay on the surface and treat only symptoms.

Answer   Nothing is more deeply embedded in your psyche than your beliefs about the world, yourself, and others—in other words, your philosophy. With our approach, we are attempting to help you develop a philosophy that is life-enhancing, satisfying, and flexible enough to be able to handle any of the jolts that life dishes out. Your emotions and your behaviors are reflections of your philosophy. If we can help you challenge and reevaluate those parts of your philosophy that get you into emotional and behavioral trouble, we not only help you alter surface symptoms but also, hopefully, help you make a profound, deep, and rewarding change in your life.

Question 3   Most other approaches dig deeply into the past in order to uncover "truths" about the present. You don't seem to be very concerned about the past. Isn't it important to get at the past *first* before you can make any impact on the present?

Answer   While it is undoubtedly true that the past influences our lives, there is scant evidence that it *controls* us so rigidly that we have no hope of changing. Things our parents taught us, or failed to teach us, may have some lasting effect on us today, but that seems to be because we rehearse their teachings on a day-to-day basis and remind ourselves that we have no alternative but to think the way they taught us or to awfulize about what they failed to teach us.

Psychotherapy provides all types of insights. One variety, commonly shared by psychodynamic psychologists (a.k.a. Freudians), is that our present emotional suffering is largely a consequence of the fact that our parents, or other loved ones, failed to meet our emotional needs as children. As a result of this failure, we seem doomed to seek out replacements for these infantile needs. Once we realize this, usually after many years of treatment, we not only feel relief from the burden of the past, but presumably can recognize when we are behaving childishly and will alter our behavior accordingly.

We cognitive/behavioral psychologists (a.k.a RETers) help our clients discover other kinds of insight:

1. Blaming the past doesn't change the past or improve the present or future.
2. Change is possible even if you never figure out the puzzle of the past.
3. We are responsible for our own emotions. Other people undoubtedly serve as catalysts for our thinking, but they do not *control* our emotions or behavior.

Coping Cue Cards

Every actor knows that a *cue* is a word, phrase, or gesture that reminds him or her of what to say or do next. In the early days of television, "idiot" cards were developed to help the actors say their lines. Today not only news broadcasters but political leaders use the TelePrompTer to help them speak more effectively. To that end, we have developed Coping Cue Cards. These cards are designed to help you remember your cue for thinking clearly and acting more effectively when you are in a performance situation. Each Coping Cue Card contains a wallet-sized summary of one of the sixteen prescriptions for overcoming performance anxiety. Please feel free to cut them out of the book and use them when needed. Each card contains a review of one or more effective tools that you can use. Each card can also serve as a handy reminder of the issues that you are working on and may help you dispute the irrational beliefs that are interfering with or blocking your performance.

It has been our experience that when our clients have made up and used similar memory aids, they have made more rapid progress.

Appendix B

Coping Cue Cards

Coping Cue Card—Prescription 1
De-stress Yourself, Don't Dis-stress Yourself!

Physically

1. *Take your PDQ.*

2. *Breathe!*
   - First take a calming/cleansing diaphragmatic breath.
   - Inhale slowly, and slowly say to yourself, "calm" and "relaxed" in rhythm with your breathing.
   - Think "calm," and stretch out the word slowly, so it takes about three counts: "Caaaalm."
   - When you exhale, slowly say to yourself "re-laxed," and again stretch the word out slowly so that it takes about three counts.
   - Repeat the sequence to yourself: "calm" as you slowly inhale, "relaxed" as you slowly exhale. Remember to take that brief pause before you exhale.

3. *Warm up before public speaking or other vigorous activity.* Try a shoulder isolation and rotation:
   - Stand or sit with your arms and hands held limply by your sides.
   - Lift your shoulders and bring your arms and hands with you as you lift.
   - Now, slowly, moving only your shoulders, lift your shoulders and bring them forward, around, down, and back.

- You will appear to be rowing a boat with your shoulders.
- Repeat this isolation slowly for three to five minutes.

4. *Take your PDQ again (note the difference).*

Cognitively

1. *Take your PDQ.*

2. *Try to challenge your dis-stressing thoughts.*
   Remind yourself that:
   "It's bad enough that I did badly, or that I am nervous or anxious about doing badly. It's bad enough that I may be trembling right now as I'm trying to speak, but it's not awful, it is not the end of the world; it is *merely* bad."

3. *Throw away your crystal ball.*
   - Don't write your obituary before you are dead!
   - When you try to look into someone's mind, you may only see a mirror!
   - People will act as they want to, not as you want them to!

4. *Use the other cue cards to help you dispute, as needed.*

5. *Take your PDQ again (note the difference).*

Coping Cue Card—Prescription 2
Rehearse a Skill, Not a Symptom:

Do not remind yourself about
   How rotten you feel!
   How bad the situation is!

Try using one of these instead:

1. "I can still perform even though I am a little (greatly) worried about the outcome."

2. "I can still rehearse (perform) even though I am uncomfortable. I can stand the discomfort, and I can concentrate on what I need to do."

3. "I can still act, teach, sing, lecture, dance, paint, even though I am experiencing this symptom (trembling, shaking, nausea, dizziness, shortness of breath, etc.). I am not going to let the symptom get between me and my goal."

4. **"Given my current level of ability and experience, I can rehearse my skills, despite my symptoms."**

Objectively evaluate the skills needed for the performance situation you are in:

1. What skills are required?

2. What skills do you already have?

3. What additional skills do you need to acquire, if any?

4. Make a plan to acquire the needed skills and *try* to stick to it.

5. Dispute any irrational beliefs that may get in your way of implementing your new plan.

Coping Cue Card—Prescription 3
Don't Confuse Anxiety with Effort

Remember:

1. A hundred minutes of anxiety is not equal to one minute of preparation!

2. Shut off the anxiety switch! (See the other side of the card.)

3. Leave stewing to the chefs.

4. Don't confuse comfort with achievement.

5. Practice **sufficient frustration tolerance.**

6. Take a frustration unit evaluation (phooey) and set your frustration ceiling high enough for the task at hand.

Ideas that will do you in

1. What if something bad happens?

2. What if I fail?

3. What if I feel *very* upset physically?

Ideas that will help you perform

1. Nothing is so bad that I can't cope with it in some fashion.

2. Failure would be unfortunate, but not the end of the world. Besides, even if I fail at a task, it doesn't mean I will fail in life.

3. My physical upset is proof that I am alive and involved. I don't need to stop myself from performing, although I would much prefer to be able to perform in a calm manner.

Coping Cue Card—Prescription 4
Don't Self-Medicate

Three common irrational equations

Relaxation = Drinking/Drugging

Worthiness = zero performance stress

Good performance = mellow drug-medicated performance

More useful equations

Relaxation = being at peace

(I can create peace in many ways: by straight thinking, by meditating, by using breathing or other relaxation exercises.)

Worthiness = being on the planet.

(I am worthy just because I exist. All humans experience some performance stress; therefore, experiencing stress is proof of my humanity, *not* my lack of worth.)

Good performance = allowing myself to perform at my current level of competence, "warts and all."

(A performance is "good" just because I did it. I can always improve, if I need to, by practicing my performance skills. **Self-medication will *not* allow me to give a good performance, even though I may delude myself into thinking it is good.**)

Ideas that will do you in

1. I shouldn't feel any discomfort associated with performing. Alcohol/drugs are disinhibitory. They are relaxants. They will loosen me up so that I can perform more naturally.

2. If I feel any discomfort, it is proof that there is something wrong with me.

3. Nobody will notice if I've had a couple of drinks. I've always been able to control by drinking. Doesn't everybody drink when under stress? I can stop, at will, when the stress is over.

Ideas that will help you perform

1. Since I am alive, I should feel discomfort. When I take alcohol or drugs, I stop myself from feeling normally and naturally.

2. Discomfort is proof that I am alive and concerned.

3. The more I rely on self-medication, the greater the chance that I will sabotage my own desire to do well. There is also an increased risk that I will become tolerant of my need for the medication and become dependent upon it, thereby making it less likely that I will be able to stop using it when I want to.

Coping Cue Card—Prescription 5
Concretize, Don't Awfulize

1. **Is it awe-full or is it an onion?** Remember, onions are supposed to stink and are often associated with tears.

2. **Use the awfulness scale**
   The Awfulness Scale
   (Spot on tie) 1 _____ 50 _____ 100 (Genocide)

3. **Realistically,** what is the worst thing that could happen?

4. **Try the following coping statements:**
   a. I didn't do well. That's too bad, but it's not the end of the world.

   b. It is bad, but I can cope with it. I am not going to die as a result of having this bad thing occur, and my future is not damaged beyond belief, even though I may have to cope with the unpleasantness of the present.

   c. This is highly unpleasant, but it's not terrible, nor is it the worst thing imaginable, even though it is not pleasant.

   d. There are many more imaginably or even unimaginably worse things than doing badly at a job or doing badly at an audition.

Coping Cue Card—Prescription 6
De-sacredize, Don't Idolize

1. **De-sacredize people**

2. **De-sacredize your symptoms**

3. **De-sacredize your performance**

Don't build any idols, false or otherwise.

Ideas that build idols:
- This is a person with life-or-death control over me.
- Look, here comes a very important and powerful person. If I ever made a mistake in his or her presence, I would never be able to live it down.
- Whenever I am in this person's presence, I shake, I quake, I quiver, I am uncomfortable.
- Whenever I think about this person, I am a mass of nerves. I get so tight that I can't do anything right.

Try being an idol smasher! When you are in the presence of your monster:

1. Close your eyes, take a calming/cleansing breath, and see yourself walking into the room where the performance situation is to take place.

2. Recognize that you have created this monstrous idol.

3. See yourself bowing down; see yourself kissing its toe.

4. Then say to yourself, "*Stop.* I don't have to do this. This is not required of me; it is not *necessary.*"

5. See yourself stand up, square your shoulders, put out your leg, and kick the idol over. See yourself knocking it down and watching it crumble into dust.

6. See a fallible human being, much like yourself, rise out of the dust.

7. Now allow yourself to talk to that other human being as an equal.

Coping Cue Card—Prescription 7
Tolerate, Don't Musturbate.

Remind yourself:

1. **Musturbation is self-abuse.**

2. **If it *shouldn't* have happened, it *wouldn't* have happened!**

3. **Don't confuse forgiveness with forgetfulness.**

4. **Remember what bears do in the woods?**
   When faced with a "bear," you can:

   a. Tolerate the ordure (this is not recommended for abusive relationships).

   b. Get out of "the woods."

   c. "Sleep under another tree."

5. **I don't like it, but I can tolerate it and...**

   a. I can learn to function effectively within it.

   b. Learn how to cope better.

   c. Work to see if there's any way I can change it, if it's in the changeable category.

Ideas that will help you perform

1. I can change my behavior, but I can't insist that anyone else change.

2. The world should be the way it is, because that is how it is. This means that a fact is a fact is a fact. Blue is blue and yellow is yellow. Cats are not dogs, nor should they be.

3. I can stand something, even if I don't like it. I can learn to tolerate it, and I don't need to like it.

4. I can learn to tell myself that situations I don't like aren't intolerable, just unpleasant.

Coping Cue Card—Prescription 8
Use "Why Not?" not "Why Me?"

"Why mes" that do you in

1. "Why am I being asked to do this? I don't know how to do this. Why are they asking something so stupid of me? After all, don't they know I don't know how to improvise."

2. "Why me? Are they trying to make me feel bad? Are they trying to get me in trouble?"

3. "Why me? Why am I being singled out to do this horrible, horrendous, horrific task? Why do I get all the hard work?"

"Why nots" that help you perform

1. "I am not really quite sure why I am being asked to do this, but why not? Directors have the right to ask for any kind of silly thing they choose to. What's the worst that can happen?"

2. "Why not? I am in charge of my emotions. Even if I do poorly, I don't have to feel dysfunctionally bad. This is not required of me. I can feel like the way I choose to feel!"

3. "Why not? It's a dirty job, but someone has to do it. Scaring myself with how horrible it all is that guarantees I will do poorly. If I do it with a good will, I may get an opportunity to do more interesting things that I would prefer to do."

Remember
The words "I'll try" imply the idea that "I cannot predict the outcome, but let's see what happens. I might turn out to be very good at this or I might need some help. Either way I have learned something useful."

Coping Cue Card—Prescription 9
Act "As If"

Ideas that will do you in

1. I am anxious. Nothing will ever change. I will always be anxious.

2. There is no hope for me. I will always hate having to perform. I cannot "act" differently.

3. Other people always seem to perform better than I. I don't know how to perform as well as they do, and I will never learn.

Ideas that will help you perform

1. I can *try* to act in a nonanxious manner like _____ (fill in the blank with the name of someone who performs the way you would prefer to).

2. I may never truly like having to perform, but if I try to act in a more confident manner, I may get better results than if I succeed in convincing myself that I can never succeed.

3. While it may be true that others seem to perform better than I do now, it is not true that I can't learn to perform. When I was a child I learned how to do many things by watching people and imitating them. I can do that equally well today.

Remember, "Whistle a Happy Tune!"

Coping Cue Card—Prescription 10
Be a Participator, Not a Self-Spectator

Ideas that will do you in

1. Whenever I begin to perform, I am aware that I might fail, and so I stop myself before I begin.

2. I am very aware of my physical distress when I performed, and I would rather stop performing than have to face it.

3. It's like I have these two little observers sitting on my shoulders—you know, like in the cartoons—who tell me whether or not I should do something. Unfortunately, the message is usually negative.

Ideas that will help you perform

1. When I become aware of my self-defeating thoughts, I can try to stop myself from dwelling on them and continue with my program. I can always return to those thoughts later if I have to.

2. When I become aware of my physical symptoms, I can try to ameliorate them by (a) taking a cleansing/calming breath and (b) reminding myself that it is normal to be having these physical symptoms in a performance situation.

3. When I am aware of my "back-seat drivers," I can try to eject them from the car or ask them to sit in the audience and talk to me afterwards.

Remember
- If you want to *watch* the show, buy a ticket.
- You can't dance with one body at two weddings.
- "…and now I am picking up the can of soup…"
- Tell your back-seat driver to "shut up or go home."

Coping Cue Card—Prescription 11
Be Process-Oriented, Not Product-Oriented

Remember:

1. Staying process-oriented means *not* self-spectating
   * Don't write the review until after the performance is over.
   * Don't concentrate on winning, concentrate on running.
   * You can decide to write, but you can't decide to write a best seller.
2. There is the dance, the dancer, and the dancing
   * Your product is your performance.
   * Focus on the process: What skills do you already have that allow you to produce that product? Are there any skills that you are lacking that you might be well advised to learn in order to create that product?
   * Consider the performer: What are your unique personal assets and liabilities? What qualities or attributes do you have that you could put to good use if you were to perform? Are you at least adequately prepared? Do you have other qualities or attributes that might get in the way of your speaking up?

Remember:

* You can improve your skills, if you wish to.
* You can dispute your horror of not being perfectly prepared or of possibly being disapproved of.
* You can calm yourself down before you perform and thereby improve your chances of having the appropriate level of stress for the situation.
* You can practice recovering from your known liabilities.
* To place failure into your vocabulary and then prepare responses to it, develop Plan B.

Success is an outcome that may be elusive. Recovery from error is an ongoing process that may bring eventual success with it.

Coping Cue Card—Prescription 12
Stay in the Moment

Remember:

Staying in the moment means staying focused on the task at hand, whether it be speaking in public or doing some mundane chore.

Questions that will do you in
* "Will I do it?"
* "How am I doing?"
* "Can I do it?"
* "Will the audience accept it/me?"

These may be interesting and even useful questions to have answers to, but they are not the questions of someone who is in the moment. They are the questions of someone who is paying attention to the product before the product has been produced. You can't examine a product before it is completed. You are a performer who is making a product at this moment.

Try to stay in the moment
* You can "act as if."
* You can participate and not self-spectate.
* You can stay process-oriented.
* Staying in the moment allows you to enjoy the sensations you are experiencing and the process of manufacturing the product. Later you can play another role, that of observer, critic, or judge, if you so choose.
* If you stay in the moment, you also allow yourself to enjoy the process.
* Staying in the moment ultimately means acting as-if, not self-spectating, and staying process-oriented.

Coping Cue Card—Prescription 13
Rate Your Behavior, Not Your Soul

I am a Falllibble Human Bean

All humans are unique, and there is no one exactly like you in all ways in this world. Your uniqueness in itself bestows worth.

Remember:

1. *Self*-improvement is impossible—try for *behavioral* improvement.

2. The "tissue box dispute"
   * Are you the tissues or the box?
   * Do not confuse the contents with the container.

3. Try to use the **all-purpose "it"**
   * "I don't like 'it' [stuttering, procrastinating, feeling anxious, etc.], but I am still a worthy human being despite 'it.'"
   * "'It' [my problematic behavior] is *not* OK, but I am OK with 'it.'"

4. Try using **"it's only"**
   * It's only my stuttering I am trying to change—it's *not* my soul.
   * I am only trying to improve one specific behavior—I am not attempting to alter by entire being.

Ideas that will do you in

1. My bad performance proves that I am worthless.

2. I didn't perform as well as I wanted to. It only goes to show how totally rotten I am.

3. I really gave a great performance; now I realize how totally wonderful I am.

Ideas that will help you perform

1. Just because I acted poorly, that does not make me a bad person.

2. Just because I acted wimpishly, that does not mean that I am a wimp.

3. I can really enjoy having done well today. But, just because I performed well today, that doesn't make me a better person. (Just because I acted unselfishly, that does not make me a saint.)

Coping Cue Card—Prescription 14
Accept Yourself, Warts and All

Try quitting the S.B.B. (self-bigotry brigade)

1. **Try to accept your self with your problematic behavior**—remember that all-purpose "it."
   "I don't like 'it,' but I can accept myself with 'it' while I work on changing 'it.'"

2. **Try to accept your appearance, warts and all**
   * Beauty is in the eye of a (hopefully blind) beholder

3. **Ideas that will do you in**
   * "I won't ask for a raise because of my appearance."
   * "I won't go for an audition because I don't look the way I am 'supposed' to look."

4. **Ideas that will help you perform**
   * If I *should have had* a different appearance, I *would have had* those features.

   * It's unfortunate that I do not look the way I would like to look, and in part, I could probably make *some* adjustments to look closer to the way I want to look. Only I can decide if it's worth the hassle and the potential pain I may have to encounter in order to change my looks. A less expensive and more effective solution is to change both my attitude and evaluation relating to my looks.

5. **Try accepting yourself in the onion situation**
   * I don't like what I have to do, or I don't like this attribute, but I am able to perform even if I don't like it. Where is it written that I should avoid things I dislike?
   * I am going to see what happens. My undesirable attributes don't have to stop me from performing.
   * I can accept that performing is a requirement. If I am to get a good evaluation, I *have* to perform.

Coping Cue Card—Prescription 15
If You Must Compare, Compare Downward

Comparisons are odious, upward comparisons are noxious.

1. **Remember Pollyanna—play a *"glad game."***
   - I may not perform as well as I would like, *but at least I am performing.*
   - I do not seem to be doing as well as the people around me, *but at least I am now aware of it, and I can try to improve.*
   - I may not perform as well as some expert, *but at least I am doing better than I did before—when I first started out.*

2. **An idea that will do you in**
   "I don't sound the way I am supposed to. It is not coming as quickly and easily as it should."

3. **An idea that will help you perform**
   "If it should have been quick and easy, it would have been quick and easy. However, it doesn't seem to be that way, and that is just too bad."

4. **Try a sideways comparison**
   "How do I sound in comparison to where I was when I first started playing?"

5. **Ideas that will do you in**
   - He or she is better than I...I may as well give up.
   - Many people seem to perform better than I do. I am doomed to failure.

6. **Ideas that will help you perform**
   - "Well, it's true that he or she is better than I am in x, y, or z, but with effort I could improve."
   - "Well, so there are people who are doing better; what an interesting challenge."

Coping Cue Card—Prescription 16
Give Yourself Permission to Be

Giving yourself permission to be means not only giving yourself permission to be jittery and perform, but also giving yourself permission to rid yourself of your irrational beliefs.

I have permission to change slowly.
I have permission to be on a plateau.
I have permission to relapse and recover.
I have permission to be human!

Index